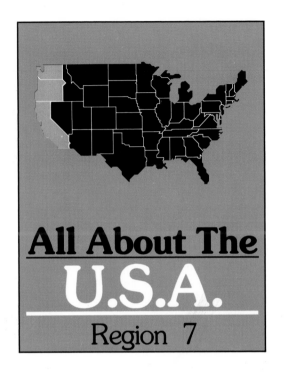

All About The
U.S.A.
Region 7

OCEAN
LANDS

by
Allan Carpenter

D1303510

ENCYCLOPAEDIA BRITANNICA EDUCATIONAL CORPORATION

Indexer and Assistant to the Author
CARL PROVORSE

Copy Preparation
VALERIE ROEBKE

Graphic Designer
ISAAK GRAZUTIS

Typography by
LAW BULLETIN PUBLISHING COMPANY

A Word from the Author — Apologia?

One of the author's favorite characters from Lewis Carroll claimed that he could do anything he pleased with words, and with language in general. Over a period of 45 years in publishing, and after 199 books bearing his name, the author at last claims the right to manipulate the language as it pleases him. If he prefers to save his text at the expense of uneven spacing of the paragraphs, he hopes he may do so. If he wants to use an incomplete sentence or to capitalize a word at some time or use a hyphen sometimes and not do either at other times, or to use a hyphen sometimes and not at others—or to use a dash—he now claims the right to do so, by virtue of age, if not senility. It is not often that an author finds editors who are willing to indulge such whims. The editors at Britannica are not only meticulous but also caring, and they have given this author carte blanche in the production of a work which is based on his 45 years of specialized study of the states. So, if such ecoentricities and inconsistencies appear in this work and if blame should fall, the author wishes it to be known that he accepts all blame as well as credit, if any.

ISBN 0-8347-3392-7
Library of Congress Catalog Card Number 86-080850

Contents

PART ONE — PACIFIC REALMS

Overview 5

Alaska 9

California 23

Hawaii 37

Oregon 51

Washington 65

American Samoa 79

Guam 82

Other Pacific Islands 85

PART TWO — THE CARIBBEAN REALM

Overview 86

Puerto Rico 87

Virgin Islands 93

Other Caribbean Islands 96

Index To This Volume 97

Acknowledgments 100

Cumulative Index to Seven Volumes 101

ALASKA

Juneau

Honolulu

HAWAII

Agana

GUAM

WAKE ISLAND

Pago Pago

AMERICAN SAMOA

WASHINGTON

Olympia

OREGON

Salem

CALIFORNIA

Sacramento

San Juan

PUERTO RICO

VIRGIN ISLANDS

PACIFIC REALMS

OVERVIEW

The various portions of the United States which touch the Pacific Ocean are spectacularly different. They have the biggest, the tallest, the coldest, the hottest, the wettest, the longest, the oldest and even the nearest.

They range from a tiny dot in the great ocean to a state which stretches wider than all the lower 48.

They have by far the greatest varieties of peoples, produce the greatest varieties of foodstuffs and sustain the widest variety of plants and animals.

Here can be found the oldest living thing, the greatest fault, the geographical center of the greater U.S.A., the world's second largest rock, the largest stands of timber, the world's most "generous" people, the most active volcano anywhere, and the world's biggest smoke rings.

Customs range from camel races to sled dog contests, from tropical feasts to a diet of blubber.

If placed in a vast box, the Pacific region would extend from the eastern boundaries of California, Oregon and Washington to Guam, which lies 3,700 miles west of Hawaii. The region would stretch from the tip of Point Barrow in the north to American Samoa, 2,600 miles southwest of Honolulu. The geographic center of this greater U.S. is found on the slopes of China Cap Mountain in northeast Oregon.

In size, the individual units range

The magical beauty of Hawaii

from Alaska's 591,004 square miles to the single square mile of Johnston Atoll.

The region contains the largest state in size, it has the smallest state west of Iowa. It also boasts the largest state in population, as well as the state with the smallest population.

In the northern section, people of the United States and people of Russia actually can see the other country. Little Diomede Island is less than three miles distant from Russia's Big Diomede Island. Mainland Alaska and mainland Russia are only fifty miles apart.

Part of the Pacific Realms freezes in the country's lowest temperature, a record minus 79.8 degrees at Point Barrow, Alaska. Part roasts in the highest — 134 degrees in Death Valley, California.

The incredible downpours that deluge Mt. Aialeale on Kauai, Hawaii, make it one of the wettest places on earth, averaging 472 inches of rain per year. As much as 624 inches of rain has fallen there in a single year. By contrast, Death Valley is one of earth's driest spots.

The five western states provide America with a wonderful gateway to the Pacific and the entire Far East. The great circle route of the world's airlines, the central hub of Hawaii and the splendid ports of the Pacific states reach out to nearly three fourths of the peoples of the world, servicing the vast commerce flowing into and out of Hawaii and the continental western states.

The great ocean routes, both ancient and modern, have brought all the races of peoples of the East to American shores.

Hawaii cherishes 64 races or combinations of races. California shelters the largest concentrations of Chinese peoples outside the Orient. The racial groups range from the Eskimos and Aleuts of the North to the Samoans on the South, from the Guamanians on the West to the Indian peoples of the Pacific Coast.

The native peoples have contributed their skills and customs to the growth of American civilization. The beautiful scrimshaw work and the amazing needlework of the Eskimos, the basket weaving of the Aleut, the totems of the Indians, the hula dances, food and legends of the Hawaiians, the buffalo and carabao races of Guam, the family customs and the sprightly siva dance of Samoa — all have been woven into the American heritage.

The attractions for tourists and travelers are everywhere in this vast area. A canyon to rival the Grand Canyon of Arizona, the pleasures of great cities, the magnificent beaches of the islands and the mainlands, interesting and unusual customs of the widest variety, craftwork of beauty and quality, sports from snow skiing to waterfall sliding — all add to the natural and manmade wonders.

When not at play the Pacific realms contribute almost every kind of product and service, from the petroleum of Alaska and California to the orchids and pineapples of Hawaii, from the coconuts of Samoa and Guam to the apples of Washington, from the salmon of the western continent to the tropical fish of Palau, from the financial mastery of San Francisco to the barter of Micronesia.

Some places in this huge area, such as Hollywood, are familiar to the whole world, while others are not even a name to most people. Here, certainly, is an opportunity to learn more about familiar regions and to experience others that remain strange and remote.

Opposite, Hawaiian girl picking flowers; overleaf, totems at Ketchikan

ALASKA

FASCINATING ALASKA

Alaska and its people have been called many things—the greatest, unique, wonderful, a little eccentric! All of these and more apply.

Here is a land where railroads "disappear," a volcano blows smoke rings, a lake empties itself on a regular schedule, where some people talk to the mountains, where the ice barks, and gigantic moose often become a hazard on the golf course.

In this "frozen land" fruits and vegetables can grow to two or three times their normal size; the family "car" becomes an airplane; one of the best-known cities was named by mistake. Alaska is the biggest, the coldest, the longest of all and can truly claim to be this country's last frontier.

THE FACE OF ALASKA

The next three states in size—Texas, California and Montana—could all be made to fit into the 570,833 square miles of this our largest state. It is the only state that reaches into the Eastern Hemisphere, and the international date-line had to be bent around it to keep Alaska from falling into two different days.

The coastline of Alaska is almost equal to that of all the other states combined. Mt. McKinley is the highest peak in North America. From its base to its peak it is taller than Mt. Everest, when measured in the same way. It is known to the native people as Denali, the Great One.

Alaska, itself, is a peninsula, one of the world's largest. Jutting out from it into the ocean are several other peninsulas, some of which could swallow up whole states to the south. The Alaska Peninsula extends 550 miles before it continues as the chain of Aleutian Islands. A host of other island groups add to the diversity of the land.

While in some areas the weather is not too bad, most of what is said about Alaska's weather turns out to be true.

Some areas are so cloudy that the Tlingit Indians had no word for blue sky, and the enormous storms which form in the Gulf of Alaska dominate much of the continent and sometimes even of Europe. The temperature extreme range of 179 degrees is the widest of all the states.

More than half of Alaska is covered with land which never thaws below a few feet. This is known as permafrost, which sometimes extends to a 1,200 foot depth.

Alaska's glaciers are the most spectacular evidence of the cold. If placed on top of Rhode Island, Malaspina Glacier alone would cover this smallest state entirely. The great weight of glaciers forces them to move down the slopes, and this movement creates such strange sounds that the glaciers are said to be "barking." When a glacier extends to the sea, large chunks break off to become icebergs. This is called calving.

THAT'S CURIOUS:
When Mt. Shishaldin puffs out volcanic smoke, it sometimes produces perfect smoke rings of gigantic size.

One of the world's greatest rivers is the mighty Yukon. Its three majestic tributaries—Porcupine, Tanana and Koyukuk—are principal rivers in their own right. The thousands of lakes cover 15,335 square miles and make Alaska the leader among the states in inland water. Lake Iliamna is the largest.

STIRRINGS

Alaska was perhaps the home of the first humans in the Western Hemisphere. At one time when the ocean surface was lower, land connected North America and Asia. Across this bridge of land, men and women and animals probably were able

Opposite, Anchorage; above, brown bear

to move to homes on the new continent.

Some "experts" believe people came to Alaska as long as 40,000 years ago, while others say it was only 12,000 to 15,000 years. The oldest date is much more likely. Not much is known about these earliest people, but they did leave some tools, along with some rather well made carvings, weapons and other evidence of their presence.

The earliest European visitors found four major and distinctive groups of peoples. The Eskimo and the Aleut have a distant relationship, but they are different. Indian people were divided into two major groups, the coastal Maritime Indians and the interior Athapascan.

THAT'S CURIOUS:
One of the world's most peculiar lakes is self-emptying Lake George. It is backed up by a dam of ice. As the lake water builds up behind the ice, it eventually becomes so heavy the dam is broken, and the lake empties. Another ice dam forms, and the cycle begins once again.

11

Denali, the majestic one—Mt. McKinley

The Aleuts were artistic and clever, making some of the finest boats and fashioning handsome clothing; they often embroidered using a needle crafted from a gull wing bone. Their basket weaving was especially fine, and no tools were used except the weaver's fingernail, which she let grow "until it is as sharp as a lancet."

Another cultured group were the Tlingit Indians, a Maritime people of what is now Southeast Alaska. They were known for their totems, carved from great logs. Some of these were like family crests, while others could be "read" for a message, perhaps sometimes even serving as bills or invoices.

The Tlingit were particularly proud of their handsome blankets and often used them much as others would use money. They were friendly to inanimate objects and often said "hello" to the mountains.

The Athapascan Indians were wanderers without permanent homes. They were admired for their intricate beadwork.

The Eskimo were perhaps the last of the many people to come to North America from Siberia, where, of course, many of their relatives remain. The Eskimos do not have chiefs or leaders in the way the Indian tribes were organized. Whoever is best at a given task will do it or direct others, but there is no fixed authority, although things are changing.

Eskimo art is recognized around the world. Their engravings on walrus ivory, known as scrimshaw, and their sculptured carving of ivory and wood often rank with great art anywhere. Examples of their work have been found dating back to prehistoric times.

THE RUSSIANS ARE COMING

In 1732 Michael Gvozdev may have been the first "modern" explorer to visit Alaska, but Vitus Bering, employed by the Russian czar, reached the North American mainland in 1741 and is given credit as the discoverer of Alaska.

Soon Russian fur traders began to plunder the area, treating the kindly Aleut people cruelly. The Aleut revolted in 1762 but were put down, and several thousand were murdered.

A permanent Russian settlement was not established until 1784 when Kodiak was founded. Meanwhile, other Europeans had been exploring, including British Captain James Cook in 1778.

Alexander Baranoff was sent to lead the Russian settlement in Alaska. For several years his progress was halted by the fierce Sitka Indians. After defeating the Indians at their capital, called Sitka, Barnoff made the site his own capital.

During Baranoff's rule, Sitka became known as a center of civilization in a vast wilderness. Some of the tales of fancy dress balls and casting of great bells at Sitka were probably exaggerations, but Sitka had such surprising evidences of civilization as a school, library, hospital and a cathedral—St. Michael's, dedicated in 1848.

Although the Russians were expanding their west coast empire as far as northern California, other nationals were carrying on business there. During the U.S. Civil War, a Confederate warship boldly entered Russian waters and sank a Union whale boat. Strangely, this event was the last skirmish of the Civil War.

Finally, Russia became certain that the English would take over Alaska and offered to sell the region to the United States. In a wonderful act of statesmanship, American Secretary of State William H. Seward arranged for the purchase in 1867. For $7,200,000, the U.S. gained a vast region offering undreamed of strategic and financial value.

TREASURE

For nearly twenty years, the new owners paid little attention to "Seward's Folly" or "Seward's Icebox."

Then in 1880 gold was discovered, and before long Juneau was established, named for one of the prospectors who struck it rich, Joe Juneau. Later, gold was found in Canada's Klondike, and Alaska became the jumping off place for a swarm of fortune seekers to the Klondike.

One day in 1899, when the tide went out on the beach at Nome, gold was discovered there, and another rush was on. Because the gold was found between the levels of high and low tide, it was easy to pan from the sand. The rush to Nome was one of the biggest and wildest in history. Before long, Nome's population had passed 20,000. Three years later,

THAT'S CURIOUS:

To reach Canada's gold, prospectors had to go through Alaska and climb over mountain passes that would have frightened expert mountaineers. Most of them did not even realize the terrible dangers they faced, but 22,000 eager gold hunters formed an almost continuous line over Chilkoot Pass. More than 3,000 men even crossed Valdez Glacier in a season when it was considered to be impossible.

Klondike miners

another gold discovery was made where Fairbanks now stands.

Juneau became the capital in 1906, and territorial government was finally established in 1912.

That year saw one of the most severe natural disasters, when Mt. Katmai flew apart in a volcanic eruption that for a hundred miles blotted out the sun with its ash. The cloud of ash circled the earth and cooled the entire northern hemisphere for a considerable time.

The chemical effect of the ash dissolved the hair on the famous Kodiak brown bears, and they wandered about naked and forlorn. The eruption left fumeroles puffing smoke all over one of the valleys, and this became the Valley of Ten Thousand Smokes.

After nine years of effort, the first railroad was completed from Anchorage to Fairbanks in 1923. President Warren Harding became the first president to visit Alaska when he dedicated this unbelievable road, owned by the federal government.

A MODERN STATE

Transportation of another kind brought Alaska into the news in 1935. World renowned humorist Will Rogers and famed flier Wiley Post were killed when their plane crashed near Barrow. That same year, the federal government made land available in the Matanuska Valley. Many homesteaders came in. After much hardship to the settlers, the valley became a farming wonder.

In a way, Alaska was at "war" with Japan before World War II began. Alaska

fishermen had to fend off the Japanese who were plundering the precious salmon.

The real war came soon enough when the Japanese seized and occupied Agattu, Attu and Kiska in the Aleutian Islands. From headquarters in Anchorage, U.S. forces were able to drive the invaders out in 1943. This was the only American territory in the hemisphere to be captured by the Japanese.

Much of the military power built up during the war remained and was increased after the war to face a possible new enemy just across the Bering Strait. Alaska became one of the first lines of defense against possible Russian attack.

Congress agreed to give Alaska statehood in 1958, and statehood was proclaimed on January 3, 1959.

One of the worst disasters of its kind in U.S. history struck with the earthquake of 1964, reaching as much as 8.6 on the measuring scale. Even those who saw the damage could not believe it. Centered near Anchorage, the quake almost wiped out that city. The tidal wave which followed caused further great damage in the state, and then it went on to overwhelm seaside communities as far away as Hawaii.

Despite the damage, the energetic Alaskans soon had recovered almost entirely.

In 1967 the 100th anniversary of U.S. ownership was a time for celebration with yearlong festivities.

Events of the 1970's included the Alaskan Native Land Claims Settlement Act in 1971 and the 1974 start of the pipeline designed to bring to market the products of the northern petroleum fields. Despite the protests of conservationists and others, this was completed in 1977.

With the billions of oil income, Alaska dropped its income tax, added thousands to the state payroll, provided expensive state services, built schools, airstrips, docks and highways, loaned money to residents and bought the Alaska railroad from the U.S. government.

Even more unusual, every Alaskan who applies receives a check each year, which in 1985 was $400. However, the oil reserves are diminishing, and oil incomes are declining. The bright prospects appear to be fading.

There is another fading prospect. Although the people of Alaska voted in 1976 to move the capital city to Willow, this apparently will not be done, according to anonymous officials.

PERSONALITIES

Persons associated with Alaska have generally not reached international fame, but the state has produced some interesting personalities.

One of these has been called "one of the notable women of America." She was Harriet Pullen, known as Mother Pullen. She and her family of boys arrived as pioneers at Skagway. During the day, she drove a heavy freight wagon, pulled by four horses, struggling over the danger-

THAT'S CURIOUS:
Alaskans went wild in celebration of statehood. The people of Fairbanks wanted a golden symbol, so they planned to turn the Chena River to gold, but through some unwanted chemical change, it turned a lovely green instead.

PEOPLES

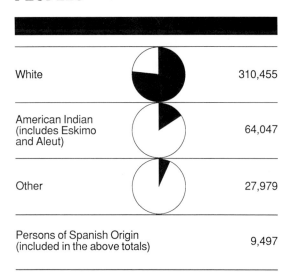

White	310,455
American Indian (includes Eskimo and Aleut)	64,047
Other	27,979
Persons of Spanish Origin (included in the above totals)	9,497

ous passes. At night she cooked fine pies for the gold seekers. She made friends with the Indians and learned several Indian languages. Later she operated a hotel, a ranch and a dairy farm—becoming a very successful businesswoman.

One of the least-known of the greatest explorers, Vitus Bering, deserves greater recognition. To get to the Pacific, he and his party had to drag their supplies across Russian Siberia. They built a ship in the eastern Siberian wilderness and explored the adjoining oceans. He and his crew finally managed to arrive at present Alaska in 1741.

Most famous of all the Russians in Alaska was Alexander Baranoff, who "ruled" the region almost as a dictator for nineteen years. By contrast, he also wrote songs and poems. His power became so great that Russian leaders grew worried that he might attempt to take away their colony. They sent a Russian navy escort to bring Baranoff back to Russia, and he died on the long voyage.

A pioneer of another type was America's John Muir. The great naturalist explored Alaska with his little dog Stickine. Another explorer/scientist was Dr. W. H. Dall. The handsome dall sheep were given his name. A third prominent natural scientist was Father Bernard Hubbard. He was known as the "Glacier Priest" because of his studies of glaciers. His studies also included volcanoes, and he gained fame as a novelist, as well.

Writers of greater fame called Alaska home for one period or another. Renowned story teller Jack London went to the Yukon in 1897, searching for gold when he was 21. He gained the background for many of his tales during his short stay in the region. Author Rex Beach lived at Stevens Village and also used the Alaska region as background for his writing.

Alaska artists include several of Eskimo heritage. The Eskimo people are well known for their artistic work. Skivoan Weyahok (Howard Rock) is admired for his sculptures and paintings of Arctic scenes. Aden Ahgupuk (known as Twok) created notable line drawings on processed reindeer skins.

A fourteen-year-old orphan at Jesse Lee Mission Home, Seward, gained fame for an unusual reason. He entered and won a contest for the design of the territorial flag. On a background of dark blue sky, Benny Benson placed the great dipper pointing at the pole star. He wrote this description, "The blue field is for the Alaska sky and the forget-me-not, an Alaska flower. The North Star is for the

future state of Alaska, the most northerly of the Union. The Dipper is for the Great Bear—symbolizing strength." Benny's prophecy of 1929 proved accurate. Thirty years later his Pole Star became the symbol of the 49th state, and his flag did become the state flag.

One of the more remarkable men of Alaska's past was the Rev. Dr. Sheldon Jackson, a missionary. His love of the region and its people made him devote much of his time to promote the interest of the American people and Congress in their remote territory.

One of Dr. Jackson's most remarkable accomplishments was bringing the reindeer back to Alaska, where it had become almost extinct. Russian Eskimo herders raised reindeer as domestic animals. Dr. Jackson managed to bring in a small stock of reindeer, with Russian helpers to teach their methods of herding. Soon great reindeer herds were flourishing; the Eskimo had a prospect of prosperity.

A WEALTH OF NATURE

Reindeer and caribou still flourish in Alaska. Even more impressive are the majestic moose, with their broad antlers. Just as impressive in a different way are the Alaska brown bears. These are the largest of all the carnivores or meat-eating animals, more massive even than tigers and lions. Most Americans have seen them on television as they cavort in the Alaskan rivers, fishing for salmon during the run of those wonderful fish.

The great polar bears are equally interesting and almost as large. Alaska also has all of the other familiar bears of the lower 48 states. Strange but true most of those animals seem to grow bigger in Alaska than in the other 48. The native musk ox became extinct, but they were brought back and now are numerous, along with buffalo (bison).

Sea otters and fur seals were almost exterminated for their beautiful skins, but with protection they have made a strong comeback. Of the same general family, the walrus has provided food and many other necessities for the Eskimo.

Salmon, king crab, razor clams, and Petersburg cocktail shrimp are among the sea creatures greatly prized worldwide. The demand has been so great that numbers of the creatures have been much reduced.

Alaska contains all but one of the 33 minerals listed as critical to modern life. New discoveries of other minerals continue at a rapid pace on a nearly regular basis.

Forests in Alaska now exceed 140 million acres. Forests extend more than 50 miles farther north than they did only forty years ago. This indicates the climate may be becoming warmer.

USING THE WEALTH

Most glamorous of Alaskan minerals is gold. Over the years, it has brought more than a billion dollars to the state and is still accounting for a modest income.

However, oil and gas are now the mineral leaders. Commercial production of petroleum began in 1957. Great new

THAT'S CURIOUS:

An Alaskan dog once ate a 20,000-year-old piece of meat without any bad effects. This was possible because the flesh of some prehistoric animals has been preserved in Alaska's "deep-freeze." Such discoveries of flesh along with bones have been of great value to scientists.

Fishing off Ketchikan

While most Americans would not think of Alaska as an "agricultural" state, more than a million acres of land are suitable for agriculture, but only a small portion of this has been cultivated. Wherever crops are grown, the products are remarkable for their huge size and good quality. Single heads of cabbage have been known to exceed 60 pounds. Individual strawberries can be sliced to make an entire serving.

Creatures of the waters still add to Alaskan wealth. Despite the diminished supplies of many species, Alaska fisheries still yield half a billion dollars a year to the state's income. Alaska continues to lead all other states in value of its marine products.

Transportation has always been a great problem in Alaska. The distances are huge and the terrain often difficult. Rivers and the ocean provided waterways, but walking and dog sledding were the only means of overland travel. Today railroad mileage is small but highway miles are increasing. However, air travel often provides the only answer to getting somewhere. The airplane is said to be the "family car." Many communities cannot be reached in any other way. Nearly a thousand communities have regular air service.

Alaska's mainline railroad was built and owned by the federal government but was purchased by the state. It runs for about 470 miles from Seward and Whittier to Fairbanks.

The most romantic form of transport in Alaska has always been the dog sled. Now this picturesque transport is mainly used in sledding contests.

Venturesome tourists from the lower 48 states can drive to Fairbanks by way of Canada over the Alaska Highway—or

fields have come into production, and petroleum exploration is fiercely competitive today. Alaska is now third among the states in value of its petroleum production. This has exceeded twelve billion dollars a year.

The problem of bringing these precious fuels to market was a thorny one. At great danger, labor and expense, the Alaska pipeline was constructed. Unusual problems, such as melting permafrost, made the project even more uncertain. Environmentalists feared the pipeline would destroy much of the natural region. Today the controversial line carries the product of the wells for 800 miles from Prudhoe Bay in the north to Valdez, where it is shipped out by tanker.

The timber and pulp industry is growing at a very rapid rate.

even take the bus. Alaska's marine "highway" up the coast is one of the most popular for tourists. The unique state ferries carry cars and passengers along much of the rugged Alaska shore, where popular cruise ships also travel.

Modern communication techniques have probably meant more to the remote communities of Alaska than any other single improvement. Through radio and radio telephone, TV and satellite nearly everyone now can keep in touch over the vast empty distances of the state. However, Alaska had cable communication with the rest of the country by 1903.

GETTING AROUND

Alaskan tourists have the widest possible choice of travel forms—from reindeer sled to 747 plane, from skimobile and dogsled to luxury liner. For variety they may pan for gold, experience perpetual daylight, marvel at glaciers, and learn about the local cultures.

Tourists who come by cruise ship or state ferry up the Inside Passage marvel at some of the world's most spectacular coastline—looming cliffs, dashing waterfalls and stupendous glaciers. They may catch glimpses of mountain goats jumping nimbly and seals and sea lions cavorting in the water. The shy and elusive sea otter might even appear.

At Ketchikan tourists reach the southernmost Alaskan port. There the houses climb up the seaside much like the mountain goats. A principal attraction is the world's largest collection of authentic Indian totem poles.

THE ECONOMY

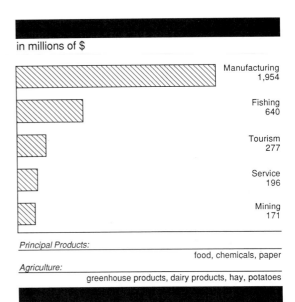

in millions of $

Manufacturing	1,954
Fishing	640
Tourism	277
Service	196
Mining	171

Principal Products:
food, chemicals, paper

Agriculture:
greenhouse products, dairy products, hay, potatoes

The Stikine River is named for Dr. John Muir's dog, Stikine. Tourists find the boat trips to be a thrilling adventure.

Alaska's earliest history is preserved at Sitka, where the Cathedral of St. Michael was rebuilt after a fire in 1966. Here the Russian Orthodox faith is still preserved along with a fine display of religious art. Each year Sitka re-enacts the ceremony of the flags, when Russia's is lowered and the U.S. banner is raised.

Despite the vote to move the capital to Willow, Juneau is still the capital city. The capitol was completed in 1930 and served as the federal and territorial capitol until statehood. The Historical Library and Museum has perhaps the finest collection of Alaskan materials.

THAT'S CURIOUS:
Tracks of the Wild Goose Railroad were laid from Nome to Anvil Creek. Because the permafrost partially melted each summer, the tracks would sink into the ground and often could not be found at all.

Glaciers rank high with tourists—Mendenhall Glacier

Skagway and Port Chilkoot are points of interest. Mendenhall Glacier is an icy wonder, but even more impressive is Glacier Bay, now a national monument. Here the terminals of over twenty great glaciers loom over a harbor of breathtaking beauty.

The recovery of Anchorage after the terrible 1964 earthquake had been called a miracle. The city was thoroughly restored and continues to grow. Principal annual attraction is the Fur Rendezvous. This features the fur auction, trappers and miners ball, sled dog races of world championship stature and quaint Eskimo dances.

Matanuska Valley is the famed center of a depression era agricultural experiment, where outstanding vegetables and other crops are now grown.

The port region of Valdez/Seward/Whittier offers the most northerly ice-free port on the continent. Seward has also mostly recovered from its 1964 earthquake damage. Its name honors the secretary of state who brought Alaska into the U.S. fold.

In summer the days at Fairbanks stretch almost around the clock; winter nights seem even longer. There is an annual Midnight Sun baseball game on the longest day. In order to keep the water system from freezing, Fairbank's system had to be designed with antifreeze circulated through the fire hydrants. Fairbanks' annual Golden Days Festival recalls the wild times of the gold rush. A nearby College is the University of Alaska.

In a strange twist of history the

country's highest mountain was not generally known until 1896 when it was "discovered" by W.A. Dickey. The native peoples called it Denali, but Dickey named it in honor of then President William McKinley. History does not record that the summit was reached until 1913.

The Aleutian Islands stretch far out to sea, forming a long volcanic chain. The farthest island, Attu, is very nearly as close to Tokyo as it is to Juneau.

The islands actually are the extension of the Alaska Peninsula. On Kodiak Island is the town of Kodiak, first non-native community in present Alaska.

Katmai National Monument covers almost two and a quarter million acres and is the largest U.S. national preserve. The glacier inside Mt. Katmai formed after the eruption of 1912. This icy sheet has given scientists a unique opportunity to study the beginning of a glacier.

Tiny Little Diomede Island brings U.S. territory almost within shouting distance of Russia on the Russian Diomede side.

Nome has a peculiar problem. Built on the permafrost, its buildings are turned and skewed as the upper surface of the ground melts in the warmer months. When the frost returns, the buildings have to be readjusted.

Much of the finest Eskimo artwork is traditionally brought up to Nome for sale.

To the north, Kotzebue is said to be the largest Eskimo community in the world. Its celebration of July 4th is one of the country's most unusual. Blanket

Moose, Alaska, an animal lover's wonderland

tossing, kayak races and a contest to pick Miss Arctic Circle liven the festivities.

Still farther north is Barrow, within the Arctic Circle, most northerly town in the U.S. It is a vital center of trade for the vast area and a site of Arctic research.

COMPAC-FACS

ALASKA
(no official nickname)

HISTORY
Statehood: January 3, 1959
Admitted as: 49th state
Capital: Juneau

THAT'S CURIOUS:
Nome was given its name by accident. A map maker did not know the name of a cape, so he wrote "name?" on his map. His draftsman thought the word was Nome, and the accidental name stuck.

The practical capitol has a splendid interior, with fine murals and decoration

OFFICIAL SYMBOLS
Motto: North to the Future
Bird: Willow ptarmigan
Fish: King salmon
Flower: Forget-me-not
Tree: Sitka spruce
Song: "Alaska's Flag"
GEO-FACS
Area: 570,833 sq. mi.
Rank in Area: First
Length (n/s): 800 miles (not including Aleutian and Alexander archipelagos)
Width (e/w): 900 miles (not including Aleutian and Alexander archipelagos)
Geographic Center: 60 mi. nw of Mt. McKinley
Highest Point: 20,320 ft. (Mt. McKinley, highest point in N. America)
Lowest Point: Sea level (Pacific Ocean)
Mean Elevation: 1,900 ft.
Temperature, Extreme Range: 179.8 degrees

Number of Boroughs: 10
Coastline: 5,580 mi.
Mountain Ranges: Alaska, Brook, Pacific, Aleutian
POPULATION
Total: 479,000 (1983)
Rank: 50th
Density: 1 person per sq. mi.
Principal Cities: Anchorage, 174,432; Fairbanks, 22,645; Juneau, 19,528; Sitka, 7,803; Ketchikan, 7,198; Kodiak, 4,756
EDUCATION
Schools: 477 elementary and secondary
Higher: 15
VITAL STATISTICS
Births (1980/83): 33,000
Deaths (1980/83): 6,000
Hospitals: 25
Drinking Age: 19
INTERESTING PEOPLE
Vitus Bering, Alexander Baranoff, William Dall, Dr. Sheldon Jackson, John Muir, Harriet Pullen, Sidney Laurence, Rex Beach, Joe Juneau, Ernest Gruening
WHEN DID IT HAPPEN?
1728: Vitus Bering discovers Bering Strait
1741: Bering first touches mainland
1784: First permanent settlement, Kodiak Island
1799: Baranoff founds old Sitka; first American fur trade agreement
1867: U.S. purchases Alaska from Russia
1880: Juneau founded by gold seekers
1899: Gold rush to Nome
1912: Alaska gains territorial status; Mt. Katmai explodes
1923: Completion of Alaska Railroad
1935: Will Rogers, Wiley Post killed
1942: Japanese occupy Attu, Kiska and Agattu Islands
1959: Statehood
1964: Worst earthquake
1977: Trans-Alaska pipeline completed
1985: People share in oil revenue; prospects diminish

THAT'S CURIOUS:
At Nenana one of the most unusual gambling events is held. In the Ice Sweepstakes, bets are taken as to the exact minute the ice will break up on the Tanana River.

CALIFORNIA

FASCINATING CALIFORNIA

California is "the most favored spot on earth," exclaimed a great naturalist. So many people have agreed with him that the state has become by far the largest of all in population. Yet others look on California as a place of weirdoes and cranks, where bizarre religions flourish, of strange experiments, such as using monkeys as orange pickers.

Whatever the individual feelings, few will argue, however, that California possesses far more than its share of varied wonders. Even now new discoveries are being made about the wonderful animals, birds, flowers, and the world's tallest and biggest trees. There are many such novelties as the butterfly trees, sea otters, abalone and the swallows of Capistrano.

Millions of visitors a year come to enjoy these and many other attractions.

THE FACE OF CALIFORNIA

As the third largest state, California stretches 770 miles in length and reaches a width of 250 miles. It descends to the lowest point on the continent and soars to the highest point in the conterminous U.S.

Its great length places the state in three distinct geographic regions and gives it a shoreline of almost 3,500 miles. That shore is broken by two of the world's finest harbors, the bays of San Francisco and San Diego. The Sierra and Coastal mountain ranges tower almost the length of the state, providing moun-

tain recreation only a few miles from the great centers of population.

Two California valleys—the huge Central and wealthy Imperial—rank among the richest on earth, while a third great depression—Death Valley—is one of the most desolate.

The state has more national sites than any other; these include such different wonders as the Devil's Postpile, the great national parks, such as the former home of the Yo Semite Indians, and the only Russian colonial settlement in the lower forty-eight.

On the negative side, California worries uneasily about its many "faults." These faults, however, are not human ones. They are the enormous cracks which separate various segments of the earth's crust. Whenever one of these segments slips down, an earthquake occurs. California is criss-crossed with some of the biggest of these faults. Many of the worst earthquakes in U.S. history already have marred the California landscape. Experts say new major quakes may be only days away, or they may not come for decades.

In prehistoric times, other mighty forces shaped the California landscape. Greatest of all was the unbelievable might that pushed up a block of granite to form the lofty Sierra Mountain range.

Much of the land was covered by the various glaciers, and fiery volcanoes changed much of the surface.

Before all of this, the land rose and fell many times; ancient seas came and went as the elevations changed.

EARLY DWELLERS

Human beings have lived in California for perhaps 40,000 years. The oldest human relics found so far are those from

Santa Rosa Island—the remains of a 30,000 year old barbecue. Later peoples have carved pictures into rocks or painted them on cliffs. These petroglyphs and pictographs probably had meaning to the artists, but we do not yet know fully what they meant.

When Europeans first came to the region, they found large numbers of various Indian tribes. We believe now that even in those days California had the largest population in what is now the United States.

The lives these Indians led were much more simple than those of the East Coast. They did not have large confederations of tribes or the sophisticated government found in the East within some tribes and tribal groups.

The Indians of the north were quite different from those of the South. Few of the tribes could make pottery, although they crafted beautiful, finely woven baskets. They fed on the things that came to hand easily, like caterpillars.

In many sections acorns provided flour for bread or mush. Pinon nuts, beans, snakes, crows, and coyotes were staples of the diet. All kinds of insects provided food. Roasted mashed grasshoppers were a great delicacy.

The Indians of California were generally peace-loving; the terrible inter-tribal wars of the East were almost unknown.

STIRRINGS

Suddenly, all this began to change when the white gods arrived in big canoes.

Opposite, the "very great" Greater Los Angeles

As early as 1510, California had been described in a novel as paradise, but it was then considered to be an island.

In 1542 the Portuguese leader named Juan Rodriguez Cabrillo and his followers sailed into present San Diego Bay in the name of the King of Spain.

English explorer Sir Francis Drake's exploration added to the world's knowledge of California.

In 1602 Sebastian Vizcaino spent a year on the coast, discovering and naming many geographic features, including San Diego, Santa Barbara, Santa Catalina, and the region he named in honor of his sponsor the Count of Monte Rey.

Following that, for almost a century and a half California had little attention from Europeans. Then came the man who has been called the "founder" of California, one of the greatest Californians—Father Junipero Serro. In 1769 he founded Mission San Diego Alcala, around which grew California's first permanent European settlement, now San Diego.

A MISSION TO SAVE

Much of the early history of California is found in the 21 missions founded by Father Serra and others, including Mission San Francisco de Asis in 1776, just as the British colonies were declaring their independence.

In 1781 not much fuss was made about the founding of El Pueblo de Nuestra Senora la Reina de Los Angeles de Porciuncula, but it was to become the second largest city in the United States.

Mission San Diego mural shows a scene of the Mexican period

Today the long name has become L.A.

The Indians were quickly herded to the missions, to work almost as slaves. They became very skillful in all the work of household and field, as well as crafts, but often they were terribly treated and repressed.

In spite of Spain's laws, ships of other nations began to trade with the California communities. Russia actually claimed a large area and in 1812 built Fort Ross north of Bodega Bay to enforce its claims. There was a great market in the Orient for the wonderful sea otter fur. Russian and other hunters killed so many of these exceptional animals they were thought to be extinct.

MEXICO TAKES OVER

After Mexico became independent of Spain in 1825, the Mexican flag officially flew over Monterey, which remained the capital.

Favored Mexicans were given huge grants of land, called ranchos. There were as many as 800 major ranchos in California. The Indians worked on as laborers and continued to be terribly mistreated by the Rancheros. They were freed in 1831 when the missions were taken over by the Mexican government, but conditions became little better.

The Mexican government in California was generally inefficient. Power struggles, Indian raids and revolutions were common.

By 1841, when the first U.S. wagon train arrived, the American influence was growing. To keep California out of the hands of other nations, a group of Americans took control and proclaimed what they called the California Republic, with a flag showing a star and a bear. This came to be called the Bear Flag Republic.

UNCLE SAM ARRIVES

Americans John C. Fremont, Kit Carson, Navy Lieutenant Edward Beale and Colonel Stephen Watts Kearny all took part in military actions which consolidated the American position during the war with Mexico.

When Mexican Governor Pio Pico surrendered, the Bear Flag Republic ended, and California officially came under American rule through the treaty of Guadalupe Hidalgo, signed in 1848.

Just before that a dramatic event took place. A piece of metal no larger than a pea was found on the property of John Sutter, who was then probably the

wealthiest man in California. This discovery turned out to be a gold nugget. Beginning in 1849, the movement of tens of thousands of people in a stampede for golden riches probably has never been equalled. Some came overland, or by boat around Cape Horn. Others took boats to Panama, struggled over the Isthmus and took Pacific based ships to California. Some succeeded; many did not.

Whatever the method of travel, the journey was terribly hard; no one knows how many thousands died. Some found great wealth, and many of them lost everything; others had no luck at all; many others prospered by providing the food and provisions gold seekers needed.

California had become populated almost overnight. For example, in less than a year, San Francisco mushroomed from a tiny village to more than 25,000 population. Only two years after American control, California was ready for statehood and admitted September 9, 1850.

State government did not immediately bring law and order; few other areas have suffered the banditry, confiscation of property, mistreatment of minorities, and other hardships, and still people swarmed into California, making matters even worse in some ways.

Of course, things gradually were brought under control, and such events as grand opera at San Francisco in 1851 indicated the stability and culture that were to come. In 1854 Sacramento became the capital.

California helped elect Lincoln president by the narrow margin of 1,000 votes; the state remained loyal to the North, and the wealth of gold and other minerals helped the Union finance the Civil War. By 1861 California enjoyed the "instant news" when the telegraph lines reached the coast. Eight years later the first transcontinental railroad brought the entire continent together as never before.

Famed travel writer Isabella Bird described an early train: "First came two great gaudy engines, the Grizzly Bear and the White Fox, their tenders loaded with logs, the engines with great solitary reflecting lamps, comfortable glass houses and well-stuffed seats for the engine drivers. Next came a baggage car, a mail car, and Wells Fargo and Company's express car, loaded with peaches and grapes; then two 'silver palace' cars, then a smoking car, at that time mainly occupied by Chinamen; and then five ordinary passenger cars, making a train about 700 feet in length."

The university with the largest student body in the country today, the University of California, started in 1868.

A pathetic war with the Indians marred the early 1870's when a handful of Indians held off several thousand soldiers for 6 months. By the 1880's visitors from all over the world were experiencing the joys of California travel, and others were trying to get in on the great land boom.

A MODERN STATE

Valuable mineral strikes continued, but the most important of all started with the oil rush at Bakersfield in 1899. San

Bartenders with big hands were in demand during the gold rush. Since the going rate for a drink was a pinch of gold dust, the bigger fingers could capture more gold.

Francisco endured one of the country's worst natural disasters in the terrible earthquake and fire of 1906.

Various reforms in government, including the vote for women, helped the people to recover from many of the injustices of the past.

A world's fair at San Francisco, the capture of the state vote by Woodrow Wilson and the tribulation of World War I were events preceding the boom period of the 1920's. In the ten years of that decade the population rose by 65 percent.

More newcomers flooded in during the depression years; they found that California was not the paradise they expected; times were hard everywhere. However, progress in the 1930's continued in many ways such as the opening of the great bridges at San Francisco Bay and the 1939 World's Fair in that city.

World War II came directly to California's shore when the oil refinery at Goleta was shelled by a Japanese submarine. The large population of Japanese Americans endured being herded into guarded camps because the government felt they could not be trusted. Many of them lost everything they had. The war carried off thousands of Californians into military service and thousands died.

Important events came ever faster—the founding of the United Nations at San Francisco in 1945, the establishment of the great telescope at Mount Palomar and the first appearance in the state of two very different groups. In 1956 the Republicans became the first party to hold a national convention in California, with their meeting at San Francisco, and in 1957 the Dodgers became the first of California's major league baseball clubs.

Sometime in the 1960's California gained first rank in population, as reported in the 1970 census. The Los Angeles area experienced a severe earthquake in 1971.

The 1980's found the state hosting the 1984 Olympics at Los Angeles, and the city went wild with patriotic and athletic fervor. The Olympic opening and closing ceremonies again demonstrated the power of Hollywood to put on a show. Also in that year the Democratic Convention at San Francisco held international attention for almost a week and nominated the ticket of Walter Mondale and Geraldine Ferraro.

PERSONALITIES

In 1986 actor Clint Eastwood started on a career, which many feel has national possibilities, when he was elected mayor of Carmel by the Sea.

Richard Nixon, born in Yorba Linda, has been the only native of California to become president to date, although Herbert Hoover long called the state his home. President Ronald Reagan made his reputation as a public administrator during his terms as governor of California, where he earlier gained prominence for the first time for his films and as a labor administrator.

Although he is not very well known outside of California, the state's founder, Father Junipero Serra, deserves wider recognition. He founded nine of the 21

missions about which California life centered for so many years. Despite continuing poor health, he taught and converted the Indians, brought in good agricultural practices and established basic industries.

His statue is one of the two from California in the Hall of Fame at the national capitol, and his grave may be seen at Mission San Carlos Borromeo de Carmelo.

The strange fate of John Sutter is not well understood. He founded Sacramento and claimed huge acreages of land, living in magnificent style in his own fortress-home. However, when gold was found on his property, the area was so overrun by prospectors that Sutter was unable to work his holdings; he lost everything and died a poor man in far-off Pennsylvania.

John C. Fremont also had much bad luck, but he overcame it. Although found guilty of insubordination in the army, he became the first senator from California. As Republican candidate for president in 1856 he lost the election; then his claims to a California land purchase were disputed. Nevertheless, after going deeply into debt to recover his land, he regained the property and sold it at a profit. Fremont is credited with being one of the most successful of all the western explorers and pioneers. He also gave the Golden Gate its name.

Early California business tycoons included Leland Stanford, Mark Hopkins, Charles Crocker and Collis P. Huntington. As railroad leaders, they were called "The Big Four." Stanford was governor of California and also made large gifts to Stanford University, named in his honor.

Some of America's most notable

Panamint Range, California

writers have been associated with California. Mark Twain realized his first great success while in the state. English writers Robert Louis Stevenson and Rudyard Kipling spent agreeable parts of their lives in California. Modern writers, all natives of the state, include Robert Frost, John Steinbeck and William Saroyan. Charles Wakefield Cadman was a noted California composer.

Perhaps the most mysterious California figure was Walter E. Scott, who became famous as Death Valley Scotty. His $2,000,000 castle in the valley and his unusual life style kept him in the public eye. Later it was found that an anonymous man of wealth had supplied Scotty's luxurious life as a strange kind of hobby.

Of course, some of the most recog-

nized California names belong to the motion picture group of Hollywood. Who can forget stars such as Mary Pickford, Clark Gable, Rudolph Valentino, Gloria Swanson and Marilyn Monroe, or producers and directors such as Cecil B. de Mille and Louis B. Meyer?

A WEALTH OF NATURE

The variety of plants and living creatures found in California is probably greater than in any other state. The unusual madrona and the Monterey pine and cypress are interesting trees. The strange Joshua tree is a type of yucca.

The yellow flower called cup of gold by the Spaniards grows so widely it has become the state flower, now named California poppy. Much more rare is the giant coreopsis, a giant sunflower only growing on the Channel Islands.

Cavorting sea lions are one of the greatest animal attractions. Equally delightful but harder to find is the clever sea otter, now saved from extinction.

Still in danger of extinction is the magnificent California condor. Desperate efforts are being made to save it.

Far from extinct are the monarch butterflies. When migrating, these beautiful insects light on the pine trees of Pacific Grove in such swarms that the trees appear to be covered with millions of orange colored blossoms.

Edible sea creatures are extremely varied, including the popular abalone. Its meat is pounded into a kind of steak, and the beautiful shell is made into jewelry.

In a state with large dry areas, the shortage of fresh water is one of the greatest problems. Although the huge mountain snows provide much water, California has had to "borrow" more and more of its water supply from other areas. This has led both to disputes with neighboring states about who should get the precious water and to ambitious and sometimes strange plans for getting water from really remote areas.

USING THE WEALTH

Each year California agriculture leads the nation in dollar value, producing nearly half of all the fruits and nuts and a fourth of all U.S. vegetables. Grapes lead the state's agricultural products in cash income, with cotton, hay and tomatoes following. The more than 200 commercial crops vary from such little known items as cherimoya to the popular navel oranges. Orange growers watched with interest when Martin Seely imported monkeys to pick oranges; the plan failed.

Ninety percent of all U.S. dates come from the Coachella Valley; Santa Cruz is the brussel sprouts capital, with Watsonville the world's strawberry center. Vast acres of bright colors herald the farms where flowers are grown for seed.

With so many valuable crops, the processing of foods and drinks ranks high in California industry. California wines have been increasing in popularity since the wine industry began in 1839.

THAT'S CURIOUS:
California can boast the highest and the oldest and biggest living things. The coastal redwood in Humboldt Redwoods State park soars to a height of 362 feet. The Giant Sequoia at Sequoia National Park is 275 feet tall and has a circumference of 83 feet 2 inches—the bulkiest living thing. The strange bristlecone pine is the oldest tree, about 4,600 years, but some of the peculiar creosote bushes now are thought to be much older.

California leads all the states in manufacturing, with the incredible annual value of shipments of nearly 200 billion dollars annually. Production includes almost every major product from the greatest concentrations of aerospace and computer science to the trousers made famous all over the world by Levi Strauss, known as levis.

An industry that made California even more famous was motion pictures, and later television. The whole world knew about Hollywood, and its stars were more famous than kings and presidents. The movie and TV industries are less concentrated in Hollywood now, but Hollywood is still a movie center.

Gold first made California a land of promise, but in later years other minerals have surpassed it. Petroleum, alone in a year, brings in more revenue than all the gold of all the past.

The state has so many attractions for visitors that tourists spend nearly thirty billion dollars a year enjoying the great variety of attractions. This provides one of the major sources of income.

GETTING AROUND

Even those tourists who know California best can still find unexpected joys in out of the way places. Innumerable things to see and do are not on the casual tourist's lists of the most important sights, but this description can only hit some of the high spots.

San Diego is a great place to start. A boat tour of the bay provides a wonderful experience and helps in orientation. The

THE ECONOMY

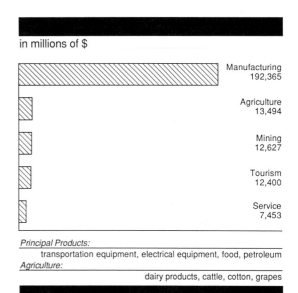

in millions of $

	Manufacturing 192,365
	Agriculture 13,494
	Mining 12,627
	Tourism 12,400
	Service 7,453

Principal Products:
transportation equipment, electrical equipment, food, petroleum
Agriculture:
dairy products, cattle, cotton, grapes

world's largest zoo, and one of the most interesting, should be on every visitor's list, as well as the many other attractions of Balboa Park where the zoo is located.

Beautiful La Jolla, a part of San Diego to the north, overlooks the sea in a spectacular way and has some of the finest shops and galleries anywhere. Nearby is the great Mt. Palomar observatory where important astronomical discoveries have been made.

To the east are rich Imperial Valley, the Salton Sea State Park and Anza-Borrego Desert State Park. Here in this arid land spring brings flowering beauty of more than 600 kinds of desert plants. In earlier years camels were brought in as work animals because they seemed logical

THAT'S CURIOUS:
Few will forget the sight of the swallows returning to Capistrano; however, this occurs only one day a year, precisely on March 19, and they leave again on September 23. No one knows how these birds manage such a feat of timing.

California beach crowded at midday

in the desert. Today Indio attracts visitors with its annual camel races, and, at another time, its annual date festival.

In the late 1800's the government settled Indians on the worthless-seeming land around what is now Palm Springs. As Palm Springs grew to be one of the country's most celebrated and elegant resorts, the Indians prospered, fortunately and unexpectedly. Today Palm Springs offers a desert wonderland.

When the Mormons saw a certain desert plant, they thought it looked like the prophet Joshua praying, so they called it the Joshua tree. These strange relatives of the yucca are preserved in Joshua Tree National Monument.

Traveling on, the tourist will want to see Inscription Canyon with its carved Indian messages, and the ghost town of Califo, now restored. Not everyone enjoys the heat and desolation of Death Valley, but many travelers find it a most interesting and unusual place.

Between San Diego and Los Angeles, Highway 101 offers many attractions.

Laguna Beach is one of the most interesting of all seaside communities and has attractions of many kinds.

Almost everyone wants to see the two transportation giants of Long Beach—the mammoth wooden plane built by Howard Hughes and the famous liner Queen Mary, now anchored and serving as a hotel. Nearby, the harbor has many points of interest.

Los Angeles has been described as "a city without a city." This is because there are so many communities which make up the total metropolis. Now, however,

downtown Los Angeles has taken on new meaning with imposing skyscrapers, great new hotels, a fine music center and many other attractions.

Nearby is Olvera Street, an interesting re-creation of the oldest part of Los Angeles, as it was founded and carried on by the Spaniards.

The head swims with the number of attractions in the 450 square miles that make up L.A. Disneyland is one of the principal magnets for young and old. A different type of amusement attraction is found at famed Knotts Berry Farm.

To the north, one of the world's notable events occurs when Pasadena holds its famous parade and Rose Bowl football game, as the first civic celebration of the New Year.

At San Marino, the Huntington Library and Museum intrigues visitors with such famous paintings as "Pinkie" and "The Blue Boy." With the greatest financial resources of any museum, the Getty art galleries may someday offer one of the world's most envied collections.

Westward lie the rather dismal areas of Hollywood Boulevard and, by contrast, the magnificent community of Beverly Hills, site of some of the most splendid homes and shops anywhere.

Off the coast, the island of Santa Catalina is well worth a visit, with its glass-bottomed boat rides and other attractions.

Santa Barbara is another wealthy community with many interesting buildings and homes in Spanish style. It is famous for its many fine shops.

A contrasting community, quaint Morro Bay, is noted for the great rock rising across the bay, nicknamed the Gibraltar of the Pacific. The tiny town is

PEOPLES

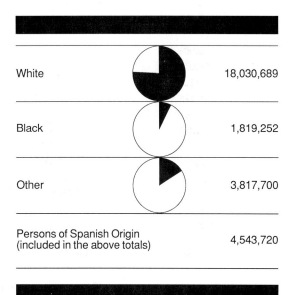

White	18,030,689
Black	1,819,252
Other	3,817,700
Persons of Spanish Origin (included in the above totals)	4,543,720

known for its crafts and art and charming seafood restaurants.

From Morro Bay, one of the most famous highways in the world makes its winding way up the coast. California highway Number One lives up to its name as the "Wonderful One." Delightful little beaches and scenic views seem to be everywhere along the highway. Each stop offers some new adventure, such as the jade which may be picked up at Jade Cove, a bluish jade found nowhere else.

Perhaps the greatest single attraction on this stretch of coast is the mighty castle with its treasures, built and assembled by publisher William Randolph Hearst. He spent millions to create an estate so splendid it is unequalled in this country. Now the enchanting palace is open to all as a state preserve.

Climbers on the trails of Pfeiffer-Big

Beautiful vistas are found everywhere on "Wonderful One"

Sur State Park catch glimpses of ocean and wilderness, lagoons and sea caves, and perhaps even a bobcat or wild pig.

Point Lobos with its twisted cypress, picturesque rocks and churning surf has been called "the greatest meeting of land and water in the world."

The Monterey Peninsula is unequalled, also. The author considers the village of Carmel to be one of the two or three most attractive communities in the United States. This view is apparently shared by the many artists and writers who call it home.

Leading from Carmel is the famous 17 mile drive which shows off the beauties of the peninsula, including the Monterey cypress, famous mansions and noted golf courses. Ocean View Boulevard has other attractions such as the renowned blooms of the ice plant and the "butterfly trees"

of Pacific Grove.

Fisherman's Wharf and Cannery Row are delights of the town of Monterey, which has interesting relics of the decades in which it was the capital of California.

Clustered around one of the world's most beautiful bodies of water, San Francisco Bay, are some of America's most talked about communities. Many consider San Francisco to be the premiere of all large cities in the country—the city that has everything in a small compact area.

After being up for repairs, the city's fabled cable cars began to clang and roll again in 1984. Visitors hang precariously to the cars going up the famed San Francisco hills to such sights as Fisherman's Wharf. New and charming wharfs and small communities of galleries,

restaurants and shops appear to be springing up everywhere almost overnight. Chinatown is said to be the largest Chinese community outside the Orient. At the center of town is Union Square, surrounded by beautiful shops and stores and luxury hotels.

The great Bay Bridge and Golden Gate Bridge are worth a visit just to be seen as marvels of their art. Across the Golden Gate, clustered on the bay at the foot of its cliff, is picturesque Sausalito, with some of the finest art galleries and gift shops. The view of San Francisco at night across the bay is one of the most breathtaking anywhere.

Many uncomplimentary words have been written about the San Francisco weather, but even the creeping, chilly fog can add glamor to this glamorous city.

Crossing under the bay by subway is another experience enjoyed by many. Oakland, Alameda and Berkeley have their own attractions, including the main campus of the University of California at Berkeley. At Mt. Diablo State Park the whole splendid vista of the Bay area opens up from the region's highest point.

Not far to the north are the centers of the wine country—Napa and Sonoma, with their wine experts and samplings.

North of San Francisco, Wonderful One becomes even more wonderful, with each of the innumerable twists and turns opening up a new view of ocean and coastal majesty.

Just past Sausalito, not far north of One, Muir Woods is a must for every visitor. Most hold their breath in awe as they walk among the gigantic, solemn redwoods preserved there. A little farther on is Point Reyes National Seashore, preserving many shore attractions.

Mendocino has one of the most interesting concentrations of art and craft shops, and its quaint old hotel should not be missed.

Mt. Shasta, Lava Beds National Monument, and Lassen Volcanic National Park with its steaming mud pots and whistling steam vents are all attractions of the inland north.

California's backbone is the mighty Sierra range, coming to its center of beauty in one of the country's foremost national parks—Yosemite. The visitor will never forget the first view of this lovely valley, with Half Dome looming in the distance and with the country's highest waterfall cascading down the cliffs to the left.

Kings Canyon and Sequoia National Parks are also unique. A living memorial to America's war dead, the General Grant tree, is one of the largest on earth.

There is much to be seen in the Central Valley, including the mammoth golden domed capitol at Sacramento. Its grounds are a showplace of more than 800 varieties of plants and trees.

The gold rush heritage is preserved at the restored town of Columbia in Columbia Historic State Park. At Marshall Gold Discovery State Park is a replica of Sutter's original mill and the site where the first alluvial gold deposit was found by Sutter's carpenter, John Marshall.

To the north and east is one of the world's most beautiful lakes—Tahoe, shared with Nevada. Emerald Bay has so much to offer it has been made a registered national landmark.

Driving across the border into Nevada, the visitor may well agree that California has provided one of the travel experiences of a lifetime.

The capitol, Sacramento

COMPAC-FACS

CALIFORNIA
The Golden State

HISTORY
Statehood: September 9, 1850
Admitted as: 31st state
Capital: Sacramento, effective 1854
OFFICIAL SYMBOLS
Motto: Eureka ("I have found it")
Animal: California grizzly bear
Bird: California valley quail
Fish: California golden trout
Flower: Golden poppy
Tree: California redwood
Song: "I Love You, California"
Stone: Serpentine
GEO-FACS
Area: 158,693 sq. mi.
Rank in Area: 3rd
Length (n/s): 770 mi.
Width (e/w): 250 mi.
Geographic Center: 35 mi. e of Madera

Highest Point: 14,494 (Mt. Whitney)
Lowest Point: 282 ft. below sea level (Death Valley)
Mean Elevation: 2,900 ft.
Temperature, Extreme Range: 179 degrees
Coastline: 540 mi.
POPULATION
Total (1984 est.): 25,550,000
Rank: First
Density: 151.4 persons per sq. mi.
Principal Cities: Los Angeles, 2,966,762; San Francisco, 678,974; San Diego, 875,504; San Jose, 636,550; Long Beach, 361,334; Oakland, 339,288; Sacramento, 275,741
EDUCATION
Schools: 6,818 elementary and secondary
Higher: 268
VITAL STATISTICS
Births: 435,019 (1982)
Deaths: 192,171 (1982)
Hospitals: 501
Drinking Age: 21
INTERESTING PEOPLE
Fr. Junipero Serra, John Sutter, John C. Fremont, Leland Stanford, Charles Crocker, Mark Hopkins, Collis P. Huntington, Mark Twain, Jack London, Helen Hunt Jackson, C. H. (Joaquin) Miller, Ambrose Bierce, John Steinbeck, Robert Frost, William Saroyan, Robert Louis Stevenson, Charles Wakefield Cadman, Herbert Hoover, Richard Nixon, Lillian Gilbreth, Earl Warren, Luther Burbank, Lee de Forest, Henry J. Kaiser, Cecil B. de Mille, D. W. Griffith, Will Rogers, Marilyn Monroe, Gloria Swanson
WHEN DID IT HAPPEN?
1542: Juan Cabrillo searches the coast
1579: Sir Francis Drake claims for English Queen
1769: Fr. Junipero Serra begins his mission
1776: San Francisco founded
1781: Los Angeles begun
1812: Russians build Fort Ross
1826: Mexican rule begins
1848: California becomes U.S. territory by treaty
1850: Statehood
1869: Railroad links California to East
1906: San Francisco earthquake and fire
1915: San Diego, San Francisco hold world's fairs
1937: Golden Gate Bridge opens
1962: California is first in population
1967: Ronald Reagan becomes Governor
1984: Olympics at Los Angeles; Democratic convention at San Francisco

HAWAII

FASCINATING HAWAII

In many ways, Hawaii is the most unusual and fascinating state. It is the only state that ever was governed by an independent non-European monarchy and recognized by international law. On its golden shores a great explorer was murdered for a "nail." Its most private and mysterious island was the site of one of the first and strangest battles fought by Americans in World War II—a battle fought by only two combatants and won by a giant sized native Hawaiian. Hawaii is a place where the weather is so perfect the original language has no word for weather.

THE FACE OF HAWAII

The strange and interesting facts about Hawaii could go on and on. Of course, its geography is unique among the states. It is the only island state and tops that by being the longest island chain in the world.

It is incredible to think that the entire island state erupted from a giant crack in the ocean bottom. All the land was formed by untold billions of tons of lava pushed up over more than 10,000,000 years. There are five major islands. Kauai is the oldest and Hawaii the youngest. Others are Maui, Oahu, and Molokai. Smaller islands add about 120 more, with the little speck of Kure 1,600 miles northwest of the southern tip of Hawaii Island the most northerly extent of the state.

Today there are still many reminders of the volcanoes. Kilauea, one of the vents on Mauna Loa, is still active. The eruption of 1868 was described by an eyewitness: "Four huge fountains boiled up with terrific fury, throwing crimson lava and rocks weighing many tons to a height from 500 to 1,000 feet...From these great fountains flowed a rapid stream of red lava, rolling, rushing and tumbling like a swollen river...surging and roaring throughout its length like a cataract with a power and fury perfectly indescribable. It was nothing less than a river of fire from 200 to 800 feet wide and twenty deep...Where it entered the sea it extended the coast-line half a mile."

Sometimes the lava cools in stringy formations called "Pele's hair," in honor of the goddess of volcanoes.

Many dead craters also help to tell the story of Hawaii's origins. The best known landmark of Oahu is Diamond Head, a volcanic crater. The crater of Haleakala is considered to be the largest inactive complex of craters in the world.

Robert Lewis Stevenson said the climate of Hawaii "sweetens one's bones." Although the Hawaiian language has no word meaning weather, the state has some of the most varied weather anywhere. Only eight inches of rain fall in the driest parts, yet Mt. Waialeale on Kauai has enormous rainfall, averaging 472 inches per year. One year 624 inches of rain drenched the mountain slopes.

The winds have a great deal to do with the climate. The slopes against which the wind blows receive tremendous rains, while the other sides, away from the wind (leeward), get little rain.

Most of the rain rushes to the sea carving deep canyons. These canyons

give the island the strange puckered look found nowhere else. So little of the water stays on land that Hawaii has the smallest area of inland water of any state. However, near the crest of Mauna Kea lies Lake Waiau, highest in the country.

The islands' slopes are so steep that no great rivers are found, but countless waterfalls leap over the many cliffs and canyons. Akaka Falls on Hawaii drops for 420 feet. Only Kauai has navigable rivers—the Hanapepe and Wailua. Most of Kauai's rivers receive their flow from the enormous Alakai Swamp. This is a thirty-square-mile morass, the catch basin of the huge rainfalls from Mount Waialeale.

The Waimea River is perhaps the most notable in Hawaii, for it has carved out stupendous Waimea Canyon. Some say this canyon rivals the Grand Canyon of Arizona, with colors as startlingly beautiful. However, Waimea is only 2,857 feet deep, 10 miles long and a mile wide.

Hawaii is noted as the only tropical state in the U.S. But there are many variations, including some surprisingly cold weather. For every 1,000 feet of rise up the mountains, the temperature drops almost four degrees. Frost is experienced every night in some places. In winter Mauna Kea and Mauna Loa are snow capped.

STIRRINGS

Many people are surprised to learn

Opposite, Honolulu, by USGS/NHAP/EROS

that Hawaii has a fascinating prehistoric culture. The legendary Menehune, only 3 feet tall, are said to have left the structures still found today, such as a 900 foot wall of carefully cut blocks forming a dam which holds back the Alekoko Fish Pond.

The ancestors of the Hawaiians found by early explorers probably came from the Marquesas Islands, perhaps as early as 400 A.D. Over the succeeding years, more Polynesians came in their light but sturdy double hulled, planked canoes. Their descendants became the people known to the first European explorers.

When the first Europeans came, they found that principal chiefs ruled the various islands, counseled by other chiefs, including women, and priests. Their lives and those of their people were greatly influenced by their gods, including Ku, Kane, Kanaloa, and Lono, along with dozens of other gods who were supposed to rule nearly every aspect of life.

Anyone who wanted to succeed in almost any enterprise had to offer prayers and sacrifices to the correct god. In some cases, human sacrifices were called for. There were strict rules against certain actions, known as kapu, from which the word tabu is taken.

Just as now, the early people of Hawaii loved water sports. They were expert surfers; they loved sliding down waterfalls and made long toboggan-like runs on grass slides covered with slippery oils. They made eating a fine art, and their manners were said to have been

THAT'S CURIOUS:

The mammoth bulk of Mauna Loa volcano makes it the largest mountain on the globe. Although it rises 13,680 feet above the ocean surface, most of its bulk lies far beneath the sea. If the underwater section of Mauna Loa is counted, it is also one of the tallest mountains in the world, about 32,000 feet.

much more refined than those of Europe at the time.

In large artificial ponds they cultivated fish for food, were skilled in making stone tools and weapons, and their artistry in creating the beautiful feather cloaks has never been surpassed. However, the birds were not killed for their feathers; they were captured alive, a few choice feathers plucked out, and the bird released.

The ancient Hawaiians made artistic clothing from a kind of felt called kapa, which was pounded from bark of trees. They loved the wonderful flowers of the islands and used them for leis and other fine designs.

STRANGERS

Into this civilization, another one, totally different, first intruded in 1778. British Captain James Cook and his men arrived in two boats which seemed big as islands to the Hawaiians. The islanders considered the men to be gods. Cook's party moved on, but the "gods" came back in 1779 to the archipelago they had named the Sandwich Islands.

In the spirit of "aloha," the Hawaiians treated strangers with courtesy and respect, but the Cook party repaid all their kindness with many injustices. The islanders were so attracted to nails and other iron objects among Cook's supplies that they began to steal. They had never known about metal and thought iron was precious. When Cook tried to punish the thieves, an angry crowd moved in and killed him. They had discovered he was a mere mortal and not a god.

Carvings of Hawaiian gods, City of Refuge

A MIGHTY KING

A young chief named Kamehameha had been very interested in the way Cook managed his ships and crew. Kamehameha began to apply some of the European organization and military techniques to his native island of Hawaii. On that island he was opposed by the great Chief Keoua. He lured Keoua to a ceremony in his honor. When the two chiefs met, dressed in their magnificent feather mantles, Keoua was killed. It is thought that Kamehameha believed he must sacrifice a great chief to the gods in order to succeed.

After securing the big island, Kamehameha conquered all of the other islands, one by one. In a battle on Maui there were so many bodies that Iao stream was said to be dammed by them.

By 1795 Kamehameha had the power to send a huge fleet of mighty war canoes carrying an army to conquer Oahu. He pushed the forces of Chief Kalanikupule over a precipice into Nuuanu Valley, where the bones of hundreds remained over the years.

Kamehameha had completed his conquest of the archipelago, and he became the first king to rule over all Hawaii. He moved his capital to Waikiki and received many foreign visitors. He asked some of these to remain and advise him.

A ROYAL LINE

His successor, King Kamehameha II ended the age-old practice of human sacrifice and other customs and improved the position of Hawaiian women. On a visit to England where he was very popular, he died of measles.

The third Kamehameha ruled for thirty years, becoming a constitutional monarch. The major powers recognized Hawaii as an independent country. The King coined the unusual motto of present day Hawaii: "Ua mau ke ea o ka aina i ka pono," which means, "The life of the land is perpetuated in righteousness."

The last descendants of the great Kamehameha were the fourth and fifth to bear that name, and the dynasty ended in 1872 after nearly eighty years. The legislature chose Prince Lunalilo king. When he died a year later, they picked David Kalakaua.

King Kalakaua became a great friend of the United States and was the first recognized ruler in history to come to U.S. shores. In fact, he died in San Francisco and was succeeded by his sister, Queen Liliuokalani, who was deposed in 1893.

After a short term as a republic under American Sanford Dole, Hawaii officially transferred authority to the United States and became a U.S. territory, with U.S. citizenship for all Hawaiians.

A MISSION TO HAWAII

One important event occurred much earlier. In 1820 a missionary ship, the

THAT'S CURIOUS:

One hundred people in one double hulled canoe! How did they live, crossing the thousands of miles of stormy ocean from their homes in the far South Pacific? How had they developed the remarkable seamanship to navigate and the know-how to store water and food and carry the right animals and seeds? The more we learn of such accomplishments, the more we must admit that the voyages of the Hawaiian pioneers rank among the greatest feats of exploration of all time!

Thaddeus, arrived on the island of Hawaii. Because of the great influence of this event, the Thaddeus is called the "Mayflower of Hawaii."

The missionaries brought not only their religion but also quickly began teaching new practical skills such as nursing, printing and dressmaking, along with the three R's. Within 40 years a large percentage of the people could read and write.

One writer declared that the missionaries, "...saved the Hawaiian race from such ravages of disease and ignorance as decimated the islanders of the South Pacific. They hitched Hawaii's wagon to a star."

A MODERN STATE

Territorial status brought rapid growth to pineapple, sugar and other industries. Ship traffic increased, and finally radio communication and air transportation drew the islands and the mainland together even more. Pan American began regular air passenger service to the islands in 1936, and Hawaii was no longer a remote land.

Because the Hawaiian islands were so important in any possible war, vast sums of money were spent on Pearl Harbor and other military installations.

In spite of this, a woeful lack of vigilance permitted the Japanese to bomb Pearl Harbor on December 7, 1941. The American fleet had been left like "sitting ducks" in the harbor, and in one blow, America's naval and air power was almost wiped out.

Recovery from the Japanese attack came with amazing speed. Because Hawaii was the key to the Pacific, the islands became the greatest war arsenal the world had ever known. Its people gave enthusiastic support to the war effort. More than 13,000 Hawaiians of Japanese ancestry fought in North Africa and Europe in a way that was said to be almost without equal. They received more decorations than any other similar group.

The Korean War again drew heavily on Hawaiian military personnel.

In 1950 Hawaiians were reminded of their volcanic origin by the eruption of Mauna Loa. During the period of 23 days, the amount of lava spewed out was estimated to be the greatest of modern times. Although Kilauea had not erupted in 100 years, abruptly in 1955 and again in 1959 it belched forth enough lava to cover six square miles.

Three years later came an event of even more lasting influence. Some Hawaiians had been hoping for statehood as early as the time of Kamehameha III. But it was not until March 12, 1959, that a proclamation of statehood became final with President Dwight Eisenhower's signature.

Hawaiian celebrations have always been notable events, but when the first fifty-star flag was raised over the capital on July 4, 1960, Hawaii really went wild.

The 1960's and 70's showed much growth and development and many changes. In 1974 George R. Ariyoshi became the first person of Japanese descent to become governor of a state.

THAT'S CURIOUS:
In spite of his treatment of them, the Hawaiians prepared Cook's body as they would other great chiefs—removing the flesh from the bones. The bones were returned to Cook's crew and buried at Kealakekua Bay on Hawaii Island.

When the new religion came to Hawaii, Chieftess Kapiolani embraced it so vigorously she defied the volcano goddess Pele by marching with her followers to the crater of Kilauea and eating the sacred ohelo berries. When no harm came to her, the missionaries were able to show how little the old religion could do.

In 1976 the state of Hawaii carried out an official project to determine how the Hawaiian ancestors were able to reach the islands. A twin-hulled, two-masted canoe called Hokule'a was built to match those of the early Polynesians. Without any modern navigation aids, the crew was able to sail the 3,000 miles to Tahiti in 35 days.

In even less time, the sturdy boat was sailed back to Hawaii. The duplication of the many ancestral voyages seemed to prove how the early settlers reached Hawaii.

On New Year's day, 1983, Kilauea's craters began to boil, and for most of that year "Madame Pele" forced out a fiery wake of lava, destroying homes, gardens and forests.

Always a magnet for tourists, Hawaii became a special attraction in 1984. The state held a year-long celebration of the 25th anniversary of statehood, culminating on August 21st with the kind of dancing, singing and partying for which the Hawaiian people have always been noted.

NOTABLE HAWAIIANS

King Kamehameha the Great does not receive the recognition and attention he deserves. Without question this unique ruler should be ranked among the world's leading conquerors and consolidators of empire—the "Napoleon of the Pacific." He needed only 28 years to complete an empire that covered the entire Hawaiian group.

His justice was stern and arbitrary, but he established laws against theft and murder and created a primitive court system. Although he retained beliefs of the traditional religion, he permitted his people to worship as they pleased. When Christian visitors urged him to accept Christianity, he suggested they throw themselves over a pali (cliff). If they could do this without harm, he would believe the power of their god and convert to their religion. Needless to say, no one did this.

Although his name means "The Lonely One" the first king was noted for mingling with his people and being aware of their needs. He was much admired in dealing with European and American representatives and for keeping foreign powers from seizing his kingdom. When he died in 1819, he was acclaimed as "...a father to the orphan, a savior to the old, a helper to the destitute, a farmer, fisherman and clothmaker to the needy."

One of his successors, King Kalakaua, declared, "In any land, in any age, he would have been a leader."

The great king's descendants were notable in many ways. Kamehameha III managed to keep his kingdom on the road to progress for more than 30 years. He, too, resisted the strong forces of the colonial powers who wanted to control the rich archipelago, and survived a British takeover by Lord George Paulet.

Among Hawaiian immigrants, one of the most famous was Elizabeth Sinclair. When she bought the entire island of

PEOPLES

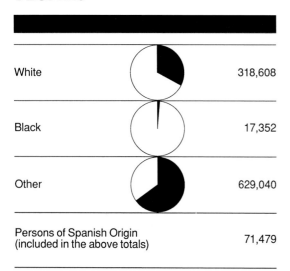

White	318,608
Black	17,352
Other	629,040
Persons of Spanish Origin (included in the above totals)	71,479

Niihau and a plantation on Kauai from King Kamehameha IV, she began a little kingdom of her own which is still owned and managed by her descendants, the Robinson family.

The Bishop family is another of the prominent Hawaiian clans. They amassed one of America's great fortunes. Other well known names are those of pineapple magnet James Dole, who devised the method of canning that favorite Hawaiian fruit, and his associate Harry Ginaca, also an inventor, who found a mechanical means of removing the shell and core from pineapples.

One of the best loved of all missionaries to Hawaii was Father Damien, who devoted sixteen years to the welfare of the sadly deprived lepers of Molokai until he himself died of the disease.

A WEALTH OF NATURE

Because of its isolation, Hawaii developed many plants and birds which were different or unique. These include the rare state bird, the Hawaiian goose called nene, which almost became extinct. Another nearly extinct bird is the 'o'o bird from which were plucked the distinctive yellow feathers for the feather robes worn only by royalty.

Another endangered species is the monk seal, found only in the Leeward Islands, now called the Hawaiian Islands National Wildlife Refuge. Here a home is preserved for birds by the millions, including the spectacular frigate bird, albatross, clownish booby birds, and delicate fairy terns.

The Hawaiian oceans are rich in natural wonders, including game fish of the greatest size, brilliant tropical fish and commercial fish of many types. The pink, gold and precious black corals are sought after all over the world. Harvesting of coral is being carefully controlled so that it will continue to grow.

With its billions of blossoms, Hawaii

THAT'S CURIOUS:
When one of the Japanese planes crash-landed on the private island of Niihau, its pilot became the only Japanese to land on Hawaiian soil during the invasion. Roaming about the island with a pistol, the pilot encountered Benihakaka Kanahele, strongman of the island, who could lift 150 pound kegs to each shoulder at one time. After being shot three times, Kanahele said, "Then I got mad." He grabbed the pilot and threw him against a wall, where he shot himself.

Volcanoes show their mighty force on the Island of Hawaii

probably has enough flowers to wrap a lei around the entire state. How could one small area possibly boast of 22,000 different kinds of orchids, just as one example? In addition to the plentiful flowers and plants, Hawaii also treasures some of the rarest. The silversword plant lifts its six foot spear only on Mt. Haleakala, and mokihana berries grow only on Kauai.

Other plants are common and useful. One of the most popular is the ti, from which comes a fermented beverage, a root product resembling candy, and leaves used for almost everything from table-cloths to "sleds" for sliding down the steep slopes on the grass.

Tara is as popular in Hawaii as potatoes in Ireland. Tara provides the famous poi, a kind of pudding.

Papaya, guavas, and of course pineapples are favorite fruits. The delicately flavored macadamia is one of the world's most expensive nut treats. Everywhere the flowers of blooming trees and wild and cultivated flowers help to make Hawaii the "Garden of the World."

USING THE WEALTH

Although pineapple is probably the

THAT'S CURIOUS:

The rulers of Hawaii have been known for their size and strength; Kamehameha the Great was said to have moved a stone weighing 4,500 pounds. His Queen Kaahumanu weighed 300 pounds. King Kaumualii's Queen Deborah also weighed 300 pounds and was six feet tall.

THE ECONOMY

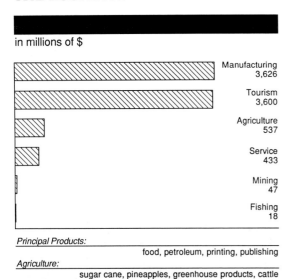

in millions of $

Manufacturing	3,626
Tourism	3,600
Agriculture	537
Service	433
Mining	47
Fishing	18

Principal Products:

food, petroleum, printing, publishing

Agriculture:

sugar cane, pineapples, greenhouse products, cattle

best-known product of Hawaii, sugarcane still brings in more income. Pineapple is not native to Hawaii but was brought there in 1886. The Dole Corporation, founded by James Dole, is now the world's largest fruit packer. The growing and harvesting of pineapple are among the most interesting processes in agriculture.

Most people would not think they eat much grass, but almost everyone does in one sense, for sugarcane is a type of grass. With their modern methods and machinery, Hawaiian cane growers achieve the world's greatest cane yields per acre.

Hawaii is the only state in the Union where conditions are right for growing coffee. Fresh flowers are another exotic crop, and Hilo is the center of America's orchid industry. Vegetables and melons add to the agricultural wealth.

Mighty Texas has the country's largest ranch, but tiny Hawaii has the second largest. The territory of the Parker ranch extends through an entire range of climate, from tropical rain forest to desert. Hawaii also has its cowboys, known as paniolos.

Manufacturing adds close to 4 billion dollars a year to the income of the state. The beautiful handmade products of the islands are becoming ever more popular.

GETTING AROUND

Many residents have become interested in reviving the old culture and traditions, and this is one of the unique attractions of the islands. One of these customs is the hula. It had almost died out but has made a strong comeback. Hula is a dance "language." The many dances tell all kinds of stories of history, tradition, romance and even jokes—simply by the moves and gestures.

Each of the islands has its own attractions.

Because Honolulu is so overcrowded, visitors are urged to sample the joys of the other islands, and many tourist facilities are being built in various areas.

MAUI

All Hawaii is noted for its great beauty, but Maui is considered special. Its west coastline is said to be one of the most beautiful anywhere.

There is also history. In Ioa Valley, Kamehameha I gained control of Maui in the shadow of a weird rock called Ioa Needle, which looms up from the valley floor to a spectacular height of 2,250 feet.

Even more spectacular is the world's largest extinct crater, now Haleakala National Park, with its unique silver-

Honolulu, with Diamond Head in the distance

sword plant and the spector of the Brocken—a rare shadow surrounded by a rainbow.

Maui also has its "capital." At Lahaina the ancient kings made their headquarters, and later the community became the "whaling capital of the world."

Lanainaluna High School claims to be the first high school west of the Rockies.

HAWAII

The "Big Island" of Hawaii gives its name to the whole chain. Hawaii is known as the Orchid Island, and Hilo as the City of Orchids.

The beaches, foliage and flowers, the ruins of ancient peoples, the little towns and friendly people all make the visitor realize that on the Big Island he really has found a tropical delight.

Dominating the scene are the two tremendous mountains, Mauna Loa and Mauna Kea. Another surprise—near the top of these there is snow and good skiing in the winter. There are frequent eruptions of Mauna Loa and of Kilauea, which is part of Mauna Loa. Kilauea's jets of lava sometimes reach 600 feet in height. Fortunately, the eruptions have caused relatively minor damage to people and property. The area is now known as Hawaii Volcanoes National Park.

There is a volcano museum, and Volcano House Hotel seems to perch on the edge of destruction. Here the lucky visitor might see the Rose Mantle, a rarely viewed shaft of pink sunlight which seems to race down the slope.

Mauna Kea forms the highest point in the state. Fortunately, it has not erupted in recent times.

The monument to Captain James Cook at Kealakekua Bay has sunken below the shoreline, but it may still be seen.

Near Kalapana visitors find a beach that contradicts all of their visions of sparkling white sand. This beach takes its black color from the particles of crushed lava washing up on shore, in marked contrast to the white foam.

One of the most unusual national parks is the City of Refuge at Honaunau. This restored 12th century temple once shielded lawbreakers and wartime refugees.

KAUAI AND NIIHAU

Each of the islands has its own most dazzling sight. On Kauai it is Waimea Canyon. Its tremendous depths and the rainbow of its colored walls make it a near rival of Arizona's Grand Canyon.

Kauai has its dramatic history, also. The old Russian fort built by Dr. George Scheffer may still be seen. Apparently, Dr. Scheffer had hoped to make this part of Hawaii a Russian territory, but he was foiled by King Kaumualii, who drove him away.

Standing beside the Wailua River, the temple of Holo-Holo-Ku Heiau recalls the war god Ku. He supposedly required a human sacrifice before each battle, and the sacrificial stone can still be seen.

At Waipahee Falls, visitors can try the popular slide down the slippery curves of a partial lava tube.

MORE ISLANDS

Molokai has kept some of the flavor of earlier days, and native Hawaiians are given incentives to homestead there.

At Kalaupapa on Molokai is a monument dedicated to devoted Father Damien, who served the leper colony there.

On the Pineapple Island of Lanai business is more important than tourism. Many improvements have been made by the island's owner, the Dole Corporation.

Kaunolu, Lanai, was known as the summer home of Kamehameha the Great, but it is now a ghost town. As a part of soldierly discipline the king made his soldiers dive into the sea from a rock sixty feet above the waters.

Kahoolawe Island has had a controversial past as a World War II bomber practice target. Other smaller islands stretch out to the west in a diminishing chain.

OAHU

Much of the state's most populated island, Oahu, can be seen from the spectacular heights of Nuuanu Pali (cliff). Kamehameha's army drove the defenders to death over the great cliff; the view must be considered among the most spectacular of all.

Many of the Oahu defenders' bones were left to bleach below the cliff, and some may still be found there, but not far away the remains of more than 17,000 other soldiers are found in famed Na-

THAT'S CURIOUS:

Offshore of Kauai the private island of Niihau is something of an island of mystery, where visitors may go only with permission of the Robinson family proprietors. The Robinsons have tried to keep the island as much as possible like early Hawaii.

tional Memorial Cemetery in Puowaina Crater's Hill of Sacrifice.

Oahu's many beaches combine to make the island one of the choicest spots for ocean sports, such as surfing, which may have originated in Hawaii. Canoe racing is another popular sport from ancient times. It is a favorite activity of women, who can paddle as much as forty miles in seven hours.

Other ocean pleasures are tours of the colorful coral gardens of Kaneoho Bay and hukilau fishing, in which visitors may help fishermen pull in their nets.

Near Honolulu is Pearl Harbor, America's premiere naval installation. Here the battleship Arizona, sunk by the Japanese in their Pearl Harbor attack, has been turned into a memorial to those who died in that tragic attack.

HONOLULU

The greatest tourist magnet of all is the capital city, home to more than 80 percent of the state's population.

Here visitors find the country's only royal palace and throne room, along with many other memories of Hawaii's past.

At Iolani Palace the last Queen, Liliuokalani, ruled and was later held prisoner. It was there as a young princess that she composed the lovely "Aloha Oe," a song known round the world.

Here is "the most unusual of all our capitols," a building designed to fit its tropical setting, as if floating in a pond.

Famed museums of the city include the Honolulu Academy of Arts, specializing in the art of the Pacific regions, the Bishop Museum, which displays much of the remains of the native culture, and the Queen Emma Museum in the summer palace of that queen.

One of the greatest displays of rare tropical plants, including the famed orchid greenhouse, may be found in Foster Botanic Garden, and Honolulu Zoo houses a similarly outstanding collection devoted to tropical fauna.

Waikiki Beach has become so famed and so popular that the many hotels and condominiums seem to overwhelm the narrow strip of land, but familiar Diamond Head landmark can still be seen, beckoning visitors to such delights as the annual Aloha Week festival of early Hawaii, the Hula Festival in Kapiolani Park, and other annual events of a bewildering variety—all of which help to make Hawaii an exotic paradise for visitors from every part of the world.

COMPAC-FACS

HAWAII
The Aloha State

HISTORY
Statehood: August 21, 1959
Admitted as: 50th state
Capital: Honolulu, named capital in 1804
OFFICIAL SYMBOLS
Motto: The life of the land is perpetuated in righteousness (Ua man ke ea ka aini i ka pono)
Marine Animal: Humpback whale
Bird: Hawaiian goose (Nene)
Flower: Hibiscus
Tree: Candlenut (Kukui)
Song: "Hawaii Ponoi" by King Kalakaua, music by Henry Berger
Official Languages: English and Hawaiian
GEO-FACS
Area: 6,425 sq. mi.
Rank in Area: 47th
Length (n/s): Extends across Pacific Ocean for 1,600 mi., se to nw
Width (e/w): 93 mi., Island of Hawaii
Major Islands: Hawaii, Maui, Oahu, Kauai, Molokai
Geographic Center: Off Maui at 20 degrees 15' N, 156 degrees 20' W
Highest Point: 13,796 ft., Mauna Kea, Island of Hawaii

The unique capitol, Honolulu

Lowest Point: Sea level (Pacific Ocean)
Mean Elevation: 3,030 ft.
Inland Water: 25 sq. mi.
Rivers: Waimea; many small streams and
waterfalls
Temperature, Extreme Range: 88 degrees
Number of Counties: 4
Coastline: 750 mi.
Shoreline: 1,052 mi.
Rainfall (annual): 22.9 in.
POPULATION
Total: 1,114,469 (1984/85 estimate)
Rank: 39th
Density: 150.1 persons per sq. mi.
Per Cent Urban: 86.5 percent
Principal Cities: Honolulu, 365,048; Ewa, 190,037;
Koolaupoko, 109,337; Wahiawa, 41,562; Hilo,
37,017; Waianae, 32,810
EDUCATION
Schools: 232 elementary and secondary
Higher: 12
VITAL STATISTICS
Births (1980-82): 60,000
Deaths (1980-83): 16,000
Hospitals: 19

Drinking Age: 18
INTERESTING PEOPLE
Kamehameha the Great, Queen Liliuokalani,
Bernice Pauahi Bishop, Father Joseph Damien,
Duke Kahanamoku, Sanford B. Dole
WHEN DID IT HAPPEN?
400 (approx): Migration begins
1778: Cook party, first European contact
1795: Kamehameha I becomes King
1797: Civil rights protection begins with Law of
Splintered Paddle
1810: Kamehameha completes conquests
1819: Kamehameha I dies
1820: American missionaries begin work in Hawaii
1843: General recognition of Hawaii as
independent nation
1893: Queen Liliuokalani's overthrow ends
monarchy
1898: United States is given control
1927: Hawaii and mainland first linked by air
1936: Regular air passenger service begins
1941: Japan attacks Pearl Harbor
1959: Hawaii becomes the 50th state
1976: Pioneer Polynesian voyages recreated
1984: 25th anniversary of statehood celebrated

OREGON

FASCINATING OREGON

Oregon is known for its many contrasts—from the dry east to the very wet west, from the wonderful coastline to the deepest canyon. It has the biggest fault, the deepest lake and the largest geyser. It can boast the biggest dunes, the greatest stands of timber and the country's only "nickel." It gave its name to the country's greatest route of migration. Although it is on the west coast, it can be said to be the center of the nation.

THE FACE OF OREGON

If the farthest tips of Alaska, Hawaii, American Samoa and Maine are taken into account, the exact center of the United States would be somewhere on the China Cap Mountain in eastern Oregon.

The land today has been shaped by the gigantic forces of nature, covered with shallow seas and drained several times, overwhelmed by the world's greatest coverings of lava, and drastically altered by vast glaciers.

The "earthquake" fault called Abert Rim, in Lake County, is 2,000 feet high and 30 miles long. It is said to be the largest of its kind on the continent.

Some of the forces beneath the earth can still be seen in the smoke that sometimes puffs from Mt. Hood. Some experts are worried that volcanic action might begin again. Underground action is demonstrated also in the many hot springs, including the geyser at Lakeview. This is considered to have the greatest flow of any continuously flowing geyser.

Most spectacular feature of Oregon is its wonderful coastline of almost 300 miles. The world's highest sand dunes, south of the Umpqua River, vie for principal attraction with the great rocks which loom out of the ocean. Haystack Rock on Cannon Beach is the third largest of its kind in the world.

Oregon claims its share of the West's greatest river—the Columbia. An amusing legend says that the river was carved by Paul Bunyan's blue ox Babe, pulling a giant plow. Greatest tributary of the Columbia, the Snake, has gouged out the deepest canyon on the continent—nearly a thousand feet deeper than the Grand Canyon of the Colorado.

The second great river of Oregon is the Willamette.

Crater Lake is considered one of the world's most beautiful. It is the deepest lake in the United States, at 1,996 feet.

Crater Lake was created when ancient Mt. Mazama blew up. Most of the mountain simply disappeared, leaving a bowl-shaped ledge around a huge crater. Over the centuries, water gathered in the crater to form the jewel-like lake.

The Coast Range looms on the west. Somewhat inland, the Cascade Range is

THAT'S CURIOUS:
When the tide comes in at Whaleshead Beach, the water spouts through a rock formation like the spout of a great whale.

capped by the nearly perfect cone of Mt. Hood. Far to the east are the Wallowa and Blue Mountains.

Oregon climate is mild and damp on the west, dry on the east. Snow falls on the heights of Mt. Hood, keeping its nine glaciers well fed.

STIRRINGS

Did the ancient Mayans of Central America make their way as far north as Oregon? Some experts believe a stone tomb found near Lexington proves there were Mayans in the region. Earlier people may have been present in Oregon for 20,000 or 30,000 years. Some of the best evidence of early peoples is found in the picture writings and carvings they placed on rocks of cliffs, such as those at Picture Gorge and Condon Day State Park.

When European explorers first came in, there were very many Indian groups in Oregon. The Chinook tribe, alone, had thirty-six branches. This group and others on the west coast lived very comfortable lives due to the wealth of salmon fishing. They hollowed huge canoes out of cedar trees and decorated some with beautifully carved and painted designs. Their large lodges were formed of cedar plank.

Indians of the east lived more like those of the great plains. In the early 1500's, the eastern Indians found a strange new animal. The horse had been introduced by the Spanish explorers. Indians bought or stole enough horses so that they quickly became of great value to Indians of the plains.

Opposite, Portland by USGA/NHAP/EROS

Indians of eastern Oregon became skilled and daring horsemen. Hunting and much of other life centered around horses and horsemanship. They became known as the Horse Indians.

Perhaps the first Europeans to see Oregon were Bartolome Ferrello and his group. Then in 1603, Martin d'Augilar did sight and name a now familiar point, Cape Blanco. Over 150 years later, Captain James Cook sailed by. Then in 1792, American Captain Robert Gray discovered the great Columbia River, entered its treacherous mouth and sailed upriver about fifteen miles to trade with the Indians. He bought two large salmon for a single nail.

The Indians called the Columbia River the Ouragon; before long the name was given to the whole region.

EARLY GROWTH

American traders were common on the west coast by 1800, but no overland party had arrived in Oregon until Meriwether Lewis and William Clark brought their doughty party to the mouth of the Columbia after terrible hardships in crossing the entire west and north. For winter quarters of 1805/06, they built Fort Clatsop on Young's Bay. Their journey helped to secure the entire region as U.S. territory.

In 1811 the fur trading company of John Jacob Astor established Astoria, first permanent European settlement in Oregon. Within six months, they had traded for 1,500 fine fur pelts, but they soon sold out to the giant Hudson's Bay Company. Under that country's local leader, Dr. John McLoughlin, they controlled the entire Northwest.

In 1834 the Rev. Jason Lee and his nephew, Daniel, set up a mission to the Indians at Salem. They came in response to a group of Indians who suffered great hardships when they traveled to St. Louis to ask for missionaries.

Only a few settlers came in, and the U.S. government took little interest in a region they thought was a desert. Then in 1842, a thousand people in one group came across the overland route. When they reached the rapids of the Columbia, they were on the point of starving. They were saved and helped to settle by Dr. McLoughlin, although he knew the settlement would probably mean his loss of the region.

Just before most of the newcomers arrived, the handful of settlers already at Champoeg had voted to be part of the U.S., and they set up a primitive government. As the thousands came in, the region began to prosper, and Oregon City was settled.

The large number of U.S. settlers helped the U.S. establish its claim to the region, and in 1846, the British gave up their claims. Dr. McLoughlin resigned and moved to Oregon City. The doctor had kept peace in the region, but the Indians now saw they would soon be overwhelmed by the newcomers. They went to war, but of course the settler tide eventually became too much for them, just as the Indians feared.

Opposite, beautiful, strange, deep—Crater Lake

MIDDLE PERIOD

The gold seekers of California to the south provided a fine market for the farm products of Oregon, and later Oregon had its own small gold rush around Jacksonville. Population skyrocketed, and Oregon Territory was created in 1853. Again, fearing the taking of their land, the Indians went on the warpath in a conflict known as the Rogue River War of 1855-1856.

By this time, the country to the east was enveloped in the struggle for and against slavery. Those for slavery did not want a new free state and kept Oregon from statehood as long as possible. However, on February 14, 1859, Oregon's admission placed the thirty-third star on the nation's flag. Oregon was now a state.

In the election of 1860, Oregon's critical vote helped send Abraham Lincoln to the presidency. This came about mainly through the efforts of Edward Dickinson Baker, who became one of Oregon's first two U.S. Senators.

During the Civil War, Baker gave up his Senate seat to join the army and became one of the first Union officers to be killed. The Civil War did not reach Oregon, but another Indian conflict, called the Modoc War, disturbed the peace.

It was not until 1883 that travelers could reach Oregon directly by rail from the East, and getting to Oregon became less difficult.

THAT'S CURIOUS:

After the first group, thousands more wagons rolled across the route which came to be known as the Oregon Trail—altogether one of the world's greatest migrations. The squeaks of the wagon wheels echoed across the countryside. The Indians thought the sound they made was like their words "chik-chik-chaile-kikash." That became the Indian name for wagon.

A MODERN STATE

In the early 1900's, Oregon was one of the pioneer states in providing more input by the people in elections. These steps included initiative, referendum and recall, primaries for presidential preference, and voting rights for women. These advantages became known as the "Oregon System" of government and have been taken up in other states.

In 1905 the Lewis and Clark Centennial Exposition was the first world's fair ever held on the west coast.

Oregon sent the first fully mobilized National Guard regiment into World War I service, and the state's shipyards built many needed vessels.

From 1933 through 1938, one of the great public works programs was the building of Bonneville Dam across the Columbia River. Salmon lovers were relieved to find that the "fish ladders" really provided a way for the great fish to swim upstream to lay their eggs.

Again in World War II, the Oregon National Guard was the first unit ready for the Pacific after Pearl Harbor. Again, too, the shipyards turned out unbelievable numbers of ships, totalling almost 1,200.

In 1960's, a storm named Frieda did more damage in Oregon than any other natural force known until then; some gusts reached 170 m.p.h.

During the 1970's, Oregon took pioneering steps in conservation. Non-returnable beverage containers were banned along with fluorocarbon aerosol cans. These and other conservation measures were widely copied.

Also in that decade, the people of Oregon felt that the state could not support more residents, and for the first time settlement was discouraged. Despite this, in the period from 1970 through 1983, the population grew by more than half a million. In 1983 the population stood at 2,662,000.

In 1985 the strange cult founded in Oregon by the Bhagwan Shree Rajneesh collapsed after the founder left the state and pleaded guilty to federal immigration fraud charges.

PERSONALITIES

One of the most remarkable of all Americans is scarcely known outside the Northwest. Dr. John McLoughlin ruled the region with an iron hand, but he also was one of the most considerate and kindly men. The Indians almost worshipped him. When the first large group of settlers arrived suffering much hardship, McLoughlin sent word, "...take what you need. Those who can pay may do so. Those who cannot must not be left to suffer...All can be paid at our house in Oregon City when your crops come in."

Ironically, it was the settlement of Oregon that forced McLoughlin out of his position when the British gave up their hold. He moved to Oregon City, where he was supposed to own property. The U.S.

THAT'S CURIOUS:

World War II came to continental U.S. shores only a few times with minor effect. On June 21, 1942, a Japanese submarine lobbed some shells at Fort Stevens. This brought the war home directly to the American people in a way not realized before.

government approved all the property claims except those of the generous doctor. He had given up his British citizenship, and the U.S. would not make him an American citizen.

This wise, brilliant and honorable man died, tired, old and without honor for his good deeds and accomplishments. However, he now is one of the two Oregon men in the National Hall of Fame in Washington.

The Rev. Jason Lee is the other Oregonian honored in the National Hall of Fame. At his pioneer mission in the Willamette Valley, he and his nephew, Daniel, taught and preached about Christianity. Like Dr. McLoughlin, Jason Lee suffered many disappointments. He lost two beloved wives and was removed from his mission post. However, he is regarded as a leading educator and as founder both of Willamette University and the capital city of Salem.

Ewing Young and Joe Gale were other interesting pioneers. Young led the first cattle drive from California to Oregon. After much hardship, he brought back the desperately needed herd of 600 animals. Before he died, Young had become one of the wealthiest men of the area.

Joe Gale made up his mind that ships could be built from the wonderful timbers of the region. Everything needed had to be cut and made by hand, even the nails. In June, 1842, they launched the "Star of

PEOPLES

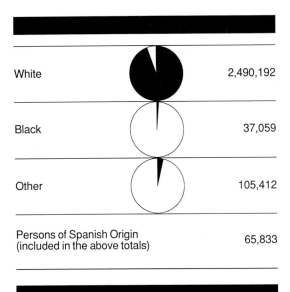

White	2,490,192
Black	37,059
Other	105,412
Persons of Spanish Origin (included in the above totals)	65,833

Oregon," the first ship ever built in the state.

The Oregon region produced one of the greatest civil and military leaders of America. However, Chief Joseph the Younger did not lead American troops. He was Chief of the Nez Perce tribe of Indians. Time after time the government promised rights to the Indians of eastern Oregon, Washington and western Idaho. Each time the Indian rights were trampled under foot. Finally Joseph's people decided to leave their lands and go to Canada, where they hoped to live in

THAT'S CURIOUS:
Nathaniel Wyeth and Dr. McLoughlin were talking about the future of Oregon: "How can they (settlers) get here, Mr. Wyeth? Even India is not so far. Oregon is the very end of the world...shut off by rock-ribbed mountains, deserts, savages, the ocean, how can they get here?" Answered Wyeth: "Overland from the United States." Dr. McLoughlin laughed, "When you have leveled the mountains, cultivated the desert, annihilated distance, then and not before." How surprised the good doctor would be today!

peace. Instead, they were forced to fight a series of battles across country until they were finally defeated in Montana.

Joseph had never wanted to battle the American forces. As he surrendered, the great chief said, "I am tired of fighting. My people ask me for food, and I have none to give. It is cold, and we have no blankets, no wood. My people are starving to death. Where is my little daughter? I do not know. Perhaps even now, she is freezing to death. Hear me, my chiefs, I have fought; but from where the sun now stands, Joseph will fight no more." With his blanket covering his face, he surrendered to the American army.

One of Oregon's best-known figures in the arts is classical composer Ernest Block, who wrote many works at his home near Agate Beach. Sculptor Ralph Stackpole and cartoonist Homer Davenport, authors Edwin Markham and Frederic Homer Balch all were Oregonians.

The writings of famed naturalists John Muir and David Douglas did much to bring favorable attention to the state and its natural resources.

A WEALTH OF NATURE

The greatest forests of virgin timber in the world enrich Oregon. Much of the timber is douglas fir, with the number two tree ponderosa pine. These vast timberlands would more than cover all of New England. In early days, the timberlands seemed so huge that no one thought about conserving them. Billions of board feet went up in smoke to clear the land, or through carelessness. Now, however, the value of this natural treasure is realized; hundreds of thousands of acres are planted every year, and new growth exceeds by several billion board feet the huge amount cut annually.

In spite of this care, in 1933 one of the worst forest fires ever in the U.S. destroyed enough timber to have constructed 5,000,000 houses.

Even redwood trees are found in Oregon although they are not usually thought of as growing so far north. There are three splendid groves.

Among living creatures, few are as useful as the mighty salmon. Most salmon migrate from their hatching place to the sea and struggle back to the birthplace to lay their eggs. Even a variety of trout is migratory; this is the seagoing steelhead. However, the Kokonee salmon cannot migrate, being landlocked. Wonderful crabs and oysters and deep sea fishing add to Oregon's ocean resources.

Animal life ranges from the Rocky Mountain elk to the ocean's great herds of seals. The only U.S. mainland seal rookery is at Sea Lion Point. At Otter Crescent, the unusual white sea lions are found, along with sea turkeys.

Although they do not have the commercial importance they once had, beaver may still be found. Fortunately, the charming sea otter has made a comeback from near extinction.

During migrations, the Tule Lake

THAT'S CURIOUS:
The madrona tree has the strange habit of shedding its bark as well as its leaves. Other unusual flora include the giant cobra lily, which captures insects with its leaves, and devours them.

Hecata Head, Oregon

National Wildlife Refuge displays the greatest concentration of waterfowl on the continent.

With a nickname of the Agate State, Oregon not surprisingly has an almost infinite variety of agates and other semiprecious stones for the pursuit of rock hounds.

Other minerals are plentiful, including much of the country's nickel. Bauxite for aluminum may exceed a hundred million short tons. There are also vast coal reserves.

Water resources are plentiful on the west and short on the east. The Columbia River has the second largest flow in the country. Underground water, hot springs and mineral springs add to the supply. Mountain runoff provides some of the purest water anywhere.

USING THE WEALTH

Oregon has led the nation in production of lumber for nearly fifty years. Production now greatly surpasses ten billion board feet a year. Forest products from Oregon have a value of $3.5 billion per year. Nearly three-fourths of the nation's plywood is produced in Oregon. Other forms of lumber, shingles, shakes, hardboard, chipboard, insulation board, paper board, paper and wood pulp all pour from the state's processing plants.

New uses for wood regularly add to the value of this tremendous natural resource.

After manufacturing, agriculture is the second greatest source of income for Oregon. Nuts and fruits and seeds are important; most bent grass seed comes

THE ECONOMY

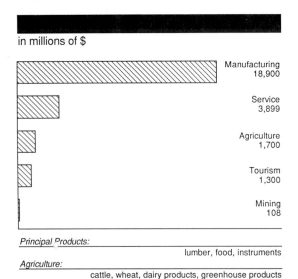

in millions of $

Manufacturing	18,900
Service	3,899
Agriculture	1,700
Tourism	1,300
Mining	108

Principal Products:
lumber, food, instruments

Agriculture:
cattle, wheat, dairy products, greenhouse products

from Oregon. Fruit growing is centered in the Hood River region. The state produces more Easter lily bulbs than any other.

In the mineral field, Oregon is the only state now producing nickel and one of the few states producing mercury ore. Reactive metals, whose use is often secret, are produced in Oregon, where processes for using these metals were discovered. These include titanium, hafnium and zirconium.

With the supply of non-renewable fuels rapidly diminishing around the world, water power becomes ever more valuable. Although Oregon ranks third in producing hydroelectric power, less than a fourth of the potential is being used.

Power from John Day Dam on the Columbia ranks second in the U.S. in capacity to produce hydroelectric power. Owyhee Lake on the Owyhee River provides valuable irrigation water to dry areas.

In industry, food processing ranks second to forest products. Food processors work with more than forty different Oregon crops. Salem ranks second in the U.S. in processing fruits and vegetables.

Oregon also has a notable dairy industry, including the world's largest cheese factory.

Portland has a flourishing electronics industry.

The ruts of the Oregon Trail may still be seen in some places, but they have been replaced by superhighways which would amaze old Dr. McLoughlin. Sailboats, steamboats and diesels have all had their place in carrying traffic on the Columbia and Willamette rivers. Portland is the only freshwater port on the U.S. Pacific coast. Much of the wheat sent by America to the Orient goes out from there. Coos Bay claims to be the greatest lumbering port in the world.

Railroads came slowly and not as extensively as in some other states. Some communities even built their own spur railroads in order to have national railroad service reach them.

GETTING AROUND

One of the joys of getting around in Oregon is its spectacular coastline. Only a few miles are not in the public domain,

Opposite, rain forest

THAT'S CURIOUS:

Even pine cones bring income to the state. Any number of students and other part-time workers have earned money by picking up the cones for seed.

so that visitors have the use of most of this natural treasure. Recreational opportunities are almost endless, including boating, fishing, clamming and just plain beachcombing. Occasionally a surprised tourist may find a glass float from a Japanese fishing boat after the sphere has floated across much of the Pacific.

Scenic highway 101 passes near dozens of attractive coves, gleaming beaches and other ocean landmarks. Astoria is the oldest city in the coastal states to be founded by Americans. Here the lofty Astor Memorial Column tells this and other facts of history in the area.

Restored Fort Stevens has its own history, as the only actual fortification on the Oregon coast. Another even more historic site is Fort Clatsop, now a national memorial. It was rebuilt in memory of the Lewis and Clark party who first built it for winter quarters at the farthest point of their exploration.

Three-hundred-foot-high Haystack Rock is one of the largest on the coast; Arch Rock at Rockaway is another interesting formation.

North of Newport, the coast has been described as "one of the most spectacular in the world." Its wildlife includes the famous white sea lions and sea turkeys. Agate Beach provides rock hounds with the intriguing prospect of finding their treasured mineral.

Portland grew quickly after it was founded in 1842. Its Rose Festival is one of the great floral fetes anywhere. The International Rose Test Gardens add even more to the community's reputation as the City of Roses.

Not to be outdone by roses, the American Rhododendron Society Test Garden boasts of thirty-five hundred rhododendron plants. Hoyt Arboretum has the largest collection of needle-foliage trees in the country.

Portland's deepwater port is the leading grain terminal west of the Mississippi and only lags behind Boston in wool shipments. Mount Tabor and Rocky Butte make Portland the only mainland community with two volcanoes within its city limits.

Beyond the city on clear days there is a dramatic view of the slender spire of beautiful Mount Hood. Striking Timberline Lodge is a center for sports and other activities around and on the mountain. Hikers now have a choice of many different routes to the summit.

Founded in 1812, the town of Salem, named state capital in 1852, was the first community in the Willamette Valley. One of the most modern of all state capitols was built at Salem after a 1935 fire destroyed the previous one. The gold-leaf covered statue of the Pioneer weighs eight and a half tons. The building displays some of the nation's finest capitol murals.

On the site of an ancient Indian village, Dr. John McLoughlin founded Oregon City in 1825. There he retired and died. His house at Oregon City has

---

THAT'S CURIOUS:
One of the more unusual "finds" of beachcombers dates back to the days of Spanish galleons. Over 200 years ago, one of those proud ships was wrecked near Manzanita. The cargo of beeswax it carried spilled out. Lumps of this wax are still being found on the shore.

The view from Crown Point looking up the Columbia River is one of the best known in the United States

been named a National Historic Site.

The gorge of the Columbia River is one of the grandest and most varied anywhere, with its great dams, mountain vistas and scenic banks, down which pour many waterfalls.

One of the best known views anywhere is that from Vista House, overlooking the Columbia. Here visitors are reminded of the historic nature of the scene. They can picture the flatboats of the pioneers or the sleek canoes of traders. However, dams and other "improvements" have made great changes. Beautiful Celilo Falls now lies beneath dammed-up waters, and the native fishermen no longer poise picturesquely waiting for salmon.

At Fort Dalles there is a museum with a fine collection of the region's pioneer past. Here too is the monument known as "The End of the Trail."

Eastern Oregon is renowned for the remains of ancient creatures found near the appropriately named town of Fossil. Crowds of visitors flock to the annual Pendleton Roundup, one of the country's best rodeos. Here visitors also find the beauty of Wallowa Lake in the territory of the Chiefs Joseph. The gorge of the Snake River is the deepest natural cut on the continent, called Hell's Canyon.

In the semi-desert east, wild horses still thrive, and there are many scenic wonders.

Perhaps the greatest wonder of the state is Crater Lake, said by many to be the world's most beautiful. Another spectacular sight is Oregon Caves National Monument.

The unusual capitol

COMPAC-FACS

OREGON
The Beaver State

HISTORY
Statehood: February 14, 1859
Admitted as: 33rd state
Capital: Salem, named as capital in 1852
OFFICIAL SYMBOLS
Motto: "The Union"
Animal: Beaver
Bird: Western meadowlark
Fish: Chinook salmon
Insect: Swallowtail butterfly
Flower: Oregon grape
Tree: Douglas fir
Song: "Oregon, My Oregon"
GEO-FACS
Area: 97,073 sq. mi.
Rank in Area: 10th
Length (n/s): 290 mi.
Width (e/w): 375 mi.

Geographic Center: In Crook County, 25 mi. sse of Prineville
Highest Point: 11,239 ft. (Mt. Hood)
Lowest Point: Sea level (Pacific Ocean)
Mean Elevation: 3,300 ft.
Temperature, Extreme Range: 173 degrees
Number of Counties: 36
Water Area: 889 sq. mi.
Coastline: 296 mi.
POPULATION
Total: 2,674,000 (1984)
Rank: 30th
Density: 28 persons per sq. mi.
Principal Cities: Portland, 366,383; Eugene, 105,624; Salem, 89,233; Springfield, 41,621; Medford, 39,603; Gresham, 33,005 Corvallis, 20,960
EDUCATION
Schools: 1,471 elementary and secondary
Higher: 45
VITAL STATISTICS
Births (1980/83): 137,000
Deaths (1980/83): 71,000
Hospitals: 83
Drinking Age: 21
INTERESTING PEOPLE
Dr. John McLoughlin, Chiefs Joseph I and II, Linus Pauling, Ernest Block, Alberto Salazar, Jason Lee, Ewing Young, Joe Gale, Edwin Markham, Frederic Homer Balch
WHEN DID IT HAPPEN?
1603: Cape Blanco named
1775: Columbia River discovered
1778: Exploration of James Cook
1792: Grey explores the Columbia River
1805: Lewis and Clark arrive
1824: Dr. John McLoughlin begins "reign"
1846: American territory established
1859: Statehood achieved
1877: War with Nez Perce
1883: Railroad arrives
1905: Portland holds Lewis and Clark Exposition
1935: Fire claims state capitol
1962: Storm Frieda devastates
1972: State pioneers in conservation measures
1983: Population reaches 2,662,000
1985: Bhagwan Shree Rajneesh leaves

WASHINGTON

FASCINATING WASHINGTON

Washington is a state where the largest city was located by a clothesline, where by land a part of the state can only be reached through Canada, where a black pioneer settler changed the course of U.S. history, where some of the native peoples tried to give away everything they owned.

The smallest of the 48 states west of Iowa, Washington has some of the greatest variety of geography, history and economics.

THE FACE OF WASHINGTON

In ancient times, much of present Washington was covered by shallow seas. The Olympic Mountains were distant islands, and the Blue Mountains were an ocean headland, now far inland. As the land rose and fell, the seas surged in and drained away many times.

Ancient volcanoes also changed the face of the land. Nearly 200,000 square miles were covered with lava, some layers nearly a mile thick. The great Cascade Mountains, Rainier, Baker, Adams, Glacier Peak and St. Helens were built by volcanic action.

Much later came the huge glaciers, covering northern Washington four different times. The last glacier left sand and gravel and rich soil, carved valleys and gouged out major lakes. When the ice melted, the ancestral Columbia River had such a flow of water that it may have been the world's greatest river. It carved out the Grand Coulee and made now Dry Falls the world's mightiest waterfall.

Today, Washington has a "split personality." West of the Cascades lie the rainy, green lands; to the east is the generally dry Columbia Plateau. The Blue Mountains loom on the east. The dramatic Olympic Mountains and the Willapa Hills dominate the far west, along with the drowned valley of Puget Sound.

Greatest river of the west is the mighty Columbia, with five times the flow of the Colorado River. Other major rivers are the Spokane, Pend Oreille, Skagit and Yakima, with a small portion of the Snake.

The world's second largest rock, Beacon Rock, rises a spectacular 900 feet from the ocean near Skamania. Z Canyon is so narrow and deep that from the bottom stars can be seen in daylight. No explanations have been found for the green oasis in the desert floor near Spokane nor for the strange bumps on the prairie near Tenino.

Western Washington boasts of its cool summers and mild winters. Eastern Washington has greater temperature extremes. One of the most interesting phases of its weather is the chinook wind, bringing abrupt changes from winter to near summer temperatures.

THAT'S CURIOUS:

Manmade geography in Washington also has some interesting twists. Point Roberts is the tip of a peninsula jutting out of the British Columbian coast. It is part of Washington, but it cannot be reached by land from the rest of the state.

STIRRINGS

Although Washington has been occupied by humans for perhaps 30,000 years, not too much is known about the earliest peoples. Basketmakers of perhaps 3000 B.C. left picture writings and carvings on rocks and canyons. They also left some carved stone images.

The Indians known to western explorers were divided into two groups—Canoe Indians of the west and Horse Indians of the east. They were quite different in the way they lived. Horse Indians moved about, living in portable lodges. Canoe Indians sometimes built permanent lodges with as many as 40 apartments.

Western Indians took their name from the canoes dug out of tree trunks, sometimes sixty feet long. Some of these are still in use after a hundred years. There were three classes, nobility, middle class and slaves. The Canoe Indians were a generally peaceful people who suffered from raids by the Haida tribes from present Canada.

Horse Indians quickly took over the raising of horses after the Spanish brought them in. They developed their own horse breeds, including the unique spotted appaloosa ponies.

All the Indians believed in spirits and that each person has his own guiding spirit. The shamans or medicine men were the spiritual leaders.

The total number of main tribal groups in what is now Washington probably did not exceed thirty-six.

GREAT EXPLORATIONS

Present Washington first came into Western annals in 1774 when the coast was spotted by Juan Perez. In 1775 Bruno Heceta and Juan de Bodega Y Quadra came on shore on the Olympic coast. In 1778 Captain James Cook named Cape Flattery, and Captain James Meares named a great mountain in honor of the Greek Mount Olympus.

In 1792 major tribal leader Chief Kitsap and his people watched in awe as a great white spirit approached. This was the ship of the English Captain George Vancouver, exploring the region he named for his friend Peter Puget. That same year found Captain Robert Gray making the most important discovery for the U.S.—the great river of the West—the Columbia.

One of the most notable explorations of all times brought the party of Meriwether Lewis and William Clark over the western mountains and down the Columbia, reaching the sea in 1805.

After being almost starved and enduring terrible hardship, the explorers relished the abundance of the west coast.

Opposite, Seattle

THAT'S CURIOUS:

All the Washington tribes observed the custom of the potlach. This strange custom consisted of elaborate parties where the host or hostess gained greater prestige the more of his possessions he presented to the guests as gifts. Some wealthy Indians reduced themselves to poverty in this way. Another peculiar custom was the use of cradle boards. These were strapped to the head to flatten it, and some of the tribes believed a flat head was a mark of beauty.

Because Lewis and Clark were so courteous to the Indians and treated their illnesses, the Nez Perce tribe remained friendly to the U.S. for over 60 years.

RULER OF THE KINGDOM OF FUR

British explorer David Thompson set up the first trading post in Washington, Spokane House, in 1810. The American Astor Company did substantial trading, setting up at Fort Okonagon the first settlement in the area to fly the American flag. Not long after, they sold out to what became the huge Hudson's Bay Company. Their headquarters at Fort Vancouver became the first permanent European settlement in Washington. They sent a physician, Dr. John McLoughlin, to manage the post. Dr. McLoughlin's fur trading covered the whole vast region.

He created a surprising civilization in the wilderness. Bagpipers sounded the arrival of guests; the long dinner tables were set with silver, fine cut glass and rare china.

Both Britain and the U.S. claimed the region. James K. Polk was elected president because he agreed with the slogan "54-40 or Fight." That is, he intended to keep the boundary at that parallel. Just when it seemed that war might break out in 1846, a settlement was reached for the boundary to lie at the present 49th parallel. Dr. Johnson resigned, and Washington went to America.

Opposite, Totemic art, Suquamish Museum

SETTLERS AND MARTYRS

Much of the U.S. victory over the border was due to wealthy George Washington Bush. Because he was black, Bush was not permitted to settle in Oregon. Finally Dr. McLoughlin gave the Bush party permission to settle on Puget Sound. He did this although he knew that this first American settlement in what is now Washington probably would clinch the American claim to Washington, as it later proved.

More and more settlers streamed in over the Oregon Trail. These included the missionaries Dr. Marcus and Narcissa Whitman, who were massacred by the Indians at their Waiilatpu Mission. The Indians had revolted because they faced the loss of their land to the hordes of newcomers, who also had brought diseases deadly to the Indians.

Indian troubles continued for several years; meanwhile, "civilization" was coming quickly. Oregon Territory was formed in 1848, including present Washington. Seattle was founded in 1851, and Washington Territory was created in 1853.

In 1855 a council of 6,000 Horse Indians met with their great chiefs to discuss their problems. There was a fairly general Indian war through 1858, which ended with the Indian defeat at the Battle of Spokane Plains.

UP-TO-DATE

Spokane Falls (now Spokane) was

THAT'S CURIOUS:
Both the U.S. and Britain claimed the San Juan Islands. Lyman Cutler shot a pig owned by a Briton. Before the British could take Cutler to trial, the U.S. sent troops to protect him. There was no fighting in this Pig War, and arbitration gave the islands to the U.S. in 1872.

founded in 1871. Coming of the railroad in 1881 brought new prosperity. Railroads were so important that when the Northern Pacific bypassed Yakima by four miles, the entire city was placed on rollers and moved to the railroad. That road reached Tacoma in 1887.

By strange and terrible coincidence, the cities of Ellensburg, Vancouver, Spokane and Seattle in 1889 were all swept by fires that destroyed their wooden buildings.

That same year saw the creation of the new State of Washington. The next decade brought the arrival of the railroad at Seattle, the prosperity of 1897 when Seattle was the supply station for the Yukon gold rush, and the creation of Mt. Rainier National Park in 1899.

Progress and expansion continued as the Columbia was first bridged and Seattle held a great fair. World War I brought inevitable changes. That war took the lives of 1,625 Washington men and women. In 1920, when Edward Hubbard flew the mail from Seattle to Victoria, British Columbia, international airmail was inaugurated. Olympic National Park was established in 1938, and the state celebrated its Golden Jubilee of statehood in 1939.

During World War II, vast numbers of bombers and ships were turned out in Washington plants, and thousands of men and women served in the armed forces.

In 1962 Seattle celebrated with a world's fair and suffered a heavy earthquake in 1965. Spokane welcomed visitors to its world's fair in 1974, and the entire Columbia-Snake river system was opened past the Washington-Idaho border in 1975.

One of the worst disasters of its kind took place in 1980, to usher in the new decade. Mt. St. Helens exploded, shattering its almost perfect cone, vaporizing nearly 1,300 feet of the mountain's top. Huge clouds of ash drifted as far as Montana. Around the mountain, 150 square miles were devastated, and there were many deaths.

By the mid 1980's, much of the region was beginning to make a comeback, but the mountain continues to threaten more destruction.

In 1985 Seattle suffered one of the longest teacher strikes in U.S. history. It lasted for six weeks.

PERSONALITIES

Dr. John McLoughlin was one of the most remarkable men in American history, yet he was mistreated in later life and has been neglected by historians. He

---

THAT'S CURIOUS:
One of the strange events of World War II was connected with the founding of Richland. Suddenly, the federal government built a city of tarpaper shacks and brought into this previously tiny community as many as 45,000 workers. In one of the most secret activities of all time, the workers prepared materials for the first atomic bomb, although, of course, only a few of them knew this. The site was selected because the bomb processes required the kind of electric power resources available from Grand Coulee. The conversion of uranium into plutonium was accomplished.

firmly but justly ruled a kingdom larger than most of those of Europe. Within four years, he had converted part of a wilderness into a center of considerable culture. To the Indians, he became almost a god. McLoughlin would never permit his men to trade rum or alcoholic drinks to the Indians. He knew how harmfully these affected the Indians.

McLoughlin kept his region at peace until he was forced from his post. After he went to Oregon to live in America, he was never able to claim the property that should have been his.

Another neglected figure is George Washington Bush. This black who had never been a slave was perhaps the wealthiest person to come over the Oregon Trail. After he and his party were permitted to settle in what he called Bush Prairie, he established a system of agriculture that helped to feed the area.

When it appeared that because Bush was black he would lose all his holdings, his friends made such a clamor that Congress passed a special law permitting him to retain his lands. He was known as a man who never neglected his friends or was neglected by them.

Two of the country's greatest Indian leaders were the Chiefs Joseph and Joseph the Younger, or Hallshallakeen, Eagle Wing. Their Nez Perce tribe was a leading group in what is now the area where Washington, Oregon and Idaho join. After years of mistreatment by the settlers and the U.S. government, the younger Joseph led his people in a tragic march across much of the West as they fought their way to what they hoped would be safety in Canada. Hallshallakeen is often ranked as one of the great military leaders of his time.

PEOPLES

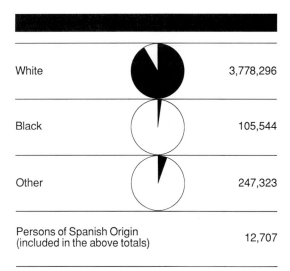

White	3,778,296
Black	105,544
Other	247,323
Persons of Spanish Origin (included in the above totals)	12,707

Another Indian leader was Chief Seattle, who gave his name to the great city. He was an eloquent speaker for his people. Chief Tslalakum of Whidbey Island was given a picture book of the Bible. Within a year, his people were singing hymns and conducting a simple version of Catholic services. Yakima Chief Kamiakin was a pioneer of irrigation in the valley. Wealthy Indian John Hoate gave away his fortune in potlaches and died poor.

Missionaries Marcus and Narcissa Whitman became martyrs to their Indian cause. Another missionary was Father Etienne de Rouge. He spent his fortune in developing St. Mary's Mission near Okanogan.

Two pioneers of the air industry were William Boeing and Moulton B. Taylor. Boeing founded the huge corporation making the planes that bear his name. Taylor developed the Aerocar.

George Washington, not to be confused with George Washington Bush, was another black pioneer of Washington State. He developed the town of Centralia.

One of the best known entertainers of all time was born in Washington. He was christened as Harry Lillis Crosby, but became known throughout the world as Bing Crosby.

A WEALTH OF NATURE

Each year enough timber grows in Washington to equal 10 percent of all the other timber growth in the U.S. Annual Washington growth is more than a billion board feet greater than is cut each year. Particularly notable is the noble douglas fir. The Olympic Peninsula contains one of the largest single stands of timber in the country outside of Alaska.

Earliest explorers admired the rhododendron, "bouquets of splendid flowers...thousands of them together," now the state flower. Much more rare is the phantom orchid. Salal, an edible berry, was used by the Indians as a syrup; they also concocted a bread from it.

Wild life is still abundant. After being almost exterminated for its fur, the beaver has made a comeback. Deer and elk, including the rare Roosevelt elk, bear, lynx, bobcat and others are found. The mountain goat population is perhaps the greatest in any state.

The bird population ranges through the sea birds to ducks and geese and inland birds of all kinds. A hundred species are found on Mount Rainier alone.

Among the fish, five varieties of salmon may be counted. One of the problems in damming the Columbia River was to find a way to protect these fish as they work their way back up stream to lay their eggs. Ingenious "ladders" were installed at the dams so that the fish could "climb" up above the dams. In some places, there are even "elevators" for the fish.

Another fish that goes out to sea and comes back like the salmon is the steelhead trout. The huge sturgeon of the Columbia are the largest fresh water fish on the continent. In order to maintain the fish population, Washington hatcheries produce and plant millions of fish each year.

More than 100 different usable minerals are found in Washington. This includes an enormous reserve of 6 billion short tons of coal.

Fresh water in streams and lakes and underground is one of the greatest natural resources of the state.

USING THE WEALTH

The flow of water in the Columbia River alone if fully utilized would satisfy the industrial power needs of the entire

nation. Despite such vast sources as the Coulee power, the wealth of waterpower has scarcely been tapped. There is thought to be more water in underground reserves than on the surface, and more of this is being used.

The Columbia Basin Project, with water from Grand Coulee, is the world's largest farm reclamation project, covering an area larger than Connecticut.

In agriculture, of course, Washington leads the world in apples. Scientists of the state have pioneered in methods of increasing and improving apple production. They also pioneer in new products such as apple candy.

An unusual crop is that of flower bulbs. There is indeed a "host of daffodils," close to a hundred million each year. Much of the country's vegetable seed also is produced in Washington.

Altogether, agriculture brings over $3,000,000,000 in income to the state each year. Wheat and fruits are the principal crops, and Washington holds third rank among the states in wheat production.

Because of its vast electric power, Washington has the greatest industrial capacity of all the states. The state holds second rank in industry among the western states. The huge Boeing plants have produced more than half of all the free world's airliners.

After World War II, Richland turned to peaceful uses of the atom, and is a center of nuclear research and reactor fuels production. The naval shipyard at Bremerton is the biggest on the Pacific.

Salmon is still king of the large Washington fishing business.

Washington has 25 ports and one of the world's largest ferryboat fleets oper-

THE ECONOMY

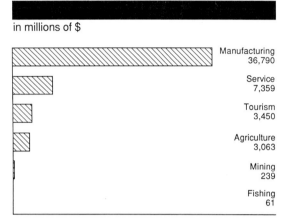

in millions of $

Manufacturing	36,790
Service	7,359
Tourism	3,450
Agriculture	3,063
Mining	239
Fishing	61

Principal Products:
transportation equipment, lumber, food, cement, sand and gravel
Agriculture:
dairy products, cattle, apples

ating in Puget Sound, which is one of the world's major transportation channels. There are three international airports and major railroad and highway networks.

GETTING AROUND

Mary Denny's clothesline was responsible for the location of Seattle. With a horseshoe tied at the end, the line was used to test the depth of the water for a port, and the present site was selected in that way.

In a little more than 100 years, Seattle has grown to be the principal metropolis of the Northwest, a center of industry, commerce and tourist magnet.

Seattle's setting provides the background for its attractions. To the east sometimes may be seen the white-

73

crowned head of Mt. Rainier. On the west are the waters of Puget Sound and the lofty bulk of the Olympic Peninsula.

The city's location makes it a unique transportation center. A complex state ferry system connects the city with dozens of other cities. A ship canal connects with the freshwater lakes, now used as sea ports. Evergreen Bridge spanning Lake Washington is the longest and heaviest floating structure anywhere.

Although it lies as far north as Newfoundland, the city's climate is moderate. Tourist attractions seem without end. Most-visited is the Seattle Center, location of the former world's fair. This is dominated by the lofty Space Needle with its revolving restaurant. Also popular there are the Pacific Science Center, the Arts and Crafts Center, and the International Fountain.

Getting to the Seattle Center is almost as much fun as being there. Visitors reach it in 90 seconds by way of the nation's first operating municipal monorail service.

King County Stadium known as Kingdome, is the second largest covered stadium anywhere. Sports lovers root for the Seattle Seahawks, Supersonics and Mariners, along with the Huskies of the University of Washington.

The skyscrapers of downtown and the restored waterfront area are other main attractions. In Seattle's Pioneer Square, community effort converted the seedy area to its original Victorian elegance. Now its fine shops and restaurants attract visitors who enjoy the impression of a bygone day.

Cultural attractions include the University of Washington campus, the Seattle Symphony and the world renowned performances of Wagner opera in both German and English. Music lovers from around the world flock to this event.

Four scenic drives lead visitors through the outlying areas of the city, variously passing Woodland Park Zoo, Green Lake, Hiram Chittenden Locks, the Seattle Art Museum, Alki Point, where Seattle was founded, and Lincoln Park, among others.

Third largest Washington city, Tacoma nestles among some of the most magnificent scenery, facing lovely Commencement Bay with Vashon Island to the north. On the western edge are the waters of Tacoma Narrows, with the Olympic Mountains glimmering in the distance.

Much of downtown Tacoma is being transformed with new shops and restaurants. The Pantages Theater has been lovingly restored as the Center for the Performing Arts.

On the waterfront, the ships carry such exotic registries as Dakar, Monrovia, Yokohama and Pireaus.

From the log palisades of Fort Nisqually the view of the Tacoma Narrows includes the suspension bridge

---

THAT'S CURIOUS:

In early Seattle days there was a shortage of females. A prominent Seattle man, Asa Mercer, went east to find some. Eleven eastern girls of good families soon went to Seattle to meet the many eligible bachelors there. A number of prominent Seattle families can still trace their history back to the "Mercer Girls."

Pacific Science Center, Seattle

that spans them. One of the disasters of the 1940's was the wind-blown destruction of the old bridge. It twisted and turned so violently in the wind, it was known as Galloping Gertie.

One of the most noticeable features of the area is the modern Tacoma Dome, decorated with an abstract design representing mountain scenery.

Only 29 miles from Tacoma is the state capital, Olympia. In spring, the cherry blossoms around the capitol burst into pink bloom. Inside the massive capitol, one of the main attractions is the chandelier by famed designer Louis Comfort Tiffany. Other Olympian attractions are the State Library, with prominent murals, sculpture, and mosaics, and the State Capitol Museum, housed in an old mansion.

Just south of Olympia at Tumwater Falls Park, late summer and early autumn days bring crowds to watch the salmon challenging the falls.

Northwest Washington is paradise for those attracted to open water. Sailboats and ferries thread their way through the 172 San Juan Islands. They visit the several small, picturesque ports.

Bellingham is the major city of the area, with its restored Whatcom County City Hall, now a museum. In the space of a morning, the visitor can drive from sea level to the foot of 10,778 foot Mt. Baker.

At Bremerton, the Naval Yard is a principal attraction.

In ancient Greece, Mt. Olympus was home of the gods. The Olympic Peninsula seems to live up to its name. It contains several Indian villages, good sized towns and Olympic National Park. Port Angeles is the largest city on the peninsula in the wettest part of continental U.S. By contrast, the east side is the driest area on the coast.

To the north and east enormously deep Lake Chelan and the vast Grand Coulee complex attract thousands of visitors. When it was built, the dam became the largest concrete structure in the world. Spokane is the capital of a region known as the Inland Empire. At Riverfront Park, a walk out on the footbridge that spans the Spokane River gives an interesting perspective of the city that stretches out on both sides of the roar and spray of the falls which are spotlighted at night.

Riverfront Park is the legacy of the world's fair of 1974. This was one of the most interesting and rewarding of the smaller fairs of the period. The building put up by the U.S. government remains as a dramatic reminder of the fair.

Many of the attractions of the city can be reached on foot from Riverfront Park. The unique French Renaissance style courthouse is said to have been "taken right out of Camelot." In downtown Spokane, enclosed overhead skywalks span the streets to connect shops and department stores.

The Lilac Festival and Spokane Interstate Fair are annual Spokane attractions. Mount Spokane State Park provides a host of recreational activities.

To the southeast, Pullman is the main business and educational center of the area where Washington, Idaho and Oregon meet. It is particularly known for Washington State University, which is located only a few miles from the University of Idaho to the east.

Until 1880, Walla Walla was the largest city in Washington Territory. In the Indian language, Walla Walla means

Riverfront Park is Spokane's legacy from the 1974 world's fair. The pillar holding a netting is the support for the U.S. Government Building at the 1974 International Environmental Exposition

many waters. Its founders said they liked it so well they named it twice.

The tri-cities of Pasco, Kennewick and Richland are in an area that might be called the tri-rivers. There, three of the nation's mightiest streams join. These are the Columbia, Snake and Yakima.

Yakima considers itself to be the center of the "Fruitbowl of the Nation." Near Goldendale is the unique soldier memorial copied from prehistoric British Stonehenge. Looming over the Cascade area are Mt. Baker and Mt. St. Helens. After St. Helens' great eruption of 1980, the area became a rather morbid attraction. Now visitors still find many attractions in the devastated region.

Vancouver is the oldest settlement in the state. The Covington House there is believed to be the state's oldest. The rebuilding of old Fort Vancouver provides an opportunity to consider the wonderful life the wilderness pioneers enjoyed under Dr. John McLoughlin.

Few would deny that the greatest scenic attraction of this particularly scenic state is its "Mount of Paradise"—Rainier. This giant rears its glaciated head to 14,410 feet. Its glaciers number 26; they feed 62 lakes and 34 waterfalls. Visitors find attractions ranging from ice caves to tiny wildflowers and giant elk. Many feel they truly have found their paradise at Paradise Inn on the mountain slope.

The capitol at night

COMPAC-FACS

WASHINGTON
The Evergreen State — Chinook State

HISTORY
Statehood: November 11, 1889
Admitted as: 42nd state
Capital: Olympia, founded 1850
OFFICIAL SYMBOLS
Motto: Alki ("By and by" in Indian language)
Bird: Willow goldfinch
Fish: Steelhead trout
Tree: Western hemlock
Colors: Green and gold
Song: "Washington, My Home"
Dance: Square Dance
Gem: Petrified wood
GEO-FACS
Area: 68,138 sq. mi.
Rank in Area: 20th
Length (n/s): 230 mi.
Width (e/w): 340 mi.
Geographic Center: 10 mi. wsw of Wenatchee
Highest Point: 14,410 ft. (Mt. Rainier)

Lowest Point: Sea level (Pacific Ocean)
Mean Elevation: 1,700 ft.
Temperature, Extreme Range: 166 degrees
Number of Counties: 39
Water Area: 1,627 sq. mi.
Coastline: 157 mi.
POPULATION
Total: 4,200,000 (1983)
Rank: 20th
Density: 65 persons per sq. mi.
Principal Cities: Seattle, 493,846; Spokane, 171,300; Tacoma, 158,501; Bellevue, 73,903; Everett 54,413; Yakima, 49,826; Bellingham, 45,794
EDUCATION
Schools: 2,041 elementary and secondary
Higher: 49
VITAL STATISTICS
Births (1980/83): 225,000
Deaths (1980/83): 105,000
Hospitals: 121
Drinking Age: 21
INTERESTING PEOPLE
Bing Crosby; Edward R. Murrow; Marcus Whitman; Narcissa Whitman; Dr. John McLoughlin; George Washington Bush; George Washington (black pioneer); Hallshallakeen (Chief Joseph the Younger); Chief Joseph, Sr.; Chief Seattle; David Douglas; William Boeing
WHEN DID IT HAPPEN?
1774: Juan Perez glimpses Olympic Mountains
1775: Heceta and Quadra claim for Spain
1778: Captain James Cook travels the coast
1792: Captain Robert Gray enters the Columbia; Captain George Vancouver reaches Puget Sound
1805: Lewis and Clark reach coast
1818: British and U.S. agree to occupy jointly
1821: Hudsons Bay Company takes over
1825: Dr. John McLoughlin at Fort Vancouver
1836: Whitmans settle Waiilatpu
1843: First great Oregon Trail crossing
1847: Most of Oregon Territory becomes U.S.
1847: Whitmans massacred
1853: Washington Territory established
1889: Statehood
1909: Alaska-Yukon-Pacific Exposition, Seattle
1928: Capitol completed, Olympia
1962: Century 21 Exposition, Seattle
1965: Eastern Washington hit by quake
1974: Inter. Environmental Expo., Spokane
1980: Mt. St. Helens explodes, devastates region
1985: Six week Seattle teacher strike

AMERICAN SAMOA

FASCINATING AMERICAN SAMOA

For most Americans, Samoa is a distant and exotic land about which they know almost nothing. One fascinating fact about American Samoa may not even be known to most of the people there. Sometime in the 1980's the people of American Samoa had their capital city "stolen."

There are many other fascinating sidelights and highlights associated with this distant paradise. The people are citizens of the United States of America, but their lives and customs are very different.

American Samoa is the only region under the American flag where the seasons are reversed from those of the states. In the capital the legislators are perhaps the only Americans who sometimes wear their native costumes.

Altogether it is a beautiful land, with unique people who have a charm all their own.

THE FACE OF SAMOA

Remote Samoa brings American rule to its most southerly point. Because it is in the southern hemisphere, the seasons are reversed, with their winter in the states' summer. The coolest months come from May to November, wafting in on the southeast trade winds. However, the pleasant south sea climate actually has little change.

From the closest American state, Hawaii, American Samoa is a distant 2,600 miles.

The American part of the Samoas is made up of six modest islands—Aunu'u, Ta'u, Olosega, Ofu (the Manu'a group), Rose and Tutuila. The islands are the tops of submerged volcanoes. On the largest island, Tutuila, the magnificent harbor of Pago Pago was formed when part of the volcano collapsed into the sea. Pago Pago is pronounced as if it were spelled Pango Pango. Its harbor is one of the world's largest and finest.

Tau Island, second largest, has the highest point of the group, Mount Lata, rising to 3,056 feet.

PAST AND PRESENT

The people of American Samoa are Polynesian. Although they have most of the modern conveniences, they have kept many of the traditions of their ancestors. Some authorities have said that they retain a larger percentage of their ancient culture than almost any other society—that they have never been "exploited, demeaned, or dispossessed."

Most of the population is still of unmixed blood lines. The Western ways they have adopted appear to be those that merge best with the traditions of their ancestors.

They are said to be a "warm, life-loving people who have found paradise and want to keep it."

European explorers first became aware of the Samoan Islands when Dutch explorer Jacob Roggeveen came to them in 1722. In 1842 U.S. Captain John Wilkes made some discoveries in the Samoas. By 1872 the U.S. had placed a naval base on the islands.

The great powers of Britain and Germany contested ownership with the United States. In 1889, just as it appeared a war might take place, a

typhoon wrecked the German and U.S. warships and sent the one British ship scurrying. Ten years later the Samoan Islands were divided between the Germans, those islands to the west, and the Americans, those to the east, now known as American Samoa. This came about through treaty with Germany and Britain. The local chiefs agreed with this arrangement in 1900 and 1904.

From 1900 until 1951, the islands were under U.S. Navy control. Then they were administered by the Interior Department, where they continue. Although Swain Island is 210 miles to the northwest, it was acquired by the U.S. in 1925 and placed under the jurisdiction of Samoa.

People of American Samoa have been American citizens since 1927. Their constitution of 1960 provided a two-house legislature for local affairs. One of the goals of that constitution is to "...protect persons of Samoan ancestry against alienation of their lands and destruction of the Samoan way of life and language." The constitution was revised in 1967.

With only a few exceptions, only those of more than half Samoan blood line may own real estate on the islands.

In 1964 the islands pioneered in teaching by television, because children and teachers were so remote and scattered from each other.

The first popular election for governor was held, and in 1978 the native islander Peter Tali Coleman was installed in that post. In 1980 the territory was permitted to send an elected, non-voting delegate to the U.S. Congress.

The Samoas to the west had been under several flags until they became the nation of Western Samoa in 1962.

There seems to be no inclination either on the side of the Samoan people or the American government to change the present relationship. Far more Samoans live in Hawaii and the west coast of the U.S. than remain in the islands.

The islands today are classified by the government as "unincorporated, unorganized territory" of the U.S.

THE ECONOMY

With soil so rich that fenceposts often take root, the islands produce bountiful crops of coconuts and bananas. Breadfruit, yams, pineapples, and oranges also are plentiful. Fine stands of grass under the coconut trees feed an increasingly large number of cattle.

The material called tapa cloth is pounded from the bark of the mulberry tree to make a kind of felt. Bright designs are inked on with wooden printing blocks. Polynesian craft traditions are carried on in some of the best work of its kind. Palm leaves provide raw materials for fine baskets and floor mats. The long boats, with many oars, are hollowed out of tree trunks, some 40 feet long.

Fishing is another vital activity, with

THAT'S CURIOUS:
The traditional capital Pago Pago is still the capital, as confirmed by the supervising Interior Department. However, some current major reference books list the section of that city known as Fagatogo as the capital. Though several of the government buildings are at Fagatogo, it is not known how the capital became "stolen."

tuna packing as the principal industry.

GETTING AROUND

Those who are searching for true tropical Pacific Island beauty would consider American Samoa their ideal territory.

Although they float on the opposite side of the globe, the islands of American Samoa have moved "closer" with the opening of Pago Pago International Airport in 1964.

A unique experience is the trip on the breathtaking cable car ride across Pago Pago Bay.

Another unusual treat of the islands is one of its favorite dishes, called palusami. This delicious food is cooked in a wrapped taro leaf and the creamy coconut delicacy is served over taro slices.

The happy considerate lifestyle of the Samoans is perhaps one of the most attractive features of the islands for visitors. Large families are common. Many people of related families are grouped together in an "extended family" known as Aiga, under a leader or matai. The typical house has no walls or doors, but mats can be dropped down during rain.

Visitors greatly enjoy the local dance called the siva, which is different from the Hawaiian hula. The Samoan language is similar to but somewhat different from Hawaiian.

Lavalava, the wrap-around garment, is still worn, sometimes in the legislature.

For those Americans from the north who want to visit a completely different land and people, yet one still proud to wave the American flag, the best advice is, "Try American Samoa."

COMPAC-FACS

AMERICAN SAMOA

HISTORY
Territorial Status: 1900
Current Status: Unincorporated, unorganized territory of the U.S.
Capital: Pago Pago
OFFICIAL SYMBOLS
Motto: Samoa Muamua le Atua ("In Samoa, God is First")
Flower: Paogo (Ula-fala)
Tree: Moso'oi
Plant: Ava
Song: "Amerika Samoa"
GEO-FACS
Area: 76 sq. mi.
Highest Point: 3,056 ft. (Mt. Lata, Tau Island)
Lowest Point: Sea level (South Pacific Ocean)
POPULATION
Total: 32,297
WHEN DID IT HAPPEN?
1722: Discovered by Jacob Roggeveen
1842: Capt. John Wilkes explores
1872: U.S. creates naval base
1889: Typhoon upsets war plans of three claimants
1899: Treaty places under U.S. control
1900: Chiefs of Tutuila and Aunu'u cede lands to U.S.
1904: King and chiefs of Manu'a cede islands of Ofu, Olosega and Tau
1925: Swains Island made part of territory
1951: Department of Interior takes jurisdiction
1960: Constitution signed
1967: Constitution revised
1978: First elected Governor, Peter Tali Coleman
1980: Delegate to Congress elected

GUAM

Visitors to Guam are on hand when day begins for the United States of America. They can climb to the top of a mountain in a few minutes, or eat a great Guamanian delicacy, roasted fanihi bat. Many enjoy their rides on the broad backs of carabao, a kind of cow.

Altogether, most outsiders find Guam a charming and completely different world, where the people are especially delightful.

THE FACE OF GUAM

Because Guam is the only American location on the eastern side of the International Date Line, the island is the first U.S. land to greet the new day. At daybreak in Guam, America "wakes up."

This westernmost territory of the United States is known as the "Gateway to the Orient." From it, Japan, the Philippines and mainland Asia can be reached easily. It lies 3,300 miles west of Honolulu, and is the largest of the island group known as the Marianas.

This kidney-bean shaped island, a speck of land on the vast ocean, is only 30 miles long and 8.5 miles wide at its widest point. However, it is the largest point of land between Hawaii and the Philippines.

On the north, the island is a coraline limestone plateau. To the south is a chain of low volcanic mountains.

The looming headlands are partly closed in by a reef of coral. From the mountain slopes, forty small streams dash toward the brilliant blues and greens of the surrounding waters.

The perfect climate of December through March heats up to a tropical summer for the rest of the year.

STIRRINGS

Was there once a great civilized continent of the Pacific? Did it suddenly sink into the ocean—leaving fragments such as Guam? Some experts believe this may have been the case. They think prehistoric objects found on Guam help to prove this.

Carved stones, topped with other stones fashioned in mushroom shape, have been found on the island. They are called latte stones. They were placed in double rows paralleling streams or the seashore. Giant human skeletons, rock carvings and other objects have been found.

Natives of historic times knew nothing about these distant people who might have been their ancestors. The native people, known as the Chamorro, may have been descendants of southern Asian residents who came to the island about 1500 B.C. Their greatest skill was in building and navigating and sailing their outrigger canoes.

PILGRIMS AND PIRATES

Into this land of a gentle and honest people came the fleet of Ferdinand Magellan in 1521. After nearly a hundred days at sea, the men were almost dead of hunger and disease. The people welcomed them with kindly deeds and were terribly treated in return.

Spain claimed Guam and the other Mariana Islands, and settlement began in 1565, but little happened to disturb the people until Jesuit priests and Spanish soldiers arrived in 1668. Then for 30 years, the people and the newcomers

clashed, until the Chamorro finally were beaten down.

The galleons of Spain called regularly; in the oceans offshore the Spanish ships were harrassed by pirates, such as Sir Francis Drake, whom they called a real pirate. With the coming of the last galleon in 1815, the island was isolated.

A MODERN LAND

Spain ceded Guam to the U.S., but aside from a military buildup, Americans paid little attention to Guam until World War II, when the Japanese captured the strategic island on December 11, 1941.

Under the Japanese, the island became practically a concentration camp. In the terrible battle to recapture Guam in July, 1944, more than 10,000 Americans lost their lives. The capital city of Agana was almost completely wiped out.

Five years after the war ended, the loyal Guamanians were made American citizens, in 1950.

In 1962 a natural disaster, typhoon Karen, proved as destructive to property as the war. Ninety percent of the buildings on Guam were wiped out, but only nine people were killed. The industrious people began to rebuild almost at once, constructing buildings to withstand the strongest blasts of weather.

In 1970 the people were able to vote for the governor and other officials. There is a single (unicameral) legislature, elected every two years. The people are not yet permitted to vote in U.S. national elections. However, in 1972, the people

began to elect a non-voting delegate to the national Congress.

In 1983 the population stood at 113,230, a 7 percent gain over the 1980 census only three years before.

THE ECONOMY

Tourism and manufacturing are the principal industries of the island. There are around 300,000 visitors each year. Manufacturing is rather generally limited to providing the products used by the island.

Agriculture produces cabbages, cucumbers, beans, tomatoes, bananas, coconuts and other crops. There are limited cattle, hogs, and poultry. Again most of the products are for home consumption.

Aquaculture is considered to have great potential for the island economy. This would consist mostly of growing fish in ponds that would be cultivated.

There is a small amount of commercial fishing.

Almost 50 percent of all those employed work for the government. The average annual income per person is about $5,000.

GETTING AROUND

Agana is one of the world's most "modern" capitals. It had to be almost completely rebuilt after each of the two catastrophes: the disasters of World War II and typhoon Karen. Built in 1958, the modern Catholic Cathedral was one of the few structures to withstand the storm of 1962.

The city is particularly well known

THAT'S CURIOUS:

In 1898 an American ship sailed in firing shots. The Spanish governor was sorry he could not return the salute for lack of ammunition. He did not know that his territory had been captured by the Americans as a far-off part of the Spanish-American War.

for its duty free shops, where fine merchandise lures many tourists.

The main highway completely circles the island. Visitors can enjoy the beaches which some say are the finest in the world. Roadways are lined with palm trees, banyans and the giant fig trees. The great buttressed roots of the fig tree were said to be home to ancestral spirits. The yoga tree grows only on the Marianas.

Around the island, visitors will find such delights as secluded waterfalls, glimpses of small deer and large lizards. Orchids of many varieties are plentiful. Shell collectors enjoy one of the world's greatest varieties of fine and often valuable shells.

One of the most unusual "pleasures" is dining on the strongly flavored roasted meat of the fruit bat, the rare fanihi. Islanders consider this a delicacy.

One of the best times to visit Guam is during one of the fiestas. The village of Inarajan holds, perhaps, the most memorable of all. Festival entertainment includes coconut husking, cockfighting, pageants and carabao racing. This bovine animal is a favorite on the island, particularly with boys of a family who love to keep the great beasts fat and sleek. Visitors are offered the "thrill" of riding these favorites.

The large number of military personnel and their families enjoy their stay on Guam, generally speaking. They have all the water sports on the lovely beaches, hunt for lost Spanish treasure, hike and fish in the lagoons and otherwise relish the advantages of a tropical paradise.

Most of all, perhaps, they and all the visitors enjoy the charm and hospitality of the people of Guam.

COMPAC-FACS

GUAM
Pearl of the Pacific

HISTORY
Discovered: 1521
Became U.S. Territory: 1898
Self-Governing: 1970
Capital: Agana
OFFICIAL SYMBOLS
Animal: Iguana
Bird: Toto (Fruit dove)
Flower: Puti tai nobio (Bougainvillea)
Tree: Ifit (Intsiabijuga)
Song: "Stand, Ye Guamanians"
GEO-FACS
Area: 209 sq. mi.
Length (n/s): 30 mi.
Width (e/w): 8.5 mi.
Highest Point: 1,334 ft. (Mt. Lamlam)
Lowest Point: Sea level (Pacific Ocean)
Mean Elevation: 500 ft.
POPULATION
Total (1983): 113,230
Density: 521.5 persons per sq. mi.
EDUCATION
Schools: 27 elementary; 9 secondary
Higher: 1
VITAL STATISTICS
Births (1983): 3,184
Deaths (1983): 462
Life Expectancy at Birth: 72 yrs.
WHEN DID IT HAPPEN?
1500 B.C. (approx.): First southeast Asians arrive
1521: Magellan discovers
1565: Spain starts modest settlement
1668: Priests and soldiers bring conflict
1815: Last galleon leaves
1898: Ceded to U.S.
1917: World War I skirmish
1941: Conquered by Japan
1944: Recaptured by U.S.
1950: People made American nationals
1962: Typhoon Karen devastates
1970: Local vote given to the people
1972: Elected, non-voting delegate sent to Congress

OTHER PACIFIC ISLANDS

WAKE ISLAND

Wake and its sister islands of Wilkes and Peale have been important links between Hawaii and the Asian mainland. They lie 2,000 miles west of Hawaii and 1,300 miles east of Guam.

Altogether the islands cover only about 3 square miles of territory.

The U.S. claimed possession on January 17, 1899. The Air Force has been the administrative agent for the population of only about 300.

THE MARIANAS

Until recently the United States has administered a trusteeship over the entire group called Micronesia.

These were the Caroline Islands and atolls, Marshall Islands and atolls and the Marianas. Guam is part of the Marianas, with a separate government.

At this writing, the Marianas are in the process of becoming a self-governing commonwealth freely associated with the United States. This will be very similar to the relationship of Puerto Rico to the United States.

In 1975 the residents voted 78 percent in favor of this Commonwealth. In 1977 the voters elected a governor, lieutenant governor and members of a bicameral legislature. This gave the people control of their domestic affairs.

The federal United States government continues to manage international and military affairs.

The Commonwealth will be fully effective when the United Nations dissolves the Trusteeship.

Most critical time in the islands' history was their recapture from the Japanese during World War II. The world remembers the bitter battles of Saipan and Tinian.

The estimated 1980 population was 16,600. They occupy a total land area of 181.9 square miles.

CAROLINES AND MARSHALLS

These island groups were offered commonwealth status with the United States, but this was rejected by their leaders. A compact of free association was agreed upon. This gives the groups full freedom of government, but the U.S. would retain responsibility for their defense.

At this writing the compact awaits both the approval of the U.S. Senate and the United Nations dissolution of the trusteeship.

Islands of the groups made famous during the terrible battles of World War II are Palau, Peleliu, Truk, Yap, and Kwajalein. Bikini and Eniwetok were renowned for their nuclear tests by the U.S.

A sad note in the history of the new nation—in June, 1985, the president of Palau was assassinated.

DISPUTED ISLANDS

At one time the U.S. disputed ownership of 18 Southwest Pacific islands with Britain, and of 7 claimed by New Zealand. In 1979 and 1980, the U.S. signed treaties relinquishing these claims. The treaty was approved by the Senate. The various islands either became independent or continued an association with New Zealand.

Carnival, St. Thomas, Virgin Islands

THE CARIBBEAN REALM

OVERVIEW

On first thought, the hundreds of islands which dot the sparkling Caribbean might appear to be very much alike. However, each has its own individuality, and those islands under American authority boast distinct personalities.

As would be expected, the weather in America's Caribbean realm is generally perfect. In the American Virgin Islands, if the temperature dips below seventy degrees many hotels give a free night's stay. Yet storms can be so severe that the worst of them takes its name from the Caribbean god Jurucan, a hurricane.

One of the rarest of all birds is the bare-legged owl of the Virgin Islands; this rare bird has been seen only twice in more than 60 years. By contrast, the miniature tree frog is found almost everywhere. At night it utters a hauntingly beautiful bell-like call, echoing the most talented of birds. This trilling song can be heard almost all night.

In population the islands range from the most densely peopled area under U.S. control to Navassa, with no permanent residents at all.

These islands possess the oldest European civilization under U.S. control, the oldest European city, the oldest continually inhabited European house and the oldest executive mansion.

At one time the region was known as the "sugarbowl of Europe." Today, a growing number of manufacturers and service groups has supplemented the agricultural base of the economy. Ever-increasing tourism is a backbone of the islands' prosperity.

The American islands include the most popular tourist destination in the Caribbean, and all have a multitude of sights and activities for tourists, including the formidable remains of the two mightiest fortresses in the hemisphere. Baseball is a popular sport, as are the legal cockfights in some areas.

Music lovers will find one of the world's most respected musical events—the Casals Festival, named in honor of the renowned cellist/conductor Pablo Casals.

The people who call the islands home and those who visit, even for the first time, generally agree that despite their many problems, the U.S. realms in the Caribbean have much to offer, whether for a day or for a lifetime.

PUERTO RICO

FASCINATING PUERTO RICO

It is spring all year round in Puerto Rico, a land which someone has said is, "More than half Spanish and more than half American." The island and its offshore islands are places where the frogs sing in trees, tobacco farmers become mountaineers, baseball is the number one sport, and cockfighting is legal and popular.

Puerto Rico boasts the oldest European style city under the U.S. flag, and the hemisphere's oldest European house.

THE FACE OF PUERTO RICO

Puerto Rico is the lesser of the greater. That is, it is the smallest of the larger islands of the Caribbean which are known as the Greater Antilles. Called "Paradise" by some, it lies between the Atlantic Ocean to the north and the blue Caribbean to the south. It is only about 100 miles long and 36 miles wide.

The nearest neighbors are the Dominican Republic on the west and the American group of the Virgin Islands on the east. Some geographers claim that the Virgin Islands should be considered a part of the Puerto Rico archipelago.

That archipelago does include a number of smaller islands. Nine miles to the east is Vieques, the largest of the associated isles. Culebra is also on the east and has a fine harbor called Puerto Grande. Mona Island lies west of the main island.

Puerto Rico is surprisingly rough and mountainous. Mountain chains extend almost across the island from east to west, but they are broken up by valleys and passes. Massive El Yunque towers above its forest canopy near the east coast. Cerro de Punta near the island center is the highest mountain. The northern shore also has many low hills.

Of the many small rivers, the chief is La Plata. This flows into the Atlantic west of San Juan.

The island has an almost ideal climate. Average temperatures vary only about 6 degrees from "winter" to "summer." The heat is never terrible, and nights are cool. Few people even notice the rains which come on suddenly but last only a short time. On El Yunque, however, 160 inches of rain descend every year, making the region a tropical rain forest. By contrast, parts of the island are very dry.

Worst weather comes with the hurricanes. The earliest was recorded in 1515. The natives of Puerto Rico are responsible for naming this most striking of all weather features. Their great god Jurucan (Hoo-roo-can) was said to be the cause of the terrible storms that often devastated the region.

We know these storms as "hurricanes" in honor of Jurucan. In Puerto Rico these storms are given the names of the saints on whose day they fall.

STIRRINGS

Ancient peoples once lived in the many caves of Puerto Rico, but not much is known about them. However, they did leave paintings and carvings on the walls of their caves.

At some time, native peoples from South America began to come up the string of Caribbean islands and reached Puerto Rico. These were the Arawak. Also somewhat later newcomers to the

islands were the dreaded Carib. They gave their name to the Caribbean. The Carib were very fierce, perhaps cannibals. They terrorized all the peoples they encountered. They had not quite reached the main island of Puerto Rico when Europeans first arrived.

The native people of the island were known by the Spanish as Borinqueno. They called the island Borinquen. For centuries the people had built towns of grass huts set on stilts. They grew crops and hunted small animals, such as the iguana, for food. Turtles and fish also provided much of the diet. The hated Caribs were known for their dugout canoes, in which they roamed the seas, attacking and capturing weaker peoples.

Borinquen was found by Christopher Columbus on his second voyage to the New World in 1493, but where he landed is not quite certain.

First Spanish settlement was made by noted explorer Don Juan Ponce de Leon. He gave the island its present name when he exclaimed, "Que rico puerto." This means what a rich port, and the island has been a "rich port" ever since.

As early as 1511, the island became the first recognized Spanish colony in the New World.

Over the years the Spanish settlers practically enslaved the native peoples, making them labor almost without rest. The native population of about 30,000 dropped almost to nothing due to hardship and disease.

GROWTH

Other countries were envious of Spain's ownership. Sir Frances Drake of England attacked and was driven off. The British Earl of Cumberland captured San Juan in 1598, but he could not keep control. The great fortresses of El Morro and San Cristobal were built to fend off attacks by French and Dutch as well as English pirates and other invaders. The old city was surrounded by a formidable wall to make it further impossible of capture.

Over the generations the people of Puerto Rico remained loyal to Spain. A small revolutionary movement in 1868 failed. Slavery was outlawed in 1873.

After nearly 400 years of Spanish rule, in 1898 Spain responded to many requests and gave the island a kind of self-government known as La Carta Autonomica, or dominion status.

However, that independence did not last for long. That same year the United States went to war with Spain. U.S. forces bombarded and then invaded Puerto Rico. Not long after, Spain ceded the island to the U.S. as a possession.

For the Puerto Ricans who had worked for dominion status, "the work of 400 years was blown away." Only gradually were the freedoms returned, until now some authorities say the islanders enjoy "the best of both worlds"—the benefits of their U.S. ties minus a number of the responsibilities.

MODERN TIMES

In 1917 Puerto Ricans received U.S. citizenship. Two world wars and later wars saw thousands of Puerto Ricans serving faithfully in U.S. forces. This and many other events and circumstances strengthened the ties with the mainland. A constantly growing number of islanders went freely to the United States to live, with the hope of making their fortunes or finding, at least, a better living.

With the great depression and rapidly growing population, economic conditions on the island grew worse. The people did not wait for the mainland government to help. They decided "that poverty was intolerable." They set up a program called "Operation Bootstrap." They gave it this name because they said they were going to raise themselves by their own bootstraps, as the old saying goes.

The program was designed to encourage outside factories and businesses to come to the island with new jobs and opportunities. It hoped to teach the people how they could help themselves by learning new skills and changing many of the old ways. It broke up many of the large farms and let small farmers buy land on easy credit.

This program became so successful that experts from all over the world came to the island to learn how to imitate that success.

Meanwhile, the question of the relationship of Puerto Rico and the United States has not yet been finally decided. In 1959 the people chose their first popularly elected governor, Luis Munoz Marin. Congress ratified a Puerto Rican constitution in 1951. Then, in 1952, the island was recognized as the Commonwealth of Puerto Rico. The new form of U.S.-Puerto Rican relationship was to be called Estado Libre Asociado, which means Associated Free State.

By mutual consent, and apparently by the will of a large majority, the people remain citizens of the United States in this self-governing community. Some want this to be changed to statehood. A small percentage of others desperately, and sometimes violently, strive to make Puerto Rico independent.

Old San Juan, Morro Castle at upper left, top

PEOPLE

Although millions of Puerto Ricans have left the island for what they hoped would be a better life on the mainland, island conditions have improved so that a goodly number have returned to their home island once more. One indication of improvement is illustrated by the increase of the islanders' average life span from 46 to over 70 years during a period of about twenty years.

In addition to Operation Bootstrap, the people have been active in another program designed to improve their lives. This was called Operation Serenidad. Through it they worked to restore historic structures, bring in more music and drama, improve education, increase higher education opportunities and otherwise look forward to a good life.

They had some unusual help in this

89

from a world renowned musician, cellist/conductor Pablo Casals. That music master fled Spain's rightist government to come to his mother's homeland. He established the Casals Festival. This continued after the beloved musician's death in 1973, as one of the great musical attractions worldwide.

In a different field of art, Francisco Oller has been honored in the Louvre in Paris. Jose Campeche and Julio Rosado are other noted artists.

Manuel Alonso, Manuel Zeno Gandia and Eugenio Maria de Hostos are prominent for their writing.

In recent years several Puerto Ricans have become distinguished in politics and statesmanship. Luis Munoz Marin was accepted at Georgetown University at the age of 14. He served as Puerto Rico's governor from 1949 to 1965 and then returned to the island Senate. His father, Luis Munoz Rivera, was also a notable statesman.

Winning political leadership for women has not been easy in Spanish speaking countries. This did not daunt Dona Felisa Rincon de Gautier, who was the successful mayor of San Juan for twenty years.

An earlier politician of note was Marshal Alejandro O'Reilly. He was renowned for the many reforms in military administration and law.

THE GIFTS OF NATURE

The greatest gift of nature to Puerto Rico is its natural beauty. The rugged mountains covered with tropical foliage, including more than 200 varieties of trees, the countless orchids, flitting birds, magnificent beaches, sparkling seas and moderate climate—all combine to form a great asset.

Nature has not been very liberal with mineral treasures, and the wonderful forests have long since diminished, although new growth is coming in fast. The brilliant red poinciana trees and the magnificent palms add to the beauty.

There are many birds but few animals and no "wild" animals such as bears or jaguars. Perhaps the most attractive "animal" is the tiny tree frog. Found everywhere, this creature's bell-like call echoes throughout the night in both city and countryside.

The greatest natural treasure of all is the "spectacularly fertile" soil. But in the rugged countryside less than a million acres of this is useful for crops.

USING THE GIFTS

With tax-free years and other incentives, Operation Bootstrap succeeded in attracting substantial new industries, developing more than 1,600 new manufacturing plants. Principal products are pharmaceuticals, petrochemicals, food products, and apparel.

Total annual value of manufactured products is about ten billion dollars.

Sugar is still the chief crop, with coffee next. Some of the tobacco is grown on such steep slopes that the workers have to be roped together like mountain climbers.

THAT'S CURIOUS:
One of the animals of Puerto Rico has been developed there. This is an aristocratic animal known as paso fino—bred locally to become one of the distinctive trotting horses of the world.

Other crops are plantains (a kind of banana), other bananas, yams, taniers, pineapples, pidgeon peas, peppers, pumpkins, coriander, lettuce and tobacco.

Cement, crushed stone, sand and gravel and lime provide a total annual income from minerals of over $2 million.

Tourism brings in almost a billion dollars of much-needed revenue.

GETTING AROUND

Tourists find a wide variety of attractions, including the palm-fringed beaches and old world charm.

San Juan, founded in 1508, is the oldest European style city under the American flag. The White House (Casa Blanca) has the distinction of being the oldest house in the hemisphere with a record of continuous occupation. Even older are some of the original foundations, perhaps even of the house of the founder, Ponce de Leon.

One of the most attractive aspects of Puerto Rico to outsiders is the easy mingling of Spanish and mainland customs. The people have become great baseball fans, and the island has produced such notable stars as Orlando Cepeda, 1958 Rookie of the Year, and Roberto Clemente, whose "fabulous" career was cut short by his death in a plane crash while on his way to help victims of a Nicaraguan earthquake.

On the side of Spanish influence, fiestas are numerous and popular. The celebration of Christmas is typically hispanic and extends from early December to January 8. Another custom not found in continental U.S., except illegally, is the legal cockfight. Some of the roosters are very valuable and are said to seldom be killed in combat.

Smaller towns and villages retain much of their old-time Spanish charm. Each town adores its own patron saint, such as the choice of St. Patrick by the town of Loiza Aldea. That saint drove the snakes from Ireland, and Loiza Aldea credits him with driving out a plague of ants.

The old town section of San Juan is one of the most attractive old Spanish style cities anywhere. Its narrow streets with overhanging balconies lead to the great bulks of El Morro and San Cristobal. The old grey forts are the finest attractions of their kind.

The parts of old San Juan that have not already been restored also will eventually be changed back so that visitors will have the experience of looking back to a community of another age. They will have a good idea of what life must have been like when the great wall that still surrounds the city served a useful purpose in fending off attackers.

Both old and new San Juan have many fine specialty shops. The port welcomes a constant procession of cruise ships with their eager tourists. One of the interesting side trips carries the visitor across the harbor by ferry. In new San Juan one of the most interesting places to visit is the splendid campus of the University of Puerto Rico.

The beaches of San Juan are all public and are always crowded with people basking in the warm sun, almost in the shadow of great modern hotels.

Outside San Juan there are beauty and interest all along the many fine roads. The brilliant blossoms and tropical birds of the El Yunque rainforest should not be missed. A trip from north to south can be made by superhighway, but the

On land or under the sea, Puerto Rico fascinates visitors

back roads over the mountains provide glimpses of mountain homes, waterfalls, ancient mineral spas, and other attractions.

The cities of Ponce, Mayaguez and Arecibo all are more than worthwhile for a visit.

On the various coasts may be found attractive hotels and resorts, with many interesting visits possible on the offshore islands, as well.

COMPAC-FACS

PUERTO RICO

HISTORY
Commonwealth status: July 25, 1952
Capital: San Juan, settled 1508
OFFICIAL SYMBOLS
Flower: Maya
Bird: Reinita
Tree: Ceiba

Flag: Three red and two white horizontal stripes, with a blue triangle at the mast bearing one white star
Song: "La Borinquena"
GEO-FACS
Area: 3,515 sq. mi.
Length (n/s): about 36 mi.
Width (e/w): about 100 mi.
Highest Point: 4,389 ft. (Cerro de Punta)
Lowest Point: Sea level (Atlantic and Caribbean)
Mean Elevation: 1,800 ft.
Temperature, Extreme Range: 38 degrees
POPULATION
Total: 3,196,520
Density: 931 persons per sq. mi.
Principal Cities: San Juan, 424,600; Bayamon, 185,087; Ponce, 161,739; Carolina, 147,835; Caguas, 87,214; Mayaguez, 82,968
EDUCATION
Schools: 1,766 elementary and secondary
Higher: 39
VITAL STATISTICS
Births (1981): 71,300
Deaths (1981): 21,085
Hospitals: 62
INTERESTING PEOPLE
Pablo Casals, Orlando Cepeda, Roberto Clemente, Dona Felisa Rincon de Gautier, Luis Munoz Marin, Luis A. Ferre, Jose Ferrer, Rita Moreno, Francisco Oller, Jose Campeche, Julio Rosado, Marshal Alejandro O'Reilly
WHEN DID IT HAPPEN?
1493: Columbus discovers
1509: Claimed by Spain
1515: Sugarcane introduced
1598: Cumberland captures San Juan, cannot hold
1797: English assault fails
1868: Small revolt against Spain
1873: Slavery abolished
1898: Dominion status granted; ceded to U.S.
1940: Operation Bootstrap
1949: First popular election
1952: Commonwealth proclaimed
1977: President Ford proposes statehood

VIRGIN ISLANDS

FASCINATING ISLANDS

Those who travel to the Virgin Islands find that their visit has been "insured." They will find the home of Bluebeard and a church made with molasses. The islands gave the world the swinging bed and provided a name for the practice of eating human flesh.

THE FACE OF THE ISLANDS

There are three main islands—St. John, St. Thomas and St. Croix—six smaller islands and a large number still smaller. To the east is another group of the same chain, the British Virgin Islands.

All these were formed by volcanoes pushing up from the undersea plateaus. St. John and St. Thomas are on the same plateau. A great sea depth of 15,000 feet separates them from St. Croix, about 40 miles to the south, and slightly east.

In relation to the mainland, the archipelago lies almost 1,000 miles east of Miami. At its eastern tip, St. Croix is the most easterly point under U.S. control. The nearest neighbors of the islands are Puerto Rico to the west and the British Virgin Islands on the east. Some geographers say the Virgin Islands really should be considered as part of Puerto Rico's island group.

Altogether the islands total only 133 square miles in area, with St. Croix accounting for two thirds of this.

The trade winds of the Caribbean maintain an almost perfect climate.

There are no rivers or lakes. This means there are no major natural supplies of fresh water above ground and almost none below the surface. Rainfall must be stored in cisterns and other places. Desalting of seawater now also provides a limited fresh supply.

STIRRINGS

Earliest known inhabitants of the islands were the Siboney Indians, who came from Florida. They were displaced by the Arawak from South America. The Arawak invented the hammock, called a "swinging bed" by Columbus. The Arawak, in turn, were driven out by the fierce Carib, who gave their name to the Caribbean.

When Columbus found that they ate human flesh, he called the Carib "calibales," now cannibal, in English.

MANY MASTERS

When Columbus discovered the islands in 1493, he called them Virgins in honor of the Virgins of St. Ursula. He found that the Carib drank a kind of beer made of sweet potatoes or corn. They smoked tobacco until near collapse. They kept a strange breed of barkless dog.

Pirates, including the infamous Bluebeard, used the islands, and they have been claimed by Spain, Holland, France, England and Denmark. The French bought St. Croix in 1651 and sold it to Denmark in 1733, giving them control of

THAT'S CURIOUS:
A kind of weather "insurance" is provided by some of the island hotels. If the average temperature falls below 70 degrees on any day, the guest gets a free night's lodging.

the island group. The Danes brought a great civilization to their islands, based on sugarcane and slave labor.

By 1840, St. Thomas (now Charlotte Amalie) had become the third largest city under Danish rule.

However, the slaves were freed, and the sugar market collapsed. The great plantations and many sugar refineries faded into decay.

ENTER, THE U.S.

By 1917 the Danes were ready to sell, and the United States bought the present U.S. Islands, mainly to keep them from falling into German hands as World War I raged in Europe and on the seas.

In 1927 U.S. citizenship was granted to the people of the islands. They were given a measure of self-government in 1936, and this was increased in 1954. There is a legislature of one house (unicameral), elected every two years. The formerly appointed position of governor became an elected post for the first time in 1970. In 1972 the islands were allowed to send a non-voting representative to Congress.

Over 80 percent of the population can trace ancestry back to the black slaves who were brought to the islands. All the former colonial powers of the islands are represented by small numbers of people, and many people from the U.S. mainland now find the islands an attractive place to work or retire.

A WEALTH OF NATURE

Strangely, the only native mammal was a flying creature—the bat. Deer and mongoose have been imported. The latter have increased to become a pest.

The term "rare bird" certainly fits one of the island inhabitants. The bare-legged owl was seen only twice in fifty years. The great frigate bird is known as "king of the air." Other birds are pelicans, great blue heron and honey creeper. One of the most attractive is the tiny Antillean crested hummingbird. This fierce little creature can scare away a hawk if it tries to attack the nest.

Tropical fruits are a great attraction of the islands. Fruit trees include soursop, sugar apple, mammee, genep, mango, papaya and guava. Royal and coconut palms, sea grape, mahoe and mangroves are other trees.

Not surprisingly, the supply of game fish is one of the great attractions. Bonefish, tarpon, wahoo, kingfish and tuna bring sportsmen to the islands on an all-year basis. Snorklers and scuba divers revel in the beautiful marine life including French angelfish, rock beauties, coral fish and the gleaming fluorescent marine jewel. Shores of the islands yield over six hundred kinds of shells; more than a hundred have some degree of rarity.

No commercial minerals are found, but enough sand and gravel and stone can be mined to supply many local building needs.

Water continues to be the greatest problem. In spite of all measures, fresh supplies are still in short order.

GETTING BY

Economic conditions on the islands once were so bad that President Herbert Hoover called them a "poorhouse." The Virgin Islands Corporation, set up by the government, has helped. Now the average income, close to $6,000, is one of the highest in the Caribbean. Unemployment at 7 percent is below the national

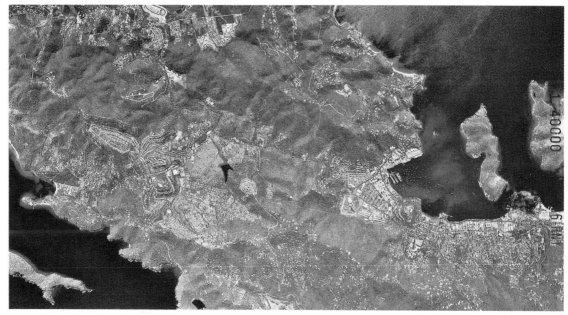

Charlotte Amalie from space

average. A million visitors a year now bring in nearly $400,000,000. Charlotte Amalie harbor is one of the world's leading cruise ports.

Agriculture remains the second most important source of income. Sugarcane continues to lead the list. Truck garden products also are important.

Processing of rum from sugar is the most important industry. There is some other industry, including processing of bauxite into aluminum, as well as watch assembly, textiles and perfumes.

GETTING AROUND

For beauty of scenery and variety of attractions few areas of such small size can match the American Virgin Islands.

Trunk Bay on St. John has been described as "One of the ten most beautiful beaches in the Western Hemisphere." Beyond the beaches stretch crystal clear waters with such fascinations as Buck Island Reef National Monument, with an underwater "trail."

On St. Thomas Island a point of particular beauty is the harbor of Charlotte Amalie, now the capital city. Hordes of tourists roam the streets, which bear picturesque and "flowery" names such as Orchid Row, Jasmine Lane and Hibiscus Alley. One of the best of all island views may be had from Skyline Drive, almost 1,200 feet above the harbor.

In the capital an old warehouse district is now a fine shopping center, with some of the finest shops. The administration building is said to be "candy pink," which contrasts with the white wrought-iron railings.

The Frederick Evangelical Lutheran church is the second oldest of its denomination in the hemisphere. For another record, some authorities say that

95

St. Thomas Synagogue is the oldest Jewish congregation in U.S. jurisdiction.

A macabre tourist attraction is Bluebeard's Castle, where he was said to have kept his many wives, murdering several.

The old wharf at Christiansted on St. Croix is important enough to have been named a national historic site. Rostered by the National Park Service, the old Steeple Building now houses a good museum. Included are relics of the ancient peoples. Still open for business is the hardware store which employed a clerk named Alexander Hamilton, before he became a national U.S. figure. The airport is named in his honor.

Another interesting town of St. Croix is Frederiksted.

Throughout the islands a main attraction is the number of old plantations, some in ruins and some beautifully restored.

A good example of the local color is found in the festivals of the islands. Accompanied by the drum bands, the people celebrate their Christmas Festival and Carnival on St. Croix. Throughout the islands, Transfer Day, on March 31st, commemorates the U.S. acquisition.

COMPAC-FACS

U.S. VIRGIN ISLANDS
Islands Of Contentment

HISTORY
Discovery: By Columbus in 1493
Became U.S. Territory: March 21, 1917
Capital: Charlotte Amalie, St. Thomas, since 1917
OFFICIAL SYMBOLS
Bird: Yellow breast
Flower: Yellow elder or yellow cedar
Song: "Virgin Islands March"

GEO-FACS
Area: 133 sq. mi.
Water Area: 1 sq. mi.
Highest Point: 1,556 ft. (Crown Mt. on St. Thomas)
Lowest Point: Sea level (Atlantic Ocean)
POPULATION
Total: 99,670 (1982)
Density: 757.6 persons per sq. mi.
Urban: 25 percent
St. Croix: 15,830
St. Thomas: 45,350
St. John: 2,490
EDUCATION
Schools: 33 elementary and secondary
Higher: One
WHEN DID IT HAPPEN?
1493: Columbus discovers on second voyage
1596: Virtually uninhabited, Caribs disappear, perhaps taken as slaves
1642: Dutch Nieuw Zeeland, first colony on islands
1651: St. Croix bought for Knights of Malta
1733: Denmark purchases St. Croix
1840: Danish prosperity at peak
1866: U.S. makes first attempt to buy islands
1917: U.S. buys from Denmark
1927: People become American Nationals
1936: Limited self-government achieved
1954: Self-rule expanded
1964: Tourist trade becomes first in income
1970: Population 62,468
1980: Population 95,000
1982: Population 99,670 (est.)

OTHER CARIBBEAN ISLANDS

Until 1981 the U.S. had laid claim to the uninhabited islands of Quita Sueno Bank, Roncador and Serrana. In that year, the U.S. gave up the claim.

The two-square-mile island of Navassa lies between Haiti and Jamaica. An automatic lighthouse there is serviced occasionally, but the island has no regular inhabitants.

THAT'S CURIOUS:

The shortage of water was so acute that when the All Saints Episcopal Church was being built at Charlotte Amalie, the builders used molasses for mixing the mortar.

INDEX to this volume

Abalone, 30
Abert Rim (earthquake fault), 51
Aerocar (M. B. Taylor), 71
Agana, GU, 83
Agate Beach, OR, 58
Agates, 59
Agattu Island (AK), 15
Agriculture, 18, 20, 29, 30, 42, 46, 59, 71, 73, 80, 83, 88, 90, 91, 95
Ahgupuk, George Aden (Twok), 16
Aiga (extended family), 81
Air Force, U.S., 85
Airmail, 70
Airlines, passenger, 42
Airmail, 70
Airplanes, 18, 19, 32, 44
Airports, 15, 73, 81, 96
Akaka Falls (HI), 39
Alakai Swamp, 39
Alameda, CA, 35
Alaska (main article), 9
Alaska Highway, 18
Alaska Hist. Library and Museum, 19
Alaska Peninsula, 9, 21
Alaska Purchase, 13
Alaska brown bears, 17
Alaska pipeline, 15, 18
Alaskan Native Claims Settlement Act, 15
Albatross, 44
Alekoko Fish Pond, 39
Aleut people, 11, 12, 13
Aleutian Islands (AK), 9, 15, 21
Alki Point (WA), 74
All Saints Episcopal Church (Charlotte Amalie, VI), 96
"Aloha Oe" (song), 49
Aloha Week Festival of Early Hawaii, 49
Alonso, Manuel, 90
Aluminum, 59, 95
American Fur Co., 69
American Samoa (main article), 79
American Rhododendron Soc. Test Garden (OR), 62
American settlements, 69
Anchorage, AK, 10*, 14, 15, 20
Angelfish, French, 94
Anso-Borrego Desert State Park (CA), 31
Anvil Creek, AK, 19
Appaloosa horses, 67
Apple, sugar, 94
Apples, 73
Aquaculture, 39
Arawak Indians, 87, 93
Arch Rock (Rockaway, OR), 62
Arctic Circle, 21
Arecibo, PR, 92
Ariyoshi, George R., 42
Arizona, Battleship, 49
Artists, 16, 25, 58, 90
Arts and Crafts Center (Seattle, WA), 74
Assassinations, 85
Astor, John Jacob, 53
Astor Fur Co., 69
Astor Mem. Column, 62
Astoria, OR, 53, 62
Athapascan Indians, 11
Atomic bomb, 70
Atomic weapons, 80
Attu Island (AK), 15, 21
Aunu'u Island (AS), 79
Authors, 16, 29, 58, 90
Aviation, 14, 18, 19, 71
Babe (Bunyan's blue ox), 51
Bahgwan Shree Rajneesh, 56
Bakersfield, CA, 27
Balboa Park (San Diego, CA), 31
Balch, Frederic Homer, 58
Bananas, 80, 83, 91
Banyan trees, 84
Barelegged owl, 94
Barker, Edward Dickinson, 55
Barrow, AK, 21
Baseball, 20, 28, 74, 91
Basketball, 74
Basketmakers, 67
Bats, 84, 94
Bats, fruit, 84
Battle of Saipan, 85
Battle of Spokane Plains, 69
Battle of Tinian, 85
Battleship Arizona, 49
Bauxite, 59, 95
Bays, 23, 26, 31, 48, 49, 53, 81
Beach, Rex, 16
Beacon Rock (WA), 65
Beale, Edward F., 26
Beans, 83

Bear Flag Republic (California), 26
Bears, 11*, 14, 16, 17, 72
Bears, Kodiak, 14
Beavers, 58, 72
Bellingham, WA, 76
Benson, Benny, 16
Bering, Vitus, 13, 16
Bering Strait, 15
Berkeley, CA, 35
Beverly Hills, CA, 33
Bikini Island (Pacific), 85
Bird, Isabella, 27
Bishop Museum, 49
Bishop family (HI), 44
Black coral, 44
Block, Ernest, 58
"Blue Boy, The" (painting), 33
Blue Mts., 53, 65
Blue heron, 94
Blue ox, Babe, 51
Bluebeard (pirate), 93, 96
Bluebeard's Castle (VI), 96
Bobcats, 33, 72
Bodega Bay, 26
Bodega Y Quadra, Juan de, 67
Boeing, William, 71
Boeing Co., 73
Bonefish, 94
Bonneville Dam (OR), 56
Booby birds, 44
Borders, 69
Boringuino (PR natives), 88
Borinquen (PR), 88
Boston, MA, 62
Boundaries, 69
Breadfruit, 80
Bremerton, WA, 73, 76
Bridges, suspension, 34
Bristlecone pines, 30
British Columbia (Canada), 70
British Virgin Islands, 93
Brocken (shadow), 47
Brown, John (Lean John), 27
Brussel sprouts, 30
Buck Island Reef Nat. Mon., 95
Buffaloes (bison), 17
Bulbs, flower, 73
Bunyan, Paul, 51
Bush, George Washington, 69, 71, 72
Bush Prairie (WA), 71
Butterflies, monarch, 30
Cabbages, 18, 83
Cable cars (San Francisco, CA), 34
Cabrillo, Juan Rodriguez, 25
Cadman, Charles Wakefield, 29
Calico, CA (ghost town), 31
California (main article), 23
California 49'ers, 27
California poppies, 30
California Republic (Bear Flag Rep), 26
California poppies, 30
Camel Rock (Lauli'i, HI), 5*
Camel races, 32
Camels, 31
Campeche, Jose, 90
Cannery Row (Monterey, CA), 34
Canoe Indians, 67
Cannibals, 88
Cannon Beach (OR), 51
Cape Blanco (OR), 53
Cape Flattery (CA), 67
Cape Horn (South America), 27
Capistrano, CA, 31
Capitals, Hawaii native, 41
Capitals, Indian, 41
Capitals, state, 14, 19, 27, 34, 42, 49, 62, 76
Capitals, territorial, 14, 80, 83, 95
Capitol domes, 35
Capitol murals, 35
Capitols, state, 22*, 36*, 50*, 64*, 78*
Carabao, 84
Carib Indians, 87, 93
Caribbean islands, 87
Caribou, 17
Carmel, CA, 28, 29, 33
Carnival (St. Croix, VI), 96
Carnival (St. Thomas, VI), 8*, 86*
Caroline Islands (Pacific), 85
Carson, Christopher (Kit), 26
Casa Blanco (San Juan, PR), 91
Casals, Pablo, 90
Casals Festival, 90
Cascade Mts., 65
Cascade Range, 65
Cathedral of St. Michael (Sitka, AK), 13, 19
Caves, 63, 77, 87
Celilo Pass (OR), 63
Cement, 91

Cemeteries (nat. HI), 49
Centennial celebration (AK), 15
Center for the Performing Arts (Tacoma, WA), 74
Central Valley (CA), 23, 35
Cepeda, Orlando, 91
Cerro de Punta, 87
Chamorro (people), 82, 83
Champoeg, OR, 55
Channel Islands (CA), 30
Charlotte Amalie, VI, 94, 95*, 96
Charlotte Amalie Harbor, 95
Chena River, 15
Cherimoya, 30
Chilkoot Pass (AK), 13
China Cap Mt., 51
Chinatown (San Francisco, CA), 34
Chinook Indians, 53
Chinook winds, 65
Christiansted, VI, 96
Christiansted Nat. Hist. Site, 96
Christmas Festival (VI), 96
Chronology, 22, 35, 50, 64, 78, 81, 84, 92, 96
City of Refuge Nat. Hist. Park (HI), 40*, 48
Civil War, 13, 27, 55
Civil rights, 69, 71
Clark, William, 53, 62, 67, 68
Clemens, Samuel L. (Mark Twain), 29
Clemente, Roberto, 91
Coachella Valley (CA), 30
Coal, 59, 72
Coast Range, 51
Coastal Mts., 23
Coastal redwoods, 30
Cockfights, 91
Coconut palms, 94
Coconuts, 80, 81, 83
Coffee, 46, 90
Coleman, Peter Tali, 80
College, AK, 20
Colorado River, 65
Columbia, CA, 35
Columbia Basin Project, 73
Columbia Plateau, 65
Columbia River, 51, 53, 56, 59, 60, 63, 63*, 65, 67, 70, 72, 73, 76
Columbia-Snake River Navigation System, 70
Commencement Bay (WA), 73
Commerce, 73, 80, 83
Communications, 17, 19, 42
Compac-Facs, 21, 22, 35, 49, 50, 64, 78, 81, 84, 92, 96
Composers, 29, 58
Computers, 31
Concentration camps, 28, 83
Condon Day State Park (OR), 53
Condors, California, 30
Conservation, 56, 58
Conservationists, 15
Constitution (AS), 80
Conventions, 28
Conventions, political, 28
Cook, James, 13, 40, 41, 42, 48, 53, 67
Coos Bay, OR, 60
Coral, 44, 49, 82, 92
Coral fish, 94
Coral reefs, 92
Cotton, 30
Count of Monte Rey, 25
Covington House (Vancouver WA), 77
Crabs, 58
Crafts, Polynesian, 80
Crater Lake, 51, 54*, 63
Creosote bushes, 30
Crocker, Charles, 29
Crosby, Harry Lillis (Bing), 72
Crown Point (OR), 63*
Cruise ships, 19, 91
Cucumbers, 83
Culebra Island (Caribbean), 87
Cumberland (Earl of), 88
Customs, Hawaiian native, 39, 43, 46, 48
Customs, Indian, 12, 25, 67, 93
Customs, prehistoric, 39, 43, 46, 48
Cutler, Lyman, 69
Cypress, Monterey, 30, 33
D'Aguilar, Martin, 53
Dairy products, 60
Dall, W. H., 16
Dall sheep, 16
Damien, de Veuster, 44
Date Festival, 32
Dates, 30
Davenport, Homer, 58
De Gautier, Dona Felisa Rincon, 90
De Hostos, Eugenio Maria, 90
De Mille, Cecil B., 30

De Rouge, Etienne, 71
Death Valley (CA), 23, 32
Death Valley Scotty (Walter E. Scott), 29
Deborah of Hawaii, 45
Deer, 72, 84, 94
Democratic Party, 28
Denali (Mt. McKinley), 9, 12*, 21
Denny, Mary, 73
Depression of 1929, 28, 89
Deserts, 31, 32, 46, 55, 65
Devil's Postpile Nat. Mon., 23
Diamond Head (HI), 37, 47*, 49
Dickey, W. A., 21
Disasters, 62, 70
Disasters, natural, 14, 15, 20, 28, 56, 58, 62, 70, 76, 80, 83
Disneyland (CA), 33
Dodgers (baseball), 28
Dog sleds, 18
Dogs, 93
Dole, James, 44, 46
Dole, Sanford, 41
Dole Corp., 46, 48
Domes, capitol, 35
Douglas, David, 58
Drake, Francis, 25, 83, 88
Dry Falls (WA), 65
Earthquakes, 15, 20, 23, 28, 51, 70, 91
Easter lily bulbs, 60
Eastern Hemisphere, 9
Eastwood, Clint, 28
Economy, 19, 31, 46, 60, 73, 80
El Morro (San Juan, PR), 88, 91
El Pueblo de Nuestra Senora la Reina de Los Angeles de Porci (LA, CA), 25
El Yunque (Mt.), 87
El Yunque rainforest (PR), 91
Electric power, 70
Electronics industry, 60
Elevators, fish, 72
Elk, 72, 77
Ellensburg, WA, 70
Emerald Bay Nat. Landmark, 35
"End of the Trail, The" (Monument), 63
Eniwetok Island (Pacific), 85
Entertainers, 28, 30, 72, 90
Environmentalists, 18
Eskimo customs, 12
Eskimo leaders, 12
Eskimo settlements, 21
Eskimos, 12, 16, 17, 21
Estado Libre Asociado, 89
European settlements, 25, 53, 69
Evergreen Bridge (WA), 73
Explorers, 13, 16, 25, 29, 40, 67, 68, 72, 82, 88
Fagatogo, AS, 80
Fairbanks, AK, 14, 15, 18, 20
Fairy terns, 44
Fanihi bats, 84
Ferraro, Geraldine, 28
Ferrello, Bartolome, 53
Ferryboats, 19, 73, 74, 76, 91
Festivals, 20, 21, 32, 49, 62, 76, 84, 90, 91, 96
Fig trees, 84
Fires, 28, 58, 62, 70
Fires, forest, 58
Fish, 18, 44, 49, 58, 83, 94
Fish elevators, 72
Fish farming, 44
Fish ladders, 72
Fisherman's Wharf (Monterey, CA), 34
Fisherman's Wharf (San Francisco, CA), 34
Fishing, commercial, 18, 58, 83
Fishing, hukilau, 49
Fishing, sport, 44, 94
Flags, 16, 17, 19, 26, 55, 80
Flower bulbs, 73
Forests, 58, 87, 90
Forget-me-not (flower), 16
Fort Clatsop, 53, 62
Fort Dalles, 63
Fort Nisqually, 74
Fort Okonagon, 69
Fort Ross, 26
Fort Stevens, 56, 62
Fort Vancouver, 69, 77
Forty-niners, 27
Fossil, OR, 63
Fossils, 63
Foster Botanic Garden (HI), 49
Frederick Evangel. Luth. Ch. (Charlotte Amalie, VI), 95
Frederiksted, VI, 96
Freedom of religion, 43
Fremont, John C., 26, 29
"Frieda" (storm), 56

Frigate bird, 44, 94
Frost, Robert, 29
Fruit bats, 84
Fur rendezvous, 20
Fur trade, 26, 53, 69
Gable, Clark, 30
Gale, Joe, 57
Galloping Gertie (Tacoma Narrows Bridge), 76
Gandia, Manuel Zeno, 90
Gas and oil, 15, 17, 27, 31
Geese, 72
Gemstones, 59
General Grant tree, 35
Geography, 9, 23, 37, 39, 46, 51, 65, 79, 82, 85, 87, 93, 96
Geology, 23, 37, 51, 65, 91, 93
Georgetown Univ., 90
Getty art galleries (CA), 33
Giant Sequoias, 30
Giant cobra lilies, 58
Giant coreopsis (sunflower), 30
Gibralter of the Pacific, 33
Ginaca, Harry, 44
Glacier Bay (AK), 20
Glacier Bay Nat. Mon., 20
Glacier Peak, 65
Glacier Priest (Bernard Hubbard), 16
Glaciers, 9, 16, 19, 20*, 21, 23, 51, 65
Gold, 13, 14, 15, 19, 20, 27, 29, 31, 35, 55, 62, 70
Gold coral, 44
Gold Days Festival, 20
Gold Discovery State Park (CA), 35
Golden Gate (CA), 28, 29, 34
Golden Gate Bridge, 28, 34
Golden Jubilee of Statehood (WA), 70
Goldendale, WA, 77
Goleta, CA, 28
Grand Canyon of the Colorado, 39, 48, 51
Grand Coulee Dam, 70, 73, 76
Grand Coulee gorge, 65
Granite, 23, 25
Grapes, 30
Gray, Robert, 53
Greater Antilles, 87
Green Lake, 74
"Grizzly Bear" (locomotive), 27
Guadalupe Hidalgo, Treaty of, 26
Guam (main article), 82
Guavas, 45, 94
Gulf of Alaska, 9
Gvozdev, Michael, 13
Hafnium, 60
Haida Indians, 67
Haleakala (HI), 37
Haleakala Nat. Park, 46
Half Dome (Yosemite Nat. Pk.), 35
Hall of Fame, U.S., 29, 57
Hallshallakeen (Joseph the Younger), 71
Hamilton, Alexander, 96
Hanapepe River, 39
Harbors, 23, 32, 42, 47, 79, 87, 95
Harding, Warren G., 14
Hawaii (main article), 37
Hawaii Island, 37, 39, 42, 47
Hawaii Royal palace and throne room, 49
Hawaii native customs, 39, 43, 46, 48
Hawaii native recreation, 39
Hawaii native wars, 41
Hawaiian gods, 37, 40*
Hawaiian Islands Nat. Wildlife Ref., 44
Hawaiian goose (nene), 44
Hawaiian hulu, 49, 81
Hawks, 94
Haystack Rock (OR), 51, 62
Hearst, William Randolph, 33
Hearst San Simeon State Hist. Mon. (CA), 33
Hecata Head (OR), 59*
Heceta, Bruno, 67
Hell's Canyon (Snake River), 63
Heron, blue, 94
Herons, 94
Hibiscus Alley (Charlotte Amalie, VI), 95
Highways, 15, 18, 32, 33, 60, 62, 73, 84, 91
Hill of Sacrifice (HI), 49
Hilo, HI, 47
Hilo Island (HI), 46
Hiram Chittenden Locks, 74
Historic districts, 33, 34, 35
Hoate, John, 71
Hokule, 43
Hollywood, CA, 28, 31
Hollywood Boulevard (LA, CA), 33
Holo-Holo-Ku Heiau (temple), 48
Honaunau, HI, 48
Honey creeper, 94
Honolulu, HI, 38*, 46, 47*, 49, 82
Honolulu Zoo (HI), 49
Hood River, 60
Hoover, Herbert, 28, 94

Hopkins, Mark, 29
Horse Indians, 53, 67, 69
Horses, 53, 63, 67, 90
Hoyt Arboretum, 62
Hubbard, Bernard, 16
Hubbard, Edward, 70
Hudson's Bay Co., 53, 69
Hughes, Howard, 32
Hula Festival, 49
Hulu, Hawaiian, 81
Humboldt Redwoods State Park (CA), 30
Humingbird, 94
Huntington, Collis P., 29
Huntington Library and Museum (CA), 33
Hurricanes, 87
Huskies (Univ. of WA football), 74
Iao stream (HI), 41
Ice Sweepstakes, 22
Iguanas, 88
Imperial Valley (CA), 23, 31
Indian capitals, 13
Indian customs, 12, 25, 67, 93
Indian population, 25
Indian rights, 57, 71
Indian wars, 26, 55, 69
Indians, 9, 12, 16, 23, 25, 29, 32, 53, 55, 56, 67, 69, 71, 72, 93
Indians, displacement, 58, 69
Indio, CA, 32
Industrialists, 29, 30, 44, 71
Industry, 30, 42, 60, 73, 80, 89, 90
Inscription Canyon (CA), 32
Insects, 30
Inside Passage, 19
Insurance, 93
Interior, U.S. Dept. of, 80
International Fountain (Seattle, WA), 74
International Rose Test Gardens (OR), 62
International dateline, 9, 82
Ioa Needle (HI), 46
Ioa Valley (HI), 46
Iolani Palace (Honolulu, HI), 49
Islands, 9, 15, 21, 25, 33, 37, 39, 40, 42, 44, 46, 47, 48, 65, 79, 80, 81, 82, 87, 93, 94, 96
J. Paul Getty Museum, 33
Jackson, Sheldon, 17
Jacksonville, OR, 55
Jade Cove (CA), 33
Japanese-Americans, 28, 42
Jasmine Lane (Charlotte Amalie, VI), 95
Javelina (wild pig), 94
Jesse Lee Mission Home (Seward, AK), 16
Jesuits, 82
Jewish congregations, 96
John Day Dam, 60
Joseph the Elder (chief), 63, 71
Joseph the Younger (chief), 57, 58, 63, 71
Joshua Tree Nat. Mon., 32
Joshua trees, 30, 32
Juneau, AK, 13, 14, 19, 21
Jurucan (PR native god), 87
Kaahumanu of Hawaii, 45
Kahoolawe Island (HI), 48
Kalakaua (David) of Hawaii, 41, 43
Kalanikupule (HI chief), 41
Kalapana, HI, 47
Kalaupapa, HI, 48
Kamehameha I (The Great), 41, 43, 45, 46, 48
Kamehameha II, 41
Kamehameha III, 41, 42, 43
Kamehameha IV, 41, 44
Kamehameha V, 4
Kamiakin (chief), 71
Kanahele, Benihakaka, 48
Kanaloa (Hawaiin diety), 39
Kane (Hawaiian diety), 39
Kaneoho Bay (HI), 49
Kapiolani (HI chiefess), 43
Kapiolani Park (Honolulu, HI), 49
"Karen" (typhoon), 83
Katmai Nat. Mon., 21, 44
Kauai Island (HI), 37, 39, 44, 48
Kaumaulii of Hawaii, 45, 48
Kaunolu (Lanai), HI, 48
Kealakekua Bay (HI), 42, 48
Kearny, Stephen Watts, 26
Kennewick, WA, 77
Keoua (HI chief), 41
Ketchikan, AK, 7, 18, 19
Kilauea (Mauna Loa), 37, 43, 47
King County Stadium (Kingdome, WA), 74
Kingdome (King County Stadium, WA), 74
Kingfish, 94
Kings Canyon Nat. Park, 35
Kipling, Rudyard, 29
Kiska Island (AK), 15
Kitsap (chief), 67
Klondike (Canada), 13
Klondike miners (1899), 14*
Knotts Berry Farm (CA), 33

Kodiak, AK, 13
Kodiak Island (AK), 21
Kodiak bears, 14
Kokonee salmon, 58
Korean War, 42
Kotzebue, AK, 21
Koyukuk River, 11
Ku (HI god of war), 39, 48
Kure Island (HI), 37
Kwajalein Island (Pacific), 85
La Carta Autonomica, 88
La Jolla, CA, 31
La Plata River, 87
Ladders, fish, 72
Lago, Daniel, 65
Laguna Beach, CA, 32
Lahaina, HI, 47
Lake Chelan, 76
Lake County, OR, 51
Lake George, 11
Lake Iliamna, 11
Lake Tahoe, 35
Lake Waiau, 39
Lake Washington, 74
Lakes, 11, 35, 39, 51, 54*, 55, 74, 76, 77
Lakeview, OR, 51
Lanai Island (HI), 48
Lanainaluna High School (HI), 47
Land bridge, 11
Land grants, 26
Lassen Volcanic Nat .Park, 35
Lava Beds Nat. Mon., 35
Lavalava (garment), 81
Lee, Jason, 55, 57
Leeward Islands (HI), 44
Legends, 51
Legislatures, unicameral, 83, 94
Leis, 49
Leprosy, 44
Levis (trousers), 31
Lewis, Meriwether, 53, 62, 67
Lewis and Clark Centennial Exposition, 56
Lewis and Clark expedition, 53, 62, 67
Lexington, OR, 53
Lilac Festival (Spokane, WA), 76
Lilies, 58, 60
Liliuokalani, of Hawaii, 41, 49
Lily, giant cobra, 58
Lincoln, Abraham, 27, 55
Lincoln Park (Seattle, WA), 74
Little Diomede Island (AK), 21
Livestock industry, 80, 83
Lizards, 94
Loiza Aldea, PR, 91
London, Jack, 51
Long Beach, CA, 32
Long Beach Harbor, 32
Lono (Hawaiian diety), 39
Los Angeles, CA, 24*, 25, 28, 32
Louvre (Paris, France), 90
Lumber and wood products, 18, 59, 71
Lumbering, 58, 59, 71
Lunalilo, of Hawaii, 41
Lynx, 72
Macadamia nuts, 45
Madrona tree, 30, 58
Magellan, Ferdinand, 82
Malaspina Glacier, 9
Mango, 94
Mangroves, 94
Manu Islands (HI), 79
Manufacturing, 31, 46, 59, 83, 90
Manzanita, OR, 62
Mariana Islands (Pacific), 82, 84, 85
Marin, Luis Munoz, 89, 90
Marine jewel (fish), 94
Maritime Indians, 11
Markham, Edwin, 58
Marquesas Islands Pacific), 39
Marshall, CA, 35
Marshall, John, 35
Marshall Islands and Atolls (Pacific), 85
Massacres, 69
Matai (family leader), 81
Matanuska Valley (AK), 14, 20
Maui Island (HI), 37, 41, 46, 47
Mauna Kea, 39, 47
Mauna Loa, 37, 39, 42, 43, 47
Mayaguez, PR, 92
Mayan civilization, 53
Mayer, Louis B., 30
McKinley, William, 21
McLoughlin, John, 53, 54, 56, 57, 60, 62, 69, 70, 71, 77
McLoughlin House Nat. Hist. Site, 62
Meares, James, 67
Medicine men (shamans), 67
Mendenhall Glacier (AK), 20*
Mendocino, CA, 35
Menehune (prehistoric Hawaiians), 39
Mercer, Asa, 74
"Mercer Girls", 74
Mercury ore, 59

Mexican period (CA), 26*
Miami, FL, 93
Micronesia, 85
Midnight Sun baseball game, 20
Mills, 35
Minerals and mining, 27, 59, 72, 90, 94, 95
Miss Arctic Circle, 21
Mission San Carlos Borromeo de Carmelo (Carmel, CA), 29
Mission San Diego Alcala, 25, 26
Mission San Diego Alcala (mural), 26*
Mission San Francisco de Asis, 25
Mississippi River, 62
Modoc War, 55
Mokihana berries, 45
Molokai Island (HI), 37, 48
Mona Island (Caribbean), 87
Monarch butterflies, 30
Mondale, Walter, 28
Mongoose, 94
Monkeys, 30
Monorails, 74
Monroe, Marilyn, 30
Monte Rey (Count of), 25
Monterey, CA, 26
Monterey Bay, 25
Monterey Peninsula, 25, 33
Monterey cypress, 30, 33
Monterey pine, 30
Monuments, 20, 21, 32, 33, 35, 48, 49, 62, 63, 77, 95
Mormons, 32
Morro Bay, CA, 33
Morro Castle (San Juan, PR), 88*
Motion picture industry, 28, 31
Mountain goats, 65
Mountains, 9, 12*, 14, 21, 23, 25, 28, 31, 35, 37, 39, 40, 42, 43, 45, 47, 51, 53, 62, 63, 65, 67, 70, 74, 76, 77, 79, 81, 82, 90, 91, 867
Mountains, prehistoric, 51
Mt. Adams, 65
Mt. Baker, 65, 76, 77
Mt. Diablo State Park (CA), 35
Mt. Everest (Nepal), 9
Mt. Haleakala, 45
Mt. Hood, 51, 53, 62
Mt. Katmai, 14, 21
Mt. Lata, 79
Mt. Malafao, 81*
Mt. Mazama (prehistoric), 51
Mt. McKinley (Denali), 9, 12*, 21
Mt. Olympus, 67
Mt. Olympus (Greece), 67, 76
Mt. Palomar observatory, 28, 31
Mt. Rainier, 65, 72, 74, 77
Mt. Rainier Nat. Park, 70
Mt. Shasta, 35
Mt. Shishaldin, 9
Mt. Spokane State Park (WA), 76
Mt. St. Helens, 65, 70, 77
Mt. Tabor, 62
Mt. Waialeale, 37, 39
Muir, John, 16, 19, 58
Muir Woods (CA), 35
Muir Woods Nat. Mon., 35
Mulberry tree, 80
Murals, capitol, 18*, 62
Museums, 19, 33, 47, 63, 76, 96
Musk ox, 17
Names, origin, 16, 21, 32, 53, 67, 87, 93
Napa, CA, 35
National Guard (OR), 56
National Hall of Fame, 1
National Mem. Cemetery of the Pacific, 49
Naval oranges, 30
Navassa Island (Caribbean), 96
Nenana, AK, 22
Nene (Hawaiian goose), 44
Newport, OR, 62
Nez Perce Indians, 57, 69, 71
Nickel, 59, 60
Niihau Island (HI), 48
Nixon, Richard M., 28
Nome, AK, 13, 19, 21
Northern Pacific RR, 70
Nuclear research, 73
Nuclear tests, 85
Nuuanu Pali cliff (HI), 48
Nuuanu Valley (HI), 41
O'o bird, 94
Oahu Island (HI), 37, 41, 48
Oakland, CA, 35
Oakland Bay Bridge, 28, 34
Ocean View Blvd. (Pacific Grove, CA), 33
Ofu Island (SA), 79
Ohelo berries, 43
Oil and gas, 15, 17, 27, 31
Oil industry, 28, 90
Okanogan, WA, 71
Oller, Francisco, 90
Olosega Island (SA), 79

Olvera Street (Los Angeles, CA), 33
Olympia, WA, 76
Olympic Games, 28
Olympic Mts., 65, 74
Olympic Nat. Park, 70, 76
Olympic Peninsula (WA), 67, 72, 74, 76
Operation Bootstrap, 89, 90
Operation Serenidad, 89
Oranges, 30, 80
Orchid Row (Charlotte Amalie, VI), 95
Orchids, 45, 46, 49, 72, 84, 90
Oregon (main article), 51
Oregon Caves Nat. Mon., 63
Oregon City, OR, 55, 56, 62
Oregon Trail, 60, 69, 71
Otter Crescent (OR), 58
Ouragon (Columbia River), 53
Owl, barelegged, 94
Owyhee Lake, 60
Owyhee River, 60
Oysters, 58
Pacific Grove, CA, 30, 33
Pacific Science Center, 74
Pago Pago, SA, 79, 80, 81
Pago Pago Bay (SA), 81
Pago Pago International Airport, 81
Palau Island (Pacific), 85
Palm Springs, CA, 32
Palm trees, 80, 84, 90, 94
Palms, coconut, 94
Palms, royal, 94
Palusami (food), 81
Pan American Airlines, 42
Panamint Mts., 29*
Pantages Theater (Tacoma, WA), 74
Papaya, 45, 94
Paradise Inn (Mt. Rainier), 77
Parker Ranch (HI), 46
Pasadena, CA, 33
Pasco, WA, 77
Paso fino (horse), 90
Paulet, George, 43
Peale Island (Pacific), 85
Pearl Harbor (HI), 42, 49, 56
Pele (HI goddess of volcanoes), 37, 43
Pele's hair, 37
Peleliu Island (Pacific), 85
Pelicans, 94
Pend Oreille River, 65
Pendleton, OR, 63
Pendleton Roundup (OR), 63
Peoples, 16, 44, 57, 71
Perfumes, 95
Perz, Juan, 67
Petersburg cocktail shrimp, 17
Petroglyphs, 25, 53
Pfeiffer-Big Sur State Park (CA), 33
Pickford, Mary, 30
Pico, Pio, 26
Pictographs, 25, 53
Picture Gorge (OR), 53
Pig War, 69
Pigs, 33
Pigs, wild, 33
Pin coral, 44
Pine, ponderosa, 58
Pine cones, 60
Pine trees, 30, 58
Pines, bristlecone, 30
"Pinkie" (painting), 33
"Pioneer" (statue), 62
Pioneer Square (Seattle, WA), 74
Pioneers, Hawaiian, 41
Pirates, 83, 88, 93
Plantains (bananas), 91
Plantations, 94
Plants, 30, 42, 46, 58, 60, 62, 72, 80, 84, 91
Plutonium, 70
Poi, 45
Poinciana trees, 90
Point Lobos (CA), 33
Point Reyes Nat. Seashore, 35
Point Roberts (WA/Canada), 65
Polar bears, 17
Polk, James K., 69
Polynesian crafts, 80
Polynesians, 39, 79, 80
Ponce, PR, 2
Ponce de Leon, Don Juan, 88, 91
Ponderosa pine, 58
Population, 13, 23, 28, 48, 49, 55, 56, 83, 89
Porcupine River, 17
Port Angeles, WA, 76
Port Chilkoot, AK, 20
Port of Seattle, 73
Portland, OR, 52*, 60, 62
Ports, 19, 20, 60, 62, 73, 74, 76, 91, 95
Post, Wiley, 14
Potatoes, 45
Potatoes, sweet, 93
Potlach, 67, 71

Prehistoric customs, 39, 43, 46, 48
Prehistoric customs (Hawaii), 39
Prehistoric dieties (HI), 39
Prehistoric mts., 51
Prehistoric peoples, 11, 23, 39, 53, 67, 82, 87, 96
Prehistoric weapons, 11, 40
Prehistoric wildlife, 17
Prospectors, 13
Prudhoe Bay (AK), 18
Puerto Grande harbor (Culebra Island), 87
Puerto Rico (main article), 87
Puerto Rico archipelago, 87
Puget, Peter, 67
Puget Sound (WA), 65, 69, 73, 74
Pullen, Harriet (Mother), 15
Pullman, WA, 76
Puowaina Crater, 7
Quadra, Juan de Bodega Y, 67
"Queen Mary" (ship), 32
Quito Sueno Bank (Caribbean island), 96
Radio, 42
Railroads, 14, 15, 18, 19, 27, 29, 55, 60, 70, 73
Rainforest (OR), 61*
Rajneesh, (Bhagwan) Shree, 56
Ranchos, 26
Razor clams, 17
Reagan, Ronald, 28
Reclamation, 73
Recreation, 23, 33, 39, 62, 76, 84
Redwood trees, 30, 35, 58
Redwoods, coastal, 58
Reindeer, 16, 17
Religious freedom, 43
Republican Party, 28
Research, 21, 73
Resources, 18, 30, 31, 57, 58, 59, 60, 72, 83, 90, 94
Restoration, 32, 33, 62, 74, 76, 77, 91, 95
Revere, Paul, 27
Revolutionary War, 25
Rhododendrons, 61, 72
Richland, WA, 70, 73, 77
Rivera, Juis Munoz, 90
Riverfront Park (Spokane, WA), 76, 77*
Rivers, 11, 19, 22, 39, 48, 51, 55, 56, 60, 63, 65, 71, 77, 87
Robinson family (HI), 44, 48, 49
Rock, Howard (Skivoan Weyahok), 16
Rockaway, OR, 62
Rocky Butte (OR), 62
Rocky Mountain elk, 58
Rogers, Will, 14
Rogue River War, 55
Roggeveen, Jacob, 79
Roncador island (caibbean), 96
Roosevelt elk, 72
Rosado, Julio, 90
Rose Bowl Parade, 33
Rose Bowl football game, 33
Rose Festival (Portland, OR), 59*, 62
Rose Island (SA), 79
Rose Mantle (HI), 47
Royal palace and throne room (HI), 49
Royal palms, 94
Rum, 95
Russian Fort, 48
Russian settlements, 13, 23
Sacramento, CA, 29, 35
Sailboats, 76
Salal berries, 72
Salem, OR, 55, 57, 60, 62
Salmon, 15, 17, 53, 56, 58, 72, 73, 76
Salton Sea State Park (CA), 31
San Cristobal (San Juan, PR), 88, 91
San Diego, CA, 23, 25, 31, 32
San Diego Bay (CA), 23, 25, 31
San Diego Zoo, 31
San Francisco, CA, 27, 28, 35, 41
San Francisco Bay (CA), 23, 28, 34
San Francisco World's Fair, 28
San Juan, PR, 87, 88, 90, 91
San Juan Islands (WA), 69, 76
San Marino, CA, 33
Sandwich Islands (HI), 40
Santa Barbara, CA, 33
Santa Barbara Channel (CA), 25
Santa Barbara Islands (CA), 25
Santa Catalina Island (CA), 25
Santa Cruz, CA, 30
Santa Rosa Island (CA), 25
Saroyan, William, 29
Sausalito, CA, 35
Scheffer, George, 48
Scott, Walter E. (Death Valley Scotty), 29
Scrimshaw, 12
Sea Lion Point (OR), 58
Sea grapes, 94
Sea lions, 19, 30, 58, 62
Sea otters, 17, 19, 26, 30, 58
Sea turkeys, 58, 62
Seals, 17, 19, 58

Seattle, WA, 66*, 69, 70, 73, 74
Seattle (chief), 71
Seattle Art Museum, 74
Seattle Center, 74
Seattle Mariners (baseball), 74
Seattle Seahawks (football), 74
Seattle Supersonics (basketball), 74
Seattle Symphony, 74
Seely, Martin, 30
Sequoia Nat. Park, 30, 35
Sequoia trees, 30
Serra, Junipero, 25, 28, 29
Serrana Island (Caribbean), 96
Settlements, American, 69
Settlements, Eskimo, 21
Settlements, European, 25, 53, 69
Settlements, Russian, 13, 23
Settlements, Spanish, 25, 88
Seventeen Mile Drive (CA), 33
Seward, AK, 16, 18, 20
Seward, William H., 13
Seward's Folly, 13
Shamans (medicine men), 67
Shipbuilding, 56, 57
Shrimp, 17
Siberia, 12, 16
Siboney Indians, 93
Sierra Nevada Mts., 23, 25, 35
Silversword plant, 46
Sinclair, Elizabeth, 43
Sitka, AK, 13, 19
Siva (dance), 81
Skagit River, 65
Skagway, AK, 15, 20
Skamania, WA, 65
Skokomish River, 8*
Skyline Drive (Charlotte Amalie, VI), 95
Skyscrapers, 33, 74
Slavery, 55, 67, 88, 94
Snake River, 51, 63, 65, 70, 77
Sonoma, CA, 35
Southern hemisphere, 79
Space Needle (Seattle, WA), 74
Spanish settlements, 25, 88
Spokane, WA, 65, 69, 70, 76, 77
Spokane Falls (WA), 69
Spokane House (trading post), 69
Spokane Interstate Fair (WA), 76
Spokane River, 65, 76
Sports, 20, 28, 39, 49, 62, 74, 91
Spruce Goose (airplane), 32
Springs, natural, 59
St. Croix Island (VI), 93, 96
St. John Island (VI), 93, 95
St. Louis, MO, 55
St. Mary's Mission (WA), 71
St. Thomas, VI (Charlotte Amalie), 86*, 94
St. Thomas Island (VI), 93, 95
St. Thomas synagogue (Charlotte Amalie, VI), 95
Stackpole, Ralph, 58
Stanford, Leland, 29
Stanford Univ., 29
"Star of Oregon" (ship), 57
State Capitol Museum (WA), 76
State Library (WA), 76
Steamboats and steamships, 60
Steelhead trout, 58
Steeple Bldg. (Christiansted Nat. Hist. Site), 96
Steinbeck, John, 29
Stevens Village, AK, 16
Stevenson, Robert Louis, 29, 37
Stikine (John Muir's dog), 16, 19
Stikine River, 19
Stonehenge (Britain), 77
Strauss, Levi, 31
Strawberries, 18, 30
Sturgeon, 58
Subways, 34
Sugar, 90
Sugarcane, 42, 46, 94, 95
Sunflowers, 80
Suquamish Museum, 69, 75
Sutter, John, 26, 29, 35
Swain Island, 80
Swallows, 31
Swamps, 39
Swanson, Gloria, 30
Sweet potatoes, 93
Ta'u Island (SA), 79
Tacoma, WA, 70, 74
Tacoma Narrows (WA), 74
Tacoma Narrows Bridge, 74
Tahiti Island (Pacific), 43
Tanana River, 11, 22
Taniers, 91
Tapa cloth, 80
Taro plants, 81
Tarpon, 94
Taylor, Moulton B., 71
Telephones, 19
Television, 19, 31, 80

Tenino, WA, 65
Textiles, 95
"Thaddeus" (ship), 42
That's Curious, 9, 11, 13, 15, 17, 19, 22, 23, 27, 28, 30, 31, 39, 41, 42, 43, 44, 45, 48, 51, 56, 57, 58, 60, 62, 65, 67, 69, 70, 72, 74, 80, 83, 90, 93, 96
Thompson, David, 69
Ti plant, 45
Tidal waves, 15
Tiffany, Louis C., 76
Timberline Lodge (Mt. Hood), 62
Titanium, 59
Tlingit Indians, 19
Tobacco, 90, 91, 93
Tokyo, Japan, 21
Tomatoes, 30, 83
Totem poles, 7*, 15, 75*
Trade winds, 79, 93
Traders, 53, 67
Tramsways, 81
Transfer Day (VI Festival), 96
Transportation, 14, 15, 18, 19, 27, 32, 42, 55, 60, 73, 74
Trappers and trapping, 20
Treaties, 26, 57, 60
Treaty of Guadalupe Hidalgo, 26
Tree frogs, 90
Trees, 30, 35, 58, 62, 80, 84, 90, 94
Tropical rain forests, 46
Trout, 58, 72
Truk Island (Pacific), 85
Trunk Bay (St. John Island, VI), 95
Tslalakum (chief), 71
Tsunami (tidal wave), 15
Tule Lake, 58
Tule Lake Nat. Wildlife Refuge, 58
Tumwater Falls Park (WA), 76
Tuna, 94
Turtles, 88
Tutuila Island (SA), 79
Twain, Mark (Samuel L. Clemens), 29
Twenty-fifth anniversary celebration (HI), 43
Twok (George Aden Ahgupuk), 16
Typhoons, 80, 83
U.S. Air Force, 85
U.S. Dept. of Interior, 80
U.S. Senate, 85
Umpqua River, 51
Unicameral legislatures, 83, 94
Union Square (San Francisco, CA), 34
United Nations, 28, 85
University of Alaska, 20
University of California, 27, 35
University of California, Berkeley, 35
University of Idaho, 76
University of Puerto Rico, 91
University of Washington, 74
Uranium, 70
Urban restoration, 95
Valdez, AK, 18, 20
Valdez Glacier (AK), 13
Valentino, Rudolph, 32
Valley of Ten Thousand Smokes (AK), 14
Vancouver, George, 67
Vancouver, WA, 70, 77
Vieques Island (Caribbean), 87
Virgin Islands (main article), 86
Virgin Islands Corp., 94
Virgins of St. Ursula, 93
Vista House (OR), 63
Vizcaino, Sebastian, 25
Volcano House Hotel (HI), 47
Volcanoes, 14, 16, 21, 23, 37, 39, 42, 43, 45, 47, 51, 62, 65, 70, 77, 79, 82, 93
Wagner, Richard, 74
Wahoo, 94
Wailatpu Mission (WA), 69
Waikiki, HI, 41
Waikiki Beach (HI), 49
Wailua River, 39, 48
Waimea Canyon (HI), 39, 48
Waipahee River, 39
Waipahee Falls (HI), 48
Wake Island (Pacific), 85
Walla Walla, WA, 76
Wallowa Lake, 63
Wallowa Mts., 53
Walrus, 17
War with Mexico, 26, 27
Washington, D.C., 20
Washington, George (WA pioneer), 72
Washington (main article), 65
Washington State Library, 76
Water routes, 18, 60
Water supply, 20, 30, 39, 59, 71, 93, 94, 96
Waterfalls, 35, 39, 48, 63, 76, 77, 84, 91
Waterpower, 60, 73
Watersheds, 11, 39
Watsonville, CA, 30
Weapons, 11, 40, 70
Weapons, atomic, 70

Weapons, prehistoric, 11, 40
Wells Fargo and Co., 27
Western Hemisphere, 11, 95
Whaleshead Beach (OR), 51
Whatcom County City Hall (WA), 76
Wheat, 60, 73
Whidbey Island (WA), 71
"White Fox" (locomotive), 27
White House (Casa Blanco, San Juan, PR), 91
White sea lions, 58
Whitman, Marcus, 69, 71
Whitman, Narcissa, 69, 71

Whittier, AK, 18, 20
Wild Goose RR, 19
Wild pigs (javelina), 33
Wildlife, 17, 30, 33, 44, 58, 62, 72, 77, 84, 94
Wildlife, prehistoric, 17
Wilkes, John, 79
Wilkes Island (Pacific), 85
Willamette River, 51, 60
Willamette Univ., 57
Willamette Valley (OR), 57, 62
Willapa Hills, 65
Willow, AK, 15, 19
Wilson, Thomas Woodrow, 28

Women's rights, 28, 56, 90
Woodland Park Zoo (Seattle, WA), 74
Wool, 62
World War I, 28, 56, 70, 88, 94
World War II, 14, 28, 42, 44, 48, 56, 70, 73, 83, 88
World's Fairs, 28, 56, 70, 74, 76
Wyeth, Nathaniel, 57
Yakima, WA, 70, 77
Yakima Indians, 71
Yakima River, 65, 77
Yams, 80, 91
Yap Island (Pacific), 85

Yo Semite Indians, 23
Yoga tree, 84
Yorba Linda, CA, 28
Yosemite Falls (Yosemite Nat. Park), 32*
Yosemite Nat. Park, 23, 32*, 35
Young, Ewing, 57
Young's Bay (OR), 53
Yucca, 30
Yukon River, 11
Yukon Territory, 70
Yukon gold rush, 70
Zirconium, 60
Zoos, 31, 49, 74

ACKNOWLEDGMENTS

Maps, charts and graphs, EBE; G. Haislemair, 5, 45, 47; EBE; 6, 8, 14, 18, 29, 32, 40, 54, 60; USGS/ NHAP/EROS, 10, 24, 38, 52, 66, 95, 102; California Office of Tourism, 25, 30, 34; Allan Carpenter, 26, 34; Dept. of Army, 32; USDI, NPS, Joshua Tree Nat. Mon., 35; Hawaii Visitors Bureau, 50; Oregon Economic Development Dept. 55, 56, 63, 64; Click, 59; State of Washington, Dept. of Economic Development, 68, 75, 77, 78; Fofo I. F. Sunia, Samoan Delegate to Congress, 81; Peter Martin, Associates, 86, 89, 92

CUMULATIVE INDEX to seven volumes

Abalone, 7-30
Abbeville County, SC, 3-105
Abbott, Charles Greeley, 1-91
Aberdeen, SD, 5-106
Abert Rim (earthquake fault), 7-51
Abilene, KS, 5-32, 34, 39
Abingdon, VA, 2-109
"Able McLaughlins, The" (book), 4-49
Abnaki Indians, 1-59
Abraham Lincoln Birthplace Nat. His. Site, 3-67
Academy of the Fine Arts (Philadelphia, PA), 2-94
Acadia Nat. Park, 1-67
Acadian Village (LA), 5-52, 53*
Acadian Village (ME), 1-67
Acadians (Cajuns), 5-49
Accault, Michel, 4-73
Acee Blue Eagle, 5-91
Acoma Pueblo (NM), 6-87
Adak, AK, 1-10
Adams, Abigail, 2-31
Adams, Alvin, 1-122
Adams, Cuyler, 4-79
Adams, John, 1-77; 2-31, 101, 104; 3-91
Adams, John Quincy, 1-77, 81; 2-119
Adams, MA, 1-80
Adams Express Co., 1-122
Adams Mansion Nat. Hist. Site, 1-81
Addams, Jane, 1-19; 4-21
Adena estate (OH), 4-99
Adena people, 2-113; 4-28, 99
Adirondack Mts., 1-111; 2-79
Admiral of the Navy (Dewey), 1-119
Aerocar (M. B. Taylor), 7-71
Aerospace Medical Center, 5-117
Aetna Life Insurance Co., 1-53
African Methodist Episcopal Church, 2-21, 92
Afton, NY, 2-77
Agamenticus (York, ME), 1-60
Agana, GU, 7-83
Agate Beach, OR, 7-58
Agate Fossil Beds Nat. Mon., 5-67
Agate Springs Fossil Quarries, 5-57
Agates, 5-57, 67; 6-77; 7-59
Agattu Island (AK), 7-15
Agnes (hurricane), 2-90
Agnew, Spiro, 4-62
Agriculture, 1-20, 51, 65, 79, 108, 121; 2-22, 23, 43, 52, 64, 65, 78, 107, 113; 3-17, 20, 21, 23, 36, 37, 44, 46, 48, 50, 78, 79, 92, 104, 106, 107, 121; 4-22, 37, 47, 48, 49, 50, 51, 64, 79, 92, 108, 120, 121; 5-21, 29, 37, 50, 64, 72, 78, 79, 93, 106, 107, 121; 6-10, 19, 22, 37, 51, 54, 65, 89, 91, 108; 7-18, 20, 29, 30, 42, 46, 59, 71, 73, 80, 83, 88, 90, 91, 95
Agriculture, Indian, 1-59, 71, 86; 2-56; 5-72
Agriculture, prehistoric, 3-44; 6-30, 85
Ahgupuk, George Aden (Twok), 7-16
Aiga (extended family), 7-81
Aiken, SC, 3-106
Aiken, Walter, 1-91
Air Force, U.S., 5-117; 7-85
Air Force Academy, U.S., 6-83
Air Force Special Weapons Center, 6-95
Air and Space Museum, Nat., 1-25
Aircraft, 5-35*
Airlines, passenger, 3-51; 4-65, 92, 93; 7-42
Airmail, 7-70
Airplanes, 2-35; 3-5*, 89; 4-62, 66,

106; 6-118; 7-18, 19, 32, 44
Airports, 1-14, 104; 2-78, 107, 108; 3-47, 51; 4-23; 6-22, 51, 79; 7-15, 73, 81, 96
Ak-Sar-Ben Ball, 5-65
Akaka Falls (HI), 7-39
Akin, Louis, 6-17
Akron, OH, 4-107
Alabama, Battleship, 3-20
Alabama (main article), 3-13
Alabama River, 3-13, 18
Alabama Shakespeare Festival, 3-24
Alabama Space and Rocket Center, 3-25
Alabaster, 6-36
Alabaster Caverns (OK), 5-95
Alakai Swamp, 7-39
Alameda, CA, 7-35
"Alamo, Dawn over the" (painting), 5-116*
Alamo (San Antonio, TX), 3-22, 119
Alamo mission, 5-115, 116*, 118, 119, 122
Alamosa, CO, 6-39
Alarcon, Hernando de, 6-17
Alaska (main article), 7-9
Alaska Highway, 7-14
Alaska Hist. Library and Museum, 7-19
Alaska Peninsula, 7-9, 21
Alaska Purchase, 7-13
Alaska brown bears, 7-17
Alaska pipeline, 7-15, 18
Alaskan Native Claims Settlement Act, 7-15
Albacore, 2-64
Albany, NY, 1-30; 2-74, 79
Albatross, 7-44
Albemarle, NC, 3-87
Albemarle Point, 3-101
Albright-Knox Art Gallery (NY), 2-80
Albuquerque, NM, 6-87, 88, 89, 91, 93, 94, 95
Alburquerque (Duke of), 6-87
Alcoa Building (Pittsburgh, PA), 2-95
Alcott, Louisa May, 1-77
Alderman (Indian), 1-102
Aldrich, Bess Streeter, 5-63
Alekoko Fish Pond, 7-39
Aleut people, 7-11, 12, 13
Aleutian Islands (AK), 1-6, 10; 7-9, 15, 21
Alexander Archipelago (AK), 1-6
Alexandria, MN, 4-75
Alexandria, VA, 2-107, 108, 110
Alexandria Gazette (newspaper), 2-107
Alexis (Grand Duke), 5-60
Alfalfa, 5-64, 65, 79
Algoma, WI, 4-121
Algonquin Indians, 1-59, 71, 86, 100, 113, 114; 2-29, 43, 56, 83; 4-71, 114; 5-73
Ali, Muhammad, 3-64
Alibamu Indians, 3-17
Alki Point (WA), 7-74
All Indian Pow Wow, 6-23
All Saints Episcopal Church (Charlotte Amalie, VI), 7-96
Allcorn, John, 4-38
Allegheny Dam, 2-83
Allegheny Highlands, 2-113
Allegheny Mts., 2-111; 3-59
Allegheny Plateau, 2-113
Allegheny River, 2-83, 96*
Allen, Ethan, 1-48, 75, 115, 118, 119, 122
Allen, Forrest C. (Phog), 5-38
Allen, Richard, 2-21, 92
Allen, William, 2-62

Allen Island (ME), 1-60
Allen's Rangers, 1-48
Alligators, 3-36, 40, 49*, 50; 5-120
Allis, Samuel, 5-63
Allouez, Claude, 4-115
"Aloha Oe" (song), 7-49
Aloha Week Festival of Early Hawaii, 7-49
Alonso, Manuel, 7-90
Alpena, MI, 4-65
Alpine Junction, WY, 6-113
Alston, Joseph, 3-105
Alston, Theodosia Burr, 3-105
Altar Room (IN World War Mem.), 4-39
Alton, IL, 4-15
Aluminum, 2-93, 122; 3-121; 4-106, 122; 5-50; 7-59, 95
Alverno College, 1-77
Amana, IA, 4-45, 51, 52, 53
Amana Co., 4-51, 53
Amana colonies, 4-52
Amargosa River, 6-69
Amarillo, TX, 5-113, 121
Amelia Island (FL), 3-33
Amendments, constitutional, 2-35, 53, 101; 5-62; 6-74, 77
"America" (song), 1-63
"America the Beautiful" (song), 6-27
America's Cup, 1-104, 105
America's Junior Miss Pageant, 3-24
American Brass Assn., 1-50
American Embassy (Iran), 2-35
American Falls, ID, 6-43
American Forestry Assn., 1-15
American Friends Service Committee, 2-90
American Fur Co., 6-60; 7-69
"American Gothic" (painting), 4-49
American Legion, 4-39
American Museum of Natural History (NYC), 2-80
American Museum of Sci. and Energy (Oak Ridge, TN), 3-122
American Rhododendron Soc. Test Garden (OR), 7-62
American Royal Livestock and Horse Show, 4-94
American Samoa (main article), 7-79
American eagle, 5-78
American settlements, 3-33; 4-31; 5-115; 6-60; 7-69
Amherst, NH, 1-79
Amish people, 2-87
Amlung, Frederick, 2-52
Amoskeag Indians, 1-86
Amoskeag Manufacturing Co., 1-93, 95
Amstel House (New Castle, DE), 2-24
Anaconda, MT, 6-63
Anaconda mines (MT), 6-63
Anacostia River, 2-28
Anadarko, OK, 5-94
Anaho Island (Pyramid Lake), 6-77
Anasazi (ancient ones), 6-25, 100
Ancestral Appalachians, 3-113
Anchorage, AK, 1-10, 14, 20; 7-10*, 14, 15, 20
Anderson, Eugenie, 4-77
Anderson, IN, 4-37
Anderson, Marian, 2-92
Andersonville Nat. Cemetery, 3-52
Andersonville Nat. Hist. Site, 3-52
Andrew Jackson State Park (SC), 3-109
Andrew Johnson Nat. Hist. Site, 3-123
Andros, Edmund, 1-45
Androscoggin River, 1-57

Anesthesiology, 3-48
"Angeles of Mercy", 2-60
Angelfish, French, 7-94
Anheuser, Eberhard, 4-91
Anheuser-Busch Co., 4-91, 92
Anhinga (water turkey), 3-27*, 36
Ann Arbor, MI, 4-67
Annapolis, MD, 1-21, 25; 2-44, 45, 46, 51, 53, 54
"Anne" (ship), 3-45
Anne of England, 2-24
Anniversary, CT 350th, 1-46
Anniversary, MD 350th, 2-49
Antarctic Continent, 1-49
Antelope, 6-64, 91
Anthracite coal, 2-93
Antietam Nat. Battlefield, 2-53
Antillean crested hummingbird, 7-94
Antimony, 6-51
Anvil Creek, AK, 7-19
Anzo-Borrego Desert State Park (CA), 7-31
Apache Indians, 5-85, 114; 6-16, 18, 20, 86, 87
Apache wars, 4-90
Aplite, 2-106
Apostle islands (WI), 4-111, 124
Appalachian Mts., 1-7, 58, 69; 2-41, 83, 97, 115; 3-15, 43, 53, 57, 83, 113, 122; 4-30
Appalachian Plateau, 2-97
Appalachian Trail, 1-66; 3-53
Appalachian Valley, 2-55, 97
Appaloosa horses, 7-67
Apple, sugar, 7-94
Apple trees, 4-39, 51, 107
Appleby, John, 4-119
Apples, 1-79, 101; 2-22, 121; 4-51, 107; 7-73
Appleseed, Johnny (Jonathan Chapman), 4-36*, 39, 107
Appleton, WI, 4-117, 121
Appomattox Courthouse, 2-102
Aquaculture, 7-83
Aquamarine, 1-92
Aquariums, 4-23, 67
Aquia Creek, 2-99
Aquidneck Island (RI), 1-102
Aracoma (female Indian leader), 2-120
Aransas Wildlife Refuge (TX), 5-123
Arapaho Indians, 5-57, 58, 85; 6-31, 32, 58, 115
Arawak Indians, 7-87, 93
Arawak people, 3-30
Arbor Day, 5-62, 66
Arbor Lodge, 5-62
Arbor Lodge State Ht. Park (NE), 5-62, 66
Arbuckle Mts., 5-83
Arcade, (Providence, RI), 1-109
Arch Rock (Rockaway, OR), 7-62
Archaic people, 2-55; 4-85, 99
Archaic-Early Woodland people, 3-99
Archbishop of Canterbury, 3-45
Architects and architecture, 1-27, 67, 80; 2-30, 31, 95, 103; 4-20, 24, 38, 80, 109, 119, 123; 5-25; 6-109
Archives and History Bldg. (Vicksburg, MS), 3-80
Arco, ID, 6-48
Arctic Circle, 7-21
Arden, DE, 2-24, 25
Arecibo, PR, 7-92
Argall, Samuel, 2-15
Arikara (Ree) Indians, 5-72, 73, 99; 6-115
Ariyoshi, George R., 7-42
Arizona, Battleship, 7-49

Arizona (main article), 6-13
Arizona State Museum, 6-24
Arizona State Univ., 6-24
Arizona Territory, 6-18
Arizona cypress, 6-21
Arizona-Sonora Desert Museum, 6-24
Arkansas (main article), 5-13
Arkansas Development Commission, 5-22
Arkansas Post, 5-16
Arkansas Post Nat. Mon., 5-24
Arkansas River, 1-7; 5-13, 15, 16, 17*, 18, 19, 22, 29, 83, 89; 6-29, 31, 38
Arkansas Territorial Restoration, 5-25
Arkansas first Statehouse, 5-24*
Arlington Mem. Bridge, 2-34
Arlington Nat. Cemetery, 1-25; 2-36, 108; 6-64
Armstrong, Louis, 5-49
Armstrong, Neil, 4-105
Arneson River Theater (San Antonio, TX), 5-123
Arnold, Benedict, 2-73
Aroostook County (ME), 1-55, 67
Arrowmaker Indians, 6-58
Arsenal in MacArthur Park, Old (Little Rock, AR), 5-25
Arsenal of the Revolution, 2-88
Art Center (Des Moines, IA), 4-53
Art Center (Milwaukee, WI), 4-122
Art Institute of Chicago, 4-24
Arthur, Chester A., 1-117, 118; 2-76; 6-34
Articles of Confederation, 2-49, 88
Artists, 1-44, 49, 64, 65, 77, 91, 106, 119; 2-21, 24, 36, 50, 63, 74, 77, 92, 94, 95; 3-49, 52; 4-24, 36, 38, 49, 91, 92, 120; 5-38, 49, 78, 94, 104, 119; 6-35, 53, 62, 75, 91, 93, 95, 106, 119, 123; 7-16, 25, 58, 90
Arts Museum and Planetarium (Vicksburg, MS), 3-80
Arts and Crafts Center (Seattle, WA), 7-74
Asbestos, 1-121
Asheboro, NC, 3-95
Asheville, NC, 3-89, 91, 95
Ashland, KY, 3-65
Ashley, William H., 6-116
Asiatic monkeys, 3-106
Aspen, CO, 6-39
Asphalt, 6-106
Assassinations, 1-76, 77; 2-32, 33, 35, 36, 43, 60, 75, 76; 3-20, 21, 90; 4-19, 60, 106; 5-47, 48, 117, 118; 6-105; 7-85
Assembly lines, 1-48
Assiniboin Indians, 6-58
Associated Free State, 7-89
Astaire, Fred, 5-63
Astor, John Jacob, 6-60; 7-53
Astor, Mrs. William, 1-106, 107
Astor, Nancy Langhorne, 2-105
Astor, Waldorf, 2-105
Astor Fur Co., 5-74; 7-69
Astor Mem. Column, 7-62
Astoria, OR, 7-53, 62
Astrodome, 5-123
Astronauts, 1-6, 7; 3-35; 4-105
Astronomy, 2-21; 4-49
Atchison, KS, 5-36
Atchison, Topeka and Santa Fe RR, 5-38
Atchison County (KS), 5-30
Athapascan Indians, 6-16, 86, 101; 7-11
Athens, GA, 3-53
Athens, OH, 4-107
"Athens of the South" (Nashville, TN), 1-26
"Athens of the West" (Lexington, KY), 3-66
Atlanta, GA, 1-26; 3-42*, 47, 48, 49,
51, 52
Atlanta fire, 3-47
Atlantic City, NJ, 1-15, 25; 2-61, 63*, 66
Atlantic Ocean, 1-85
Atlantic Tuna Tournament, U.S., 1-107
Atomic Age, 4-20
Atomic Energy Commission, 6-74
Atomic bomb, 4-90; 7-70
Atomic power, 6-48
Atomic weapons, 6-74, 89; 7-80
Atsina Indians, 6-58
Attakullakulla (Little Carpenter), 3-114
Attu Island (AK), 7-15, 21
Attucks, Crispus, 1-80
Auburn, MA, 1-79
Audubon, John James, 5-49, 78
Augusta, GA, 3-45, 46, 51, 52
Augusta, ME, 1-31, 34, 57, 61, 67, 68
Augusta Tabor cottage (Leadville, CO), 6-39
Augusty County, VA, 2-100
Aunu'u Island (AS), 7-79
Aurora, CO, 6-32
Aurora, NE, 5-66
Austin, Moses, 5-115, 119
Austin, NV, 6-75
Austin, Stephen, 5-115, 118
Austin, TX, 1-27; 5-116, 123
Austin, Walter, 2-114
Australia, 1-105
Authors, 1-49, 62, 63, 77, 92, 119; 2-21, 36, 50, 76, 91, 106, 119, 120; 3-36, 48, 76, 91; 4-21, 35, 49, 61, 62, 78, 89, 91, 104, 107; 5-20, 35, 49, 63, 67, 94, 104, 105; 6-35, 49, 76, 90, 91, 93, 105, 119; 7-16, 29, 58, 90
Automobile industry, 4-65
Automobiles, 1-48, 79, 90, 119; 2-21; 4-37, 63, 92, 107, 117
Automobiles, Duryeas, 1-79
Avery Island (LA), 5-43, 51, 52
Avery Island preserve (LA), 5-50
Aviation, 1-46; 2-34, 61, 120, 123; 3-34, 89; 4-65, 77, 93, 104, 106; 5-36, 89, 90; 6-51, 118; 7-14, 18, 19, 71
Aviation industry, 5-34, 35, 37
Awashonks (Indian princess), 1-102
Azaleas, 3-24
Aztalan, WI, 4-113, 114
Aztec Ruins Nat. Mon., 6-93
Aztec people, 4-99, 113
B-24 Bombers, 4-62
Babbitt, Bruce E., 6-19
Babbitt, Milton, 1-92*
Babcock, Stephen M., 4-119
Babcock, VA, 2-107
Babe (Bunyan's blue ox), 4-81; 7-51
Baby Doe cabin (Leadville, CO), 6-39
Baca, Elfego, 6-90
Backbone Mt., 2-41
Bacon, Nathaniel, 2-100
Bacon Rind (chief), 5-94
Badgers (animal), 4-115, 120
Badlands (ND), 5-71*, 72, 80
Badlands (NE), 5-55, 67
Badlands (SD), 5-97
Badlands Nat. Mon., 5-103
Badlands Nat. Park, 5-108
Baha'i Temple (Wilmette, IL), 4-24
Bahgwan Shree Rajneesh, 7-56
Bailey, "Mad Ann", 2-120
Baker Library (Dartmouth College), 1-95
Bakersfield, CA, 7-27
Balance Rock (WI), 4-111*
Balboa Park (San Diego, CA), 7-31
Balch, Frederic Homer, 7-58
Balcones Escarpment (TX), 5-113
Bald Cypress, 2-21
Bald eagles, 1-31*; 2-64; 4-94; 6-120
Ball games, Indian, 3-45
Ballinger, TX, 5-114
Baltimore, Lady, 2-43
Baltimore, Lord, 2-29, 43, 44
Baltimore, MD, 1-25; 2-42*, 44, 46, 48, 50, 53; 4-55
Baltimore Clipper ships, 2-47
Baltimore Colts (football), 2-53
Baltimore Museum of Art, 2-53
Baltimore Orioles (baseball), 2-53
Baltimore Symphony Orchestra, 2-53
Baltimore orioles (bird), 2-52
Bamberger, Louis, 2-63
Bananas, 7-80, 83, 91
Bandelier Nat. Mon., 6-93
Bangor, ME, 1-56*, 65, 66, 67
"Bangor" (song), 1-67
Bankhead, John H Jr., 3-22
Bankhead, John H., 3-22
Bankhead, Tallulah, 3-22
Bankhead, William B., 3-22
Banking, 5-104, 106
"Banks of the Missouri" (painting), 5-101*
Banneker, Benjamin, 2-49
Bannock, MT, 6-60
Bannock Indians, 6-45, 47
Banyan trees, 7-84
Baptists, 1-102
Bar Harbor, ME, 1-62, 67
Baraboo, WI, 4-113, 123
Baranoff, Alexander, 7-13, 16
Barbary Pirates, 2-50
Barbed wire, 5-119
Barber, Samuel, 2-92
Barberton, OH, 4-108
Bardstown, KY, 3-66, 67
Barelegged owl, 7-94
Barges, 4-93
Barite, 4-92
Barker, Edward Dickinson, 7-55
Barkley, Alben, 3-63
Barley, 5-79; 6-92
Barlowe, Arthur, 3-86
Barnsdall, OK, 5-93
Barnum, Phineas T., 1-49, 52, 94
Barnum Festival, 1-52
Barnum Museum, 1-52
Barracks, Revolutionary, 2-66
Barratts Chapel (DE), 2-25
Barre, VT, 1-31, 121, 123
Barrell, Sally Sayward, 1-63
Barrier Canyon (UT), 6-100
Barrington, MA, 1-79
Barrington River, 1-103; 3-66
Barrow, AK, 1-10; 7-21
Barter Theater (Abingdon, VA), 2-109
Bartholdi, Frederic Auguste, 2-74
Bartlesville, OK, 5-94
Barton, Clara, 2-63
Barton, William, 1-103
Baseball, 2-51, 53, 60, 75, 80; 3-49; 4-24, 80, 91, 93, 94, 104, 109, 118; 7-20, 28, 74, 91
Baseball Hall of Fame, 2-80
Bashaba (sagamon), 1-86
Basketball, 4-24; 5-38; 7-74
Basketmakers, 5-85; 6-16, 30, 39, 85; 7-67
Baskets, Dat-So-La-Lee, 6-76*
Basque Festival, 1-29; 6-53, 81
Bass, 1-120; 2-64
Bass Islands (OH), 4-99
Batataria Island (LA), 5-46
Bates, Katherine Lee, 6-27
Bath, ME, 1-65, 66
Bath, NC, 3-87, 93
Bath Iron Works, 1-65
Bath Shipyards, 1-66
Bathhouse Row (Hot Springs, AR), 5-22, 23*
Baton Rouge, LA, 1-27; 5-42*, 46,
51, 53
Bats, 6-91; 7-84, 94
Bats, fruit, 7-84
Battell, Joseph, 1-119
Battery, The (NYC), 2-74
Battle Above the Clouds, 3-116, 117
Battle Creek, MI, 4-64
"Battle Hymn of the Republic" (song), 2-36
Battle Mt., 6-77
Battle of Alamance, 3-88
Battle of Antietam Creek, 2-48
Battle of Atlanta, 3-52
Battle of Bad Axe, 4-115
Battle of Bear's Paw, 6-61
Battle of Bennington, 1-123
Battle of Bentonville, 3-89
Battle of Big Mound, 5-74
Battle of Blair Mountain, 2-118
Battle of Bloody Marsh, 3-45
Battle of Boonesboro, 2-48
Battle of Buffington Island, 2-117
Battle of Bull Run (Manassas), 1-104; 2-33, 101, 119
Battle of Bunker Hill, 1-36*, 47, 61, 89
Battle of Camden, 3-104
Battle of Chancellorsville, 2-119
Battle of Chattanooga, 4-61
Battle of Cooch's Bridge, 2-17
Battle of Corrick's Ford, 2-117
Battle of Cowpens, 3-102
Battle of Fallen Timbers, 4-102
Battle of Flour Bag Fort, 2-87
Battle of Fort McHenry, 2-50
Battle of Fort Meigs, 4-102
Battle of Fort Moultrie, 3-8*
Battle of Fort Stephanson, 4-102
Battle of Fort Washington, 2-73
Battle of Franklin, 3-117
Battle of Gettysburg, 1-30; 2-18, 60, 89, 94; 4-61*, 75
Battle of Glorietta, 6-88, 89
Battle of Guilford Court House, 3-88
Battle of Harlem Heights, 2-73
Battle of Iuka, 4-46
Battle of Killdeer Mountains, 5-74
Battle of Kings Mountain, 3-88*, 102, 115
Battle of Lake Champlain, 1-46; 2-17
Battle of Lake Erie, 2-89; 4-60, 102, 103*
Battle of Lancaster, 3-102
Battle of Laurel Hill, 2-117
Battle of Laurel Mountain, 2-86
Battle of Lexington, 1-103; 3-66
Battle of Little Big Horn, 4-62; 5-74, 75, 105; 6-60
Battle of Long Island, 1-47; 2-16, 45, 73
Battle of Lookout Mountain, 3-116, 117
Battle of Manassas (Bull Run), 1-104; 2-33, 101, 119
Battle of Middle Creek, 3-60
Battle of Mine Creek, 5-31
Battle of Missionary Ridge, 3-117
Battle of Monmouth, 2-74
Battle of Monocacy, 2-48
Battle of Moores Creek Bridge, 3-88
Battle of New Orleans, 3-60, 74, 115, 118, 119; 5-60
Battle of Olustee, 3-34
Battle of Pea Ridge, 5-18
Battle of Philippi, 2-117
Battle of Plattsburgh, 2-74
Battle of Point Pleasant, 2-115
Battle of Prairie Grove, 5-18
Battle of Raisin River, 4-102
Battle of Rhode Island, 1-103, 108
Battle of Rich Mountain, 2-117
Battle of Round Mountain, 5-86
Battle of Saipan, 7-85
Battle of San Jacinto, 5-116

Battle of San Juan Hill, 5-77*
Battle of Saratoga, 2-73
Battle of Shiloh, 3-74, 116; 4-117; 6-20
Battle of South Mountain, 2-48
Battle of Spokane Plains, 7-69
Battle of Stones River, 3-116
Battle of Tinian, 7-85
Battle of Trenton, 2-59, 66
Battle of Valcour Bay, 2-73
Battle of Westport, 4-88
Battle of White Canyon, 6-47
Battle of Whitemarsh, 2-88
Battle of Whitestone Hill, 5-74
Battle of Wilson's Creek, 4-46
Battleship Alabama, 3-20
Battleship Arizona, 7-49
Battleship North Carolina, 3-94*
Battleship Texas, 5-123
Baum, L. Frank, 5-105
Bauxite, 3-50, 51; 5-18, 21; 7-59, 95
Baxter, Elisha, 5-18
Baxter Peak, 1-58
Baxter State Park (ME), 1-58, 66
Bay Minette, AL, 3-18
Bay St. Louis, MS, 3-81
Bayard, Thomas F., 2-20
Bayard family, 2-20
Bayonne, NJ, 2-65
Bays, 1-7, 97; 2-13, 15, 41, 46, 52, 71, 85, 97; 3-16, 28, 31, 85, 100; 7-23, 26, 31, 48, 49, 53, 81
Beach, Rex, 7-16
Beach Lake, 1-99
Beacon Rock (WA), 7-65
Beal, Barney, 1-64
Beal's Island (ME), 1-64
Beale, Edward F., 6-23; 7-26
Beale Street (Memphis, TN), 3-118
"Beale Street Blues" (song), 3-120
Bean, Roy, 5-122
Bean Blossom, IN, 4-38
Beans, 1-86, 100; 2-57, 78; 5-79; 7-83
Bear Butte (SD), 5-99, 108
Bear Flag Republic (California), 7-26
Bear Lake, 6-43, 99
Bear Mt., 2-81
Bear River, 6-43, 99, 113
Beard, Daniel Carter, 3-77
Bears, 1-27, 64; 2-77; 3-121; 5-49, 76; 6-64; 7-11*, 14, 16, 17, 72
Bears, Kodiak, 7-14
Beartooth Highway, 6-66
Beatrice, NE, 5-60, 66
Beaufort, SC, 3-109
Beaumont, TX, 5-121
Beaumont, William, 4-63, 119
Beauregard, Pierre G. T., 5-46
Beauvoir, MS, 3-81
Beaver Island (MI), 4-57, 60, 66
Beaver skins, 2-81
Beavers, 1-11, 64; 5-105; 6-60, 107; 7-58, 72
Becknell, W. H., 5-30, 31
Beckwourth, Jim, 6-32
Bedford, IN, 4-37
Bee, Barnard E., 2-119
Beech Aircraft, 5-57
Beecher, Henry Ward, 1-49
Beer, 4-121
Beets, sugar, 6-120
Belfast, ME, 1-66
Belfast and Moosehead Lake RR, 1-66
Belgravia (Louisville, KY), 3-66
Bell, NM, 6-95
Bell Fourche, SD, 5-106
Bell Laboratories, 1-24
Bell Town (East Hampton, CT), 1-50
Belle Grove Hist. Dist. (AR), 5-23
Belleville, IL, 4-22
Bellevue, NE, 5-58
Bellingham, WA, 7-76

Bellingrath Gardens and Home (AL), 3-12*, 24
Bellows Falls, VT, 1-113
Beloit, WI, 4-121
Beloved Woman of the Nation (Cherokee), 3-114
Bemidji, MN, 4-81
"Ben Hur" (book), 4-36; 6-90
Bennington, VT, 1-115, 123
Benson, Benny, 7-16
Benson, Ezra Taft, 6-106
Bent and St. Vrain trading firm, 6-31
Bentley, Wilson A. (Snowflake), 1-119
Benton, Thomas Hart (artist), 3-120; 4-87, 91
Benton, Thomas Hart (senator), 3-104; 4-90
Benton Harbor, MI, 4-28
Bentonite, 5-106; 6-120
Bentonville, AR, 5-21
Beowawe Geyser field (NV), 6-71, 79
Berea, KY, 3-67
Berea College, 3-67
Bergen, NJ, 2-57
Bergen County, NJ, 2-61
Bergen swamp (NY), 2-77
Bering, Vitus, 7-13, 16
Bering Strait, 7-15
Berkeley, CA, 1-8*, 21; 7-35
Berkeley, Lord, 2-57, 61
Berkeley County, WV, 2-117
Berkeley Riflemen, 2-115
Berkeley Square, WV, 2-116
Berkshire, MA, 1-80
Berkshire Hills,, 1-69
Berkshire Mts., 1-43, 52
Berkshire Music Festival, 1-80
Berlin, Irving, 2-77
Berlin, MD, 2-50
Berthoud Pass (CO), 6-38
Bertoia, Harry, 4-24
Beryl, 6-77
Bessemer, Henry, 3-63
Bessemer steel process, 3-63
Bessey, Charles, 5-64
Betatakin (ledge) House (Navajo Nat. Mon.), 6-25
Bethany College, 5-39
Bethel, CT, 1-47, 49
Bethlehem, PA, 2-87, 94
Bethlehem Steel Co., 2-92
Bettendorf, IA, 4-51
Beveridge, Albert J., 4-35
Beverly Hills, CA, 7-33
Bicentennial celebrations (Frankfort, KY), 3-61
Bicentennial celebrations (U.S.), 1-105; 2-75
Bienville, Celeron de, 4-100, 101
Bienville, LA, 5-44
Bienville, Sieur de, 5-44, 45
Bierstadt, Albert, 6-35
Big Basin (KS), 5-27
Big Bend (TX), 1-7; 5-120
Big Bend Dam (SD), 5-97
Big Bend Nat. Park, 5-6*, 122
Big Bone Lick (KY fossil grounds), 3-57
Big Cottonwood Canyon (UT), 6-97
Big Elk (chief), 5-58
Big Inch pipeline, 2-65
"Big Mac" (bridge), 4-12*, 62
Big Sandy River, 2-111; 3-55
Big Sioux River, 4-41, 53; 5-108
Big Springs, MO, 4-83
Big Stone Lake, 5-99
Big Thicket (TX), 5-120
"Big Three" (automobiles), 4-65
"Big Tub" (Johan Printz), 2-15, 57, 85
Bighorn Canyon Nat. Rec. Area, 6-121
Bighorn Mts., 6-116

Bighorn River, 6-59, 119
Bighorn sheep, 5-120; 6-21, 36, 77
Bikini Island (Pacific), 7-85
Bill Williams River, 6-15
Bill of Rights, 2-38, 104
Billings, MT, 6-66
Billopp, Christopher, 2-81
Billy the Kid (William H. Bonney), 6-88, 90
Biloxi, MS, 3-81; 379-0
Biloxi Lighthouse, 3-81
Biltmore House, 3-25*, 95
Bird, Isabella, 6-37, 120; 7-27
Bird, Robert Montgomery, 2-21
Bird Effigy Mound (IA), 4-43*
Birkbough, Konrad Elias, 5-78
Birmingham, Al, 3-23, 25
Biscayne Bay, FL, 3-34
Bishop, James, 1-52
Bishop Museum, 7-49
Bishop family (HI), 7-44
Bismarck, ND, 1-29; 5-70*, 74, 75, 81
Bitterroot Range, 6-41, 43, 55
Black Canyon of the Gunnison Nat. Mon., 6-39
Black Canyon of the Gunnison River, 6-29
Black Fish (chief), 3-62
Black Fork, WY, 6-123
Black Fox (chief), 5-21
Black Hawk (chief), 4-7*, 17, 115
Black Hawk War, 3-76; 4-17, 21, 115
Black Hills, 5-99, 101, 102, 104, 107, 108
Black Hills Passion Play, 5-108
Black Hills gold rush, 5-101
Black Jack Ketchum, 6-90
Black Mesa (OK), 5-83
Black Patch Tobacco War, 3-60
Black River (MO), 4-83
Black River (WI), 4-113
Black Robes (priests), 4-115
Black Warrior River, 3-15
Black coral, 7-44
Blackbeard (pirate), 2-16; 3-45, 101
Blackbird (chief), 5-58
Blackbird Creek, 2-16
Blacksburg, WV, 2-115
Blackstone, William, 1-101
Blackstone River, 1-99
Blaine, James G., 1-67
Blaine House, James G., 1-67
Blair House (DC), 2-35
Blakely, Ronald L., 5-39
Blessing of the shrimp fleet, 3-78*
Blimps, 1-48
Bloch, Henry, 5-38
Bloch, Richard, 5-36
Block, Adriaen, 1-44, 101; 2-72
Block, Ernest, 7-58
Block, Henry, 5-36
Block, Richard, 5-36
Block Brothers Tobacco Co., 2-122
Block Co., H & R, 5-36
Block Island (RI), 1-97, 99, 104, 108
Bloomer, Amelia, 4-50
Bloomers, 4-50
Bloomfield, NJ, 2-35
Blooming Grove, OH, 4-106
Bloomington, IN, 4-36, 37, 38
Bloomington, MN, 4-80
Blount, William, 3-115
Blowing Rock, NC, 3-95
"Blue Boy, The" (painting), 7-33
Blue Hen's Chickens, 2-16
Blue Mts., 7-53, 65
Blue Ridge Mts., 2-97, 100; 3-6*, 41, 97
Blue Ridge Parkway, 3-94
Blue Room, White House, 2-33, 38
Blue crabs, 1-107
Blue heron, 7-94
Blue laws, 3-104

Blue ox, Babe, 4-81; 7-51
Bluebeard (pirate), 7-93, 96
Bluebeard's Castle (VI), 7-96
Blueberries, 1-65
Bluefield, WV, 2-111, 113, 122
Blues (music), 3-118, 119, 120; 4-91
Bluff Dwellers, 5-15
Blumenschein, Ernest L., 6-94
Boardwalk (Atlantic City, NJ), 2-66
Boars, 3-121
Boatload of Knowledge, 4-32
Bobcats, 2-51; 6-64; 7-33, 72
Bodega Bay, 7-26
Bodmer, Carl, 5-78; 6-59
Boeing, William, 7-71
Boeing Co., 7-73
Bois de Sioux River, 4-69
Boise, ID, 1-29; 6-42*, 47, 49, 53
Boise Valley (ID), 6-47
Boll weevil, 3-20, 23, 25, 78, 104
Bolley, Henry L., 5-78
Bonaparte, Napoleon, 3-65; 5-45
Bond, Carrie Jacobs, 4-120
Bond, Shadrach, 4-17
Bonefish, 7-94
Bonham, James Butler, 5-118
Bonham, John, 5-119
Bonnet (pirate), 3-101
Bonnet Carre Spillway, 5-43, 44
Bonneville, B. L. E. de, 6-116
Bonneville Dam (OR), 7-56
Bonneville Salt Flats, 6-81, 97
Bonney, Ann, 3-91
Bonney, William H. (Billy the Kid), 6-88, 90
Bonsack, James A., 3-91
Booby birds, 7-44
Boomers, 5-88
Boone, Daniel, 3-58, 62, 64; 4-91, 92
Boone, IA, 4-50
Boone Tavern (KY), 3-67
Boone's Trace, 3-58
Boonesborough, KY, 3-58
Boot Hill (KS), 5-39
Booth, Sherman M., 4-116
Boothill Cemetery (Virginia City, MT), 6-66
Booz, 2-64
Boozer, Marie, 3-105
Borah, William, 6-49
Borden, Gail, 3-77
Border War, Michigan-Ohio, 4-103
Border War, NJ, 2-58
Border disputes, 1-18, 61, 89; 2-58, 102, 104; 4-44, 60, 89, 97, 103; 5-117
Borders, 1-67, 89, 91, 113; 3-13, 43; 4-57, 69, 74, 81, 89; 5-15, 81, 95; 6-15, 18, 41, 83; 7-69
Borglum, Gutzon, 3-52, 53; 5-104
Boringuino (PR natives), 7-88
Borinquen Island (PR), 7-88
Boston, MA, 1-14, 24, 35*, 67, 70*, 71, 73, 75, 77, 78, 79, 80, 81, 87, 93, 101; 2-45, 58, 87, 115; 7-62
Boston Massacre, 1-80
Boston Pops Orchestra, 1-24, 81
Boston Symphony, 1-81
Boston Tea Party, 2-45, 58
Botanical Center (Des Moines, IA), 4-53
Botanical Garden (St. Louis, MO), 4-93
Bottineau, Pierre, 4-74
Boudinot, Elias, 2-59
Bougainvillea, 3-36
Boulder City, NV, 6-74, 80, 81
Boundaries, 1-18, 41, 57, 61, 85, 88, 97, 113, 114; 2-15, 30, 41, 52, 55, 58, 69, 83, 97, 100, 102, 111; 3-13, 43, 55, 57, 69, 71, 97, 113; 4-13, 28, 31, 41, 44, 55, 57, 60, 65, 69, 74, 83, 97, 99, 103, 113; 5-15, 24, 41, 43, 55, 71, 72, 83, 113; 6-15, 29, 31, 32, 41, 55, 71, 83, 88; 7-69

Boundary Mts., 1-57
Boundary disputes, 1-18, 61, 89; 2-58, 102, 104; 4-44, 60, 89, 97, 103
Bountiful, UT, 6-104
Bouquet, Henry, 2-87; 4-101
Bourbeuse River, 4-85
Bourbon Street (New Orleans,LA), 5-52
Bouwerie (NYC Bowery), 2-72
Bow, NH, 1-92
Bowdoin College, 1-62, 66
Bowdoin College Museum of Art, 1-66
Bowers, Sandy, 6-76
Bowie, James (Jim), 5-115, 118
Bowie knife, 5-118
Bowling Hall of Fame and Museum, 4-94
Box huckleberry, 2-22, 121
Boy Scouts of America, 3-64; 6-48
Boyd, Isabel (Belle), 2-120
Boydville, WV, 2-120
Boys Town, NE, 5-63, 65
Bradbury, John, 5-64
Braddock, Edward, 2-86
Bradford, William, 1-72
Bradley, Omar M., 4-89
Bragg, Braxton, 3-60
Brahma Cattle, 5-105
Brahmalo, 5-105
Brainard, MN, 4-81
Branch Park (Newark, NJ), 2-67
Brandeis, Louis Dembitz, 3-63
Brando, Marlon, 5-63
Brandywine Creek, 2-88
Brandywine River, 2-24
Branson, Lloyd, 3-98
Brattleboro, VT, 1-114, 119
Brazito, NM, 6-88
Bread Loaf, VT, 1-119
"Breadbasket of the World, The" (ND Red River Valley), 5-79
Breakers (Newport, RI), 1-108
Breakfast food, 4-64
Breathitt County, KY, 3-61
Breckenridge, MN, 4-69
Breckenridge, MO, 4-91
Breed's Hill (MA), 1-35*, 47, 75
Bremerton, WA, 7-73, 76
Brevoort, Hendrick, 2-72
Brewster County (TX), 5-111
Bridal Veil Falls (NC), 3-95
Bridgeport, AL, 3-25
Bridgeport, CT, 1-49, 52, 53
Bridger, Jim, 5-59; 6-60, 101, 102, 116, 119, 123
Bridges, suspension, 2-75; 3-60; 7-34
Brigham City, UT, 6-109
Brigham Young Univ., 6-109
Bristlecone pines, 1-11; 7-30
Bristol, RI, 1-101
Bristol Harbor, 1-99
British Columbia (Canada), 7-70
British Virgin Islands, 7-93
Broad arrow trees, 1-61, 88
Broadmoor Hotel (Colorado Springs, CO), 6-34
Broadway (NYC), 2-72, 73, 80
Brocken (shadow), 7-47
Bromine, 5-21
Bronx, NY, 2-71
Bronx Zoo, 2-80
Brookfield Zoo, 4-23
Brookline, MA, 1-76
Brooklyn, CT, 1-47
Brooklyn, NY, 2-71, 73, 76
Brooklyn Bridge, 2-75; 3-60
Brooklyn Children's Museum, 2-81
Brooks, Gwendolyn, 4-21
Brooks-Baxter war, 5-18
Broomcorn, 6-37, 92
Brown, Bailey T., 2-117, 123
Brown, Emerson, 5-33
Brown, John, 1-49; 2-32, 116; 5-31, 32*, 39, 59

Brown, John (Lean John), 7-27
Brown, Moses, 1-106
Brown, Mrs. James J. (Molly), 6-36
Brown County, IN, 4-38
Brown House (Denver, CO), 6-39
Brown Museum, John (KS), 5-39
Brown bears, 3-121
Brown vs. Board of Education of Topeka, 5-34
Browning, John M., 6-106
Browning, Jonathan, 6-106
Browning, MT, 6-66
Browns Valley, MN, 4-71
Browns Valley Man, 4-71
Brownsville, TX, 5-116
Brule, Etienne, 2-85; 4-57
Brule River, 4-111
Brunswick, Ga, 3-51
Brunswick, ME, 1-63, 64, 66
Brush, Charles F., 4-107
Brussel sprouts, 7-30
Bryan, William Jennings, 2-108; 3-117; 5-63
Bryant, William Cullen, 1-77, 110
Bryce, Ebenezer, 1-7
Bryce Canyon Nat. Park, 1-7; 6-99, 100*, 108
Bryon, William Jennings, 4-89
Buchanan, James, 2-91; 4-116
Buck, Pearl, 2-119, 120
Buck, Pearl (home), 2-120*
Buck Island Reef Nat. Mon., 7-95
Buckeye (nickname), 4-103
Buckingham Fountain, 4-24
Buckonghanon (chief), 2-120
Buell, Don Carlos, 3-60
Buena Vista, Mexico, 5-18
Buffalo, NY, 2-69, 75, 80; 4-106
Buffalo, SC, 3-106
Buffalo Bill (William F. Cody), 4-50; 5-36, 63, 66; 6-35, 39, 119, 121, 122
Buffalo Bill Museum, 6-122
Buffalo Bill Ranch State Hist. Park (NE), 5-67
Buffalo Bill's Grave and Museum, 6-39
Buffalo Bill's Wild West Show, 5-105
Buffalo Bills (football), 2-80
"Buffalo Dance at Mishongnovi" (painting), 6-11*
Buffalo hunts, 7-30
Buffaloes (bison), 1-11, 92; 2-121; 4-22, 50, 71, 72, 92, 101; 5-29, 31, 32, 36, 49, 57, 73, 76, 81, 85, 92, 105, 108, 120; 6-4*, 12, 44, 66, 87, 101, 113, 114, 120; 7-17
Bulbs, flower, 7-73
Bulfinch, Charles, 1-53, 67, 80
Bull Bay (SC), 3-99
Bull Lake, 6-114
Bull Shoals Lake, 4-83
Bunche, Ralph J., 4-63
Bunker Hill, WV, 2-115
Bunker Hill (MA), 1-75
Bunyan, Paul, 1-66*, 67; 4-81, 113; 7-51
Burdick Tavern (CT), 1-47
Bureau of American Ethnology, 6-20
Bureau of Printing and Engraving, 2-38
Bureau of Reclamation, 6-33
Burger, Warren, 4-77
Burgoyne, John, 2-73
Burlington, IA, 4-44, 52
Burlington, NJ, 2-64
Burlington, VT, 1-112*, 117, 118, 122
Burns Harbor, IN, 4-34
Burnside, Ambrose, 1-106; 4-34
Burnsides (sideburns), 1-106
Burr, Aaron, 1-68; 2-63, 67, 104; 3-105

Burritte, Elihu, 1-49
Busch, Adolphus, 4-91
Busch Gardens, 3-39; 4-91
Busch Stadium, 4-91, 93
Bush, George Washington, 7-69, 71, 72
Bush Prairie (WA), 7-71
Bushnell Park (Hartford, CT), 1-53
Butler, Benjamin F., 5-47
Butler, Jim, 6-74
Butler-McCook House (CT), 1-46*
Butte, MT, 6-61, 62, 63, 65
Butterfat, 4-119
Butterflies, monarch, 7-30
Buxton Town, ME, 1-63
Byram River, 1-41
Byrd, Harry Flood, 2-102, 105
Byrnes, James J., 3-105
Cabbages, 2-78; 7-18, 83
Cable cars (San Francisco, CA), 7-34
Cabot, John, 1-60, 71
Cabrillo, Juan Rodriguez, 7-25
Cache, OK, 5-94
Cache la Poudre River, 6-35
Cacti, 5-92; 6-21, 92, 107
Caddo Indians, 5-16, 44, 73, 85, 114
Caddo people, 5-16
Cadillac, Antoine de la Mothe, 4-58, 67
Cadillac Mt., 1-57
Cadman, Charles Wakefield, 2-92; 7-29
Cahokia, IL, 4-15, 16
Cahokia Mounds Park, 4-25
"Cairo" (Union gunboat), 3-81
Cajuns (Acadians), 5-49
Calais, ME, 1-67
Calamity Jane (Martha Jane Canary), 5-105, 108; 6-119
Calder, Alexander, 4-24
Caldwell, NJ, 2-67
"Caleb Cushing" (ship), 1-62
Calendar Islands (ME), 1-57
Calhoun, John C., 3-102, 105
Calico, CA (ghost town), 7-32
Calico RR, 4-45
California (main article), 7-23
California 49'ers, 5-59; 6-47; 103; 7-27
California Republic (Bear Flag Rep), 7-26
California condor, 7-30
California poppies, 7-30
California redwood, 1-11
Calipatria, CA, 1-10
Calusa Indians, 3-31
Calvert, Cecil (Lord Baltimore), 2-43
Calvert, Charles (Lord Baltimore), 2-44
Calvert, George (Lord Baltimore), 2-29, 43
Calvert, Leonard, 2-43, 44
Calvert Cliffs, 2-41
Camas plant, 6-46, 50
Cambridge, MA, 1-24, 47, 81
Cambridge Univ., 1-105
Camden, NJ, 2-65
Camden, SC, 3-108
Cameahwait (chief), 6-46
Camel Rock (Lauli'i, HI), 7-5*
Camel races, 7-32
Camels, 6-22, 23; 7-31
Camels, prehistoric, 5-99
Cameron, Simon, 2-92
Camp Lee, VA, 2-102
Camp Pike, AR, 5-19
Camp Shelby (MS), 3-75
Campbell, William, 2-57
Campbell Soup Co., 2-63, 64
Campeachy (TX), 5-115
Campeche, Jose, 7-90
Campion, John F., 6-35
Canadian River, 6-85
Canal Builders, 6-16

Canary, Martha Jane (Calamity Jane), 5-105, 108; 6-119
Canby, Henry Seidel, 2-21
Candler, Asa G., 3-49
Candlewood Lake, 1-43
Candlewood Mts., 1-52
Candy, 4-23
Cane, 5-47
Cannery Row (Monterey, CA), 7-34
Cannibals, 3-99; 4-114; 7-88
Cannon, Annie Jump, 2-21
Cannon, James W., 3-91
Cannon, Joe, 2-38
Cannon, Lucretia (Patty), 2-17
Cannon, Shadrach, 2-25
Cannon, William, 2-18
Cannon Beach (OR), 7-51
Cannon Mills, 3-91
Cannonicus (sachem), 1-101
Canoe Indians, 7-67
Canon City, CO, 6-37, 38
Canton, NY, 2-77
Canton, OH, 4-108
Canyon, TX, 5-121
Canyon de Chelly Nat. Mon., 6-24
Canyon of the St. Croix River, 4-81
Canyonlands Nat. Park, 6-109
Cap Rock Escarpment (TX), 5-113
Cape Blanco (OR), 7-53
Cape Canaveral, FL, 3-30, 31, 33, 34, 35, 37
Cape Charles, VA, 2-97, 99
Cape Cod, 1-7, 24, 69, 72, 80
Cape Cod Bay (MA), 1-72
Cape Fear, NC, 3-83
Cape Flattery (CA), 7-67
Cape Hatteras Lighthouse, 3-93
Cape Hatteras Nat. Seashore, 3-93
Cape Henry (VA), 2-97, 99
Cape Horn (South America), 7-27
Cape May, NJ, 2-18, 55, 60, 66
Cape May diamonds, 2-66
Capistrano, CA, 7-31
Capital, Confederate, 2-101
Capital, U.S., 2-30, 46, 48, 88, 123
Capital Centre (St. Paul, MN), 4-80
Capitals, Hawaii native, 7-41
Capitals, Indian, 2-71, 99; 5-94; 7-13
Capitals, colonial, 2-44, 85, 100, 109; 3-94
Capitals, former U.S., 2-46, 53*, 59, 74, 88
Capitals, state, 1-24, 25, 26, 27, 29, 30, 31, 42*, 53, 61, 67, 80, 95, 98*, 104, 123; 2-0, 17, 25, 46, 56*, 59, 66, 79, 89, 94, 98*, 109, 112*, 117, 122; 3-39, 52, 67, 70*, 80, 84*, 95, 98*, 102, 109, 112*, 115, 116, 123; 4-13, 29*, 32, 39, 42*, 45, 53, 60, 67, 74, 80, 94, 103, 112*, 116, 122; 5-14*, 28*, 38, 42*, 53, 56*, 60, 67, 70, 81, 84, 88, 95, 98, 109, 123; 6-14*, 24, 28*, 39, 42*, 53, 67, 81, 84*, 85, 87, 95, 98*, 109, 112*, 117, 122; 7-14, 19, 27, 34, 42, 49, 62, 76
Capitals, territorial, 5-59, 88; 6-18; 7-14, 80, 83, 95
Capitol, U.S., 1-25, 29; 2-31, 32, 37*, 45, 46, 54; 4-95, 120
Capitol Hill (DC), 2-32
Capitol Hill (Salt Lake City, UT), 6-109
Capitol Reef Nat. Park, 6-109
Capitol Square (Raleigh, NC), 3-95
Capitol Theatre (Salt Lake City, UT), 6-109
Capitol dome, U.S., 2-37, 54
Capitol domes, 1-20, 24, 29, 80, 109, 110, 123; 2-37, 54; 4-67, 80, 122; 6-24, 67, 122; 7-35
Capitol murals, 7-62
Capitols, state, 1-11, 24, 25, 26, 27, 29, 30, 31, 40*, 54*, 67, 68*, 80, 82*, 95, 96*, 109, 110*, 123, 124*; 2-12*, 25*, 27, 31, 33, 53*, 59,

66*, 68*, 78, 79*, 89, 94*, 109*, 117, 118, 122, 124*; 3-26*, 39*, 52, 54*, 68*, 82*, 90, 95, 96*, 109, 110*, 119, 123, 124*; 4-13, 17, 25, 26*, 33, 39, 40*, 53, 54*, 67, 68*, 76, 80, 82*, 94, 95*, 109, 116, 122*; 5-24*, 25*, 32, 38, 40*, 47, 53, 54*, 61, 68*, 81, 82*, 93, 96*, 109*, 123, 124*; 6-26*, 39, 40*, 53, 54*, 68*, 81, 82*, 95, 96*, 109, 110*, 122, 124*; 7-22*, 36*, 50*, 64*, 78*
"Captain My Captain" (poem), 2-36
Capulin, NM, 6-85
Capulin Mt., 6-93
Carabao, 7-84
Caraway, Hattie W., 5-19, 20
Carbon dioxide, 2-92
Cardiff, NY, 2-74
Cardiff Giant, 2-74
Carib Indians, 7-87, 93
Caribbean islands, 7-87
Caribbean pine, 3-36
Caribou, 7-17
Carlsbad, NM, 6-92
Carlsbad Caverns Nat. Park, 6-91, 93
Carmel, CA, 6-101; 7-28, 29, 33
Carmichael, Hoagland (Hoagy), 4-36
Carnegie, Andrew, 2-79, 92
Carnegie, Dale, 4-91
Carnival (St. Croix, VI), 7-96
Carnival (St. Thomas, VI), 7-8*, 86*
Carnotite, 6-36
Caroline Islands (Pacific), 7-85
Carowinds Theme Park, 3-95
Carpenter, Scott, 6-35
Carpenter's Hall (Philadelphia, PA), 2-87, 94
Carr, Robert, 2-15
Carrizozo, NM, 6-85
Carroll, Anna Ella, 2-51
Carroll, Charles, 2-46*, 49
Carrollton, MD, 2-46
Carson, Christopher (Kit), 6-18, 35, 81, 90, 94; 7-26
Carson, Johnny, 4-50; 5-63
Carson City, NV, 1-27; 6-75, 81
Carter, James Earl (Jimmy), 1-105; 2-75; 3-47, 52, 61; 6-52
Carteret, George, 2-57, 61
Cartersville, GA, 3-44, 48
Cartoons, 2-63
Caruthersville, MO, 4-85
Carver, George Washington, 3-21; 4-49, 92
Carver Museum, 3-21
Casa Blanco (San Juan, PR), 7-91
Casa Grande, AZ, 6-16
Casals, Pablo, 7-90
Casals Festival, 7-90
Cascade Mts., 7-65
Cascade Range, 7-51
Casco (Portland, ME), 1-61, 65
Casco Bay (ME), 1-57, 63, 65
Cash register, 4-104, 106
Casimir, DE, 2-15
Casper, WY, 6-122
Casper Mts., 6-122
Cass, Gilbert, 2-122, 124
Cass, Lewis, 4-91
Castillo de San Marcos (FL), 3-33, 39
Castle Gardens (WY), 6-113
Caswell, Richard, 3-88
Cataldo, ID, 6-47, 53
Cataract Canyon (UT), 6-109
Catawba Indians, 3-99
Catawba River, 3-97
Catfish Creek, IA, 4-44
Cathedral Gorge State Park (NV), 6-72*
Cathedral of St. John the Divine (NYC), 2-81

Cathedral of St. Michael (Sitka, AK), 7-13, 19
Cathedral of St. Paul (St. Paul, MN), 4-80
Cathedral of the Holy Cross (Boston, MA), 1-80
Cather, Willa, 2-106; 5-63, 67; 6-90
Catholic Sisters of St. Francis, 4-77
Catholics, 1-60
Catlin, George, 3-33; 4-72; 5-17, 21, 30, 78
Catskill Mts., 1-30; 2-79
Catt, Carrie Chapman, 4-50
Cavanal Hill (OK), 5-85
Cavelier, Rene Robert (Sieur de La Salle), 3-73; 4-16, 28, 58, 86, 100; 5-15, 16, 17*, 44, 85, 115
Caves, 3-57; 4-83, 85, 94; 6-53, 66, 71, 91, 93, 109; 7-63, 77, 87
Cavett, Dick, 5-63
Cedar Breaks (UT), 6-109
Cedar Falls, IA, 4-53
Cedar Key, FL, 3-39
Cedar Rapids, IA, 4-51, 53
Cedar River, 4-41
Cedarville, KS, 5-53
Celeron claim plates, 4-100, 101
Celilo Pass (OR), 7-63
Cellophane, 2-22; 4-51
Cement, 4-64; 5-121; 6-78; 7-91
Cemeteries (nat. HI), 7-49
Cenotaphs, 4-39
Centennial Mts., 6-55
Centennial celebration (AK), 7-15
Centennial celebration (Nashville, TN), 3-117
Centennial celebration (U.S.), 2-90; 6-23
Center for the Performing Arts (Tacoma, WA), 7-74
Center of Science & Industry (Des Moines, IA), 4-53
Central City, CO, 6-37
Central City Nat. Hist. Dist. (CO), 6-37
Central Falls, RI, 1-99
Central High School Little Rock, AR, 5-19
Central Montana RR, 6-66
Central Pacific RR, 6-107
Central Park (NYC), 2-80, 81*
Central Plains (TX), 5-111, 113
Central Valley (CA), 1-27; 7-23, 35
Century of Progress, 4-20
Century plant, 6-21
Cepeda, Orlando, 7-91
Ceramics, 2-64; 4-36
Cerro de Punta, 7-87
Cessna, Clyde Vernon, 5-35
Cessna Aircraft, 5-35*, 37
Chaboillez, Charles, 5-73
Chaco Canyon (NM), 6-85
Chaculissa (prehistoric village), 3-113, 114*
Chadds Ford, PA, 2-88
Chagall, Marc, 4-24
Chalfant, J. D., 2-21
Chalk Pyramids (KS), 5-27
Challenger (space shuttle), 1-90; 3-35
Chamber of Commerce, 2-83, 94
Chambersburg, PA, 2-89
Chamorro (people), 7-82, 83
Champlain, Samuel de, 1-114; 2-71; 4-28
Champoeg, OR, 7-55
Chancellorsville, VA, 2-101
Chandor, Douglas, 5-119
Channel Islands (CA), 7-30
Channing, William Ellery, 1-77
Chapel Hill, NC, 1-21; 3-95
Chapman, John G., 2-11
Chapman, Jonathan (Johnny Appleseed), 4-36*, 39, 107
Charboneau, Tuissant, 6-64
Charcoal, 4-93

Chargoggagoggmanchuaggagoggchaubunagungamaugg Lake, 1-71
Charles (Prince of Wales), 5-117
Charles City, IA, 4-50, 51
Charles City County, VA, 2-104
Charles I of England, 2-44, 52; 3-97
Charles II of England, 2-44, 72, 85; 3-87
Charles II of Spain, 5-45
Charles River, 1-81
Charles Towne, SC, 3-87, 101, 108
Charles Towne Landing, SC, 3-87, 101*, 108
Charleston, IL, 4-24
Charleston, SC, 3-101, 102, 103, 105, 106, 107, 108*, 109
Charleston, WV, 1-20; 2-112*, 116, 117, 121, 122
Charleston earthquake, 3-103
Charlotte, NC, 3-93, 95
Charlotte Amalie, VI, 7-94, 95*, 96
Charlotte Amalie Harbor, 7-95
Charlottesville, VA, 2-108
Charter Oak, 1-45, 53
Charter of Liberties, 2-73
Charter of Privileges, 2-86
Chase, Salmon P., 1-91
Chateau de Mores State Mon. (ND), 5-80
Chattahoochee River, 3-13, 43, 45, 51
Chattanooga, TN, 3-47, 113, 116, 122
Chattanooga Nat. Wild and Scenic River, 3-109
Cheaha Mt. State Park (AL), 3-15*
Chemical industry, 2-65; 5-50
Chemicals, 5-121
Chena River, 7-15
Chepachet, RI, 1-101
Chequamegon Bay (WI), 4-111
Cherimoya, 7-30
Cherokee Foothills Scenic Highway, 3-109
Cherokee Indians, 2-31, 99; 3-9, 17, 18, 44, 45, 58, 88, 92, 95, 99, 101, 113, 114, 115, 116, 119; 4-87; 5-17, 86, 88, 90, 94, 117
Cherries, 4-64
Cherry Festival, 4-66
Cherry trees, 1-29; 2-34, 67
Chesapeake Bay, 1-7; 2-13, 23, 41, 46, 97, 99, 106
Chesapeake Bay Bridge & Tunnel, 2-97, 107
Chesapeake Bay retriever, 2-52
Chesapeake and Delaware Canal, 2-13, 23
Chesapeake and Ohio Canal, 2-53
Chesterfield, VA, 2-106
Chevron Corp., 6-79
Chew, Samuel, 1-25; 2-0
Cheyenne, WY, 1-29; 5-107; 6-112*, 117
Cheyenne Frontier Days, 6-122
Cheyenne Indians, 5-30, 33, 57, 58, 60, 72, 85; 6-31, 32, 58, 115
Cheyenne Mountain Zoo, 6-35, 38
Cheyenne Mt., 6-33, 34
Cheyenne River, 5-97
Chicago, IL, 1-14, 15, 19, 51; 4-3*, 13, 14*, 17, 18, 20, 23, 24, 61, 90, 93, 117; 5-39; 6-64
"Chicago Picasso" (sculpture), 4-24*
Chicago River, 4-16
Chicago Symphony Orchestra, 4-24
Chickamauga Indians, 3-114, 115
Chickamauga-Chattanooga Nat. Military Park, 3-53, 122
Chickasaw Bluffs (Memphis, TN), 3-122
Chickasaw Indians, 3-17, 18, 60, 71, 72, 73, 74, 113, 114; 5-16, 86, 94

Chickasha, OK, 5-93
Chicken, Rhode Island red, 1-105, 108
Chicken (chief), 1-52
Chicken Hill, CT, 1-52
Chickering, Jonas, 1-91
Child labor laws, 4-117
Childersburg, AL, 3-25
Children's Museum (IN), 4-39
Children's Museum of Rhode Island, 1-108
Children's Theater (MN), 4-80
Chiles, Walter, 2-114
Chili Cookoff, World's Championship, 5-122
Chili peppers, 6-92
Chilkoot Pass (AK), 7-13
Chimney (MN), 4-71
Chimney Point (VT), 1-114
Chimney Rock (NC), 3-95
Chimney Rock Nat. Hist. Site, 5-59, 67
China Cap Mt., 7-51
Chinatown (NYC), 2-80
Chinatown (San Francisco, CA), 7-34
Chinchona tree, 3-22
Chincoteague Bay (MD/VA), 2-43
Chincoteague Island (VA), 2-108
Chinook Indians, 7-53
Chinook winds, 6-114; 7-65
Chinquapin trees, 3-121
Chippewa Indians (Ojibwa), 4-28, 43, 57, 71, 72, 74, 76; 5-72
Chippewa River, 4-70, 71, 113
Chiputneticook Lakes, 1-57
Chiricahua Mts., 6-15, 21
Chisholm, A. M., 4-77
Chisholm, Jesse, 5-32
Chisholm Trail, 5-32, 93, 94, 116
Chocorua (chief), 1-87
Choctaw Indians, 3-16, 18, 71, 72, 74, 77; 5-86, 93
Cholera, 4-63
Choteau, MT, 6-62
Choupique (prehistoric fish), 5-50
Chouteau, Auguste Pierre, 4-86; 5-0
Christ Church Burial Ground (Philadelphia, PA), 2-94
"Christ of the Ozarks" (statue), 5-23
Christiansted, VI, 7-96
Christiansted Nat. Hist. Site, 7-96
Christmas Basque Sheepherders Ball, 6-53
Christmas Festival (VI), 7-96
Christmas trees, 2-87; 4-79
Chronology, 1-54, 68, 82, 96, 110, 124; 2-26, 40, 54, 68, 82, 96, 110, 124; 3-26, 40, 54, 68, 82, 96, 110, 124; 4-26, 40, 54, 68, 82, 96, 110, 124; 5-26, 40, 54, 68, 82, 96, 110, 124; 6-26, 40, 54, 68, 82, 96, 110, 124; 7-22, 35, 50, 64, 78, 81, 84, 92, 96
Chrysler, Walter P., 4-65; 5-36
Church, Benjamin, 1-102
Church, Frank, 6-49
Church Butte (WY), 6-113
Church of England, 1-105
Church of Jesus Christ of Latter Day Saints, 1-119; 2-77; 4-18, 88, 103; 6-102, 104, 105, 106, 109
Church of San Miguel (Santa Fe, NM), 6-95
Churchill, Winston, 2-35; 4-89, 90
Churchill, Winston (novelist), 4-91
Churchill Downs, 3-61*, 66
Cimarron County, OK, 5-95
Cimarron River, 5-31; 6-85
Cincinnati, OH, 3-60; 4-98*, 102, 103, 104, 106, 108, 109
Cincinnati Art Museum, 4-109
Cincinnati Bengals (football), 4-109
Cincinnati Reds (baseball), 4-104, 109

Cincinnati Symphony, 4-109
Cincinnati Zoo, 4-109
Circus World Museum, 4-123
Circus festival, 4-39
Circuses, 2-117; 4-39, 113, 123
Citicorp, 5-104
Citrus, 3-37
Citrus industry, 3-37
City Center Square (Kansas City, KS), 4-94
City Creek, 1-29; 6-102, 108
City of Refuge Nat. Hist. Park (HI), 7-40*, 48
Civic Arts & Science Center (St. Paul, MN), 4-80
Civic Square (Concord, NH), 1-95
Civil Service Act, 1-118
Civil War, 1-46, 49, 61, 62, 75, 90, 91, 104, 106, 117; 2-18, 24, 33, 48, 60, 63, 74, 89, 101, 105, 109, 117, 123; 3-19, 24, 33, 52, 53, 60, 63, 74, 75, 77, 80, 89, 91, 102, 103, 109, 116, 117, 123; 4-19, 33, 35, 45, 46, 61, 62, 67, 75, 77, 88, 89, 106, 117; 5-17, 18, 23, 31, 47, 59, 74, 86, 87, 101, 116; 6-18, 74, 88, 89, 90; 7-13, 27, 55
Civil rights, 1-75, 104, 105, 118; 3-20, 49, 90, 103, 104; 7-69, 71
Civilized Tribes, 3-17, 44, 46; 5-17, 86, 87, 88
Claiborne, William, 2-43, 44
Clams, 2-106
Claremont, NH, 1-91
Claremore, OK, 5-89, 94
Clark, George Rogers, 2-100; 3-66; 4-16, 25, 30, 31
Clark, James Beauchamp (champ), 4-90
Clark, William, 4-44, 87; 5-30, 58, 74, 81, 100; 6-46, 47, 50, 58, 59, 66, 67, 119; 7-53, 62, 67, 68
Clark, William Andrews, 6-63
Clark County, KS, 5-27
Clark Fork River, 6-57
Clark Hill Reservoir, 3-43
Clark's nutcracker, 6-50
Clarke, John, 1-102
Clarksburg, WV, 2-121
Clarksville, IN, 4-31
Clay, Henry, 3-66
Clayton, John Middleton, 2-20
Clayton-Bulwar Treaty, 2-20
Clear Lake, SD, 5-102
Clear Lake, TX, 5-117
Clearwater, FL, 3-30
Clearwater River, 6-5, 46
Cleaveland, Moses, 4-109
Clemens, Orion, 6-76
Clemens, Samuel L. (Mark Twain), 1-49, 53; 2-80; 3-65; 4-89, 91, 119; 5-15, 53; 6-76, 77, 79; 7-29
Clemente, Roberto, 7-91
Clemson, SC, 3-109
Clemson Univ., 3-109
Cleveland, Benjamin, 3-87
Cleveland, Grover, 2-20, 33, 62, 67, 76; 5-20, 62
Cleveland, OH, 4-102, 104, 107, 109*
Cleveland Health Museum, 4-109
Cleveland Symphony Orchestra, 4-109
Cliburn, Van, 5-119
Cliff Palace (Mesa Verde Nat. Park), 6-30
Cliff dwellers, 6-16, 100
Clifton, NJ, 2-65
Climax, CO, 6-39
Clinton, George, 1-115
Clinton, IA, 4-51, 52
Clipper Ships, 1-51
"Close Encounters of the Third Kind" (movie), 6-121
Cloudcroft, NM, 6-95
Clough, Enos M., 1-90

Clowes Hall (Indianapolis, IN), 4-39
Coachella Valley (CA), 7-30
Coacoochee (chief), 3-35, 36
Coahuiltecan Indians, 5-114
Coal, 1-11, 78, 99, 109; 2-93, 106, 107, 117, 118, 121, 122; 3-22, 23, 57, 64, 65, 121; 4-22, 36, 37, 50, 64, 78, 92, 93, 108; 5-18, 21, 37, 76, 78, 79, 83, 92, 93, 106, 113; 6-36, 64, 65, 77, 106, 108, 120; 7-59, 72; 43-6
Coal Hill, AR, 5-18
Coast Guard Academy, 1-52
Coast Range, 7-51
Coastal Mts., 7-23
Coastal Alluvial Plain, 3-15
Coastal Plains, 1-69; 2-55, 97; 5-113
Coastal Region, 2-41
Coastal Waterway, 5-123
Coastal redwoods, 7-30
Cobb, Tyrus R. (Ty), 3-49
Coca-Cola Co., 3-49
Cochise (chief), 6-18, 88
Cochise Man, 6-16
Cockfights, 2-16; 7-91
Coconut palms, 7-94
Coconuts, 7-80, 81, 83
Coddington, William, 1-102
Cody, William F. (Buffalo Bill), 4-50; 5-36, 63, 66; 6-35, 39, 119, 121, 122
Coeur d'Alene, ID, 6-44, 48, 53
Coeur d'Alene Indians, 6-45, 46
Coffee, 7-46, 90
Cofitachiqui (Indian princess), 3-100
Cog RR (Pikes Peak), 6-38
Cog railroads, 1-89, 94; 6-38
Colby College, 1-63
Coleman, Peter Tali, 7-80
Coleman, Sheldon, 5-34
Coles Creek people, 5-44
Colgate clock, 2-57
College, AK, 7-20
College Park, MD, 2-53
Colman's Point (Sandy Point, NJ), 2-57
Cologne, Germany, 6-67
Colorado (main article), 6-27
Colorado Heights, KS, 5-29
Colorado Heritage Center, 6-39
Colorado River, 7-6; 6-13, 15, 17, 18, 19, 20, 22, 23, 69, 71, 85, 99, 101, 106, 109; 7-65
Colorado Springs, CO, 6-34, 38
Colorado-Big Thompson project, 6-36
Colt, Samuel, 1-50
Colter, John, 6-60, 116, 119
Colter's Hell (Yellowstone Nat. Park), 6-116
Columbia, CA, 7-35
Columbia, MD, 2-49
Columbia, MO, 4-94
Columbia, SC, 1-26; 3-98*, 102, 109
Columbia, TN, 3-123
Columbia Basin Project, 7-73
Columbia Island (DC), 2-28
Columbia Plateau, 7-65
Columbia River, 6-113; 7-51, 53, 56, 59, 60, 63, 63*, 65, 67, 70, 72, 73, 76
Columbia Univ., 5-34
Columbia-Snake River Navigation System, 7-70
Columbine, 1-11; 6-36, 107
Columbus, Christopher, 1-18, 60, 71
Columbus, IN, 4-38
Columbus, KY, 3-60
Columbus, MS, 3-72, 81
Columbus, NM, 6-89
Columbus, OH, 1-20; 4-103, 109
Columnar cedars, 5-78
Comal River, 5-113
Comanche Indians, 5-85, 94, 114; 6-

31, 32, 87
Commencement Bay (WA), 7-73
Commerce, 2-69, 74; 5-19, 53, 65, 104, 106; 7-73, 80, 83
Commercial shipping, 1-51
Communal settlements, 4-52, 103
Communications, 2-65; 3-63; 4-23, 45; 6-89, 106, 120; 7-17, 19, 42
Communism, 6-19
Compac-Facs, 1-53, 67, 68, 95, 96, 109, 110, 123, 124; 2-26, 39, 54, 55, 68, 82, 95, 96, 110, 123; 3-25, 26, 40, 54, 81, 96, 109, 110, 123; 4-25, 40, 53, 54, 67, 68, 81, 82, 95, 109, 110, 124; 5-26, 39, 40, 53, 54, 68, 82, 95, 96, 109, 124; 6-25, 26, 39, 40, 53, 54, 67, 68, 82, 95, 109, 110, 123, 124; 7-21, 22, 35, 49, 50, 64, 78, 81, 84, 92, 96
Composers, 1-49, 91, 92*; 2-36, 77, 92; 3-22, 66, 77, 118, 120; 4-36, 49, 91, 107, 120; 5-49, 63, 119; 7-29, 58
Computers, 4-49; 5-121; 7-31
Comstock, NV, 6-74
Comstock Lode, 6-76, 81
Concentration camps, 7-28, 83
Concord, CA, 7-35
Concord, MA, 1-75, 77, 80
Concord, NH, 1-24, 88, 92, 95
Concord, NY, 1-90
Concord grape, 1-79
Concord stagecoaches, 1-93
Condon Day State Park (OR), 7-53
Condors, California, 1-11; 7-30
Conductors, musical, 2-36, 92
Conestoga wagons, 2-93, 122; 6-118
Coney Island, NY, 2-81
Confederate Congress, 2-109
Confederate Pageant, 3-80
Confederate States of America, 1-26; 5-47
Confederate capital, 2-101
Congamond Lakes, 1-41
Congregational church, 1-46
Congressional Medal of Honor, 3-75; 5-92, 117
Connecticut (main article), 1-41
Connecticut River, 1-43, 44, 69, 79, 85, 113; 2-72
Connecticut River Valley, 1-79
Connecticut State Library, 1-53
Connecticut colony, 1-45
Connecticut firsts, 1-50
Connelly, John B. Jr., 5-117
Conoco Oil, 2-19
Conowingo Lake, 2-41
Conservancy Act of 1914, 4-104
Conservation, 1-11, 50, 64, 92; 2-67, 76, 77; 4-50, 64, 75, 76, 94, 120; 5-37, 61, 88, 93; 6-33; 7-56, 58
Conservationists, 7-15
"Constellation" (ship), 2-53
Constitution (AS), 7-80
Constitutional amendment (state, RI), 1-104
Constitutional amendments, 2-35, 53, 101; 5-62; 6-74, 77
Constitutions, 1-45, 75, 104; 2-16, 17, 18, 30, 38, 45, 46, 49, 59, 61, 71, 83, 86, 87, 88, 89, 91, 100, 101, 102, 103, 104, 116; 4-60; 5-75; 6-62, 74
Continental Congress, 2-16, 21, 45, 46, 58, 59, 87, 92, 100, 106; 3-88, 91, 105
Continental Divide, 6-29, 31, 38, 55, 59, 66, 85, 111, 123
Contour farming, 4-121
Contreras, LA, 5-43
Convention, Constitutional (U.S.), 2-101
Convention Under the Oaks, 4-60
Conventions, 2-45, 48, 75, 90, 101; 4-18, 60, 76, 89; 6-102; 7-28
Conventions, political, 2-48, 75; 4-18, 76, 89; 7-28

Cook, James, 1-49; 7-13, 40, 41, 42, 48, 53, 67
Cook, James H., 5-57
Coolidge, Calvin, 1-75, 77, 80, 117, 118, 119; 4-47, 49; 5-102
Coolidge, John, 1-119
Coolidge Homestead, 1-123
Cooper, James Fenimore, 2-76
Cooper, L. Gordon, 5-89, 90, 91
Cooper, William, 5-49
Cooper River, 3-99
Cooperstown, NY, 2-76, 79
Coos Bay, OR, 7-60
Coosa Valley (AL), 3-15
Copland, Aaron, 1-92*
Copper, 1-11, 92, 121; 2-64; 3-121; 4-60, 64, 92; 6-50, 67, 77, 78, 91, 92, 105, 108
Copper Culture people, 4-113
Copper industry, 6-63
Coral, 1-113; 3-29; 7-44, 49, 82, 92
Coral Pink Sand Dunes, 6-100
Coral fish, 7-94
Coral reefs, 1-113; 7-92
Corbit, Charles F., 2-18
Corbon Game Preserve, 1-92
Corn, 1-86, 100; 2-57; 4-22, 37, 49, 50, 108; 5-8*, 108
Corn Hill (MA), 1-72
Corn Island (KY), 4-31
Corn Palace (Mitchell, SD), 5-108
Cornell Univ., 2-80
Corning, NY, 2-80
Corning Glass Center, 2-80
Corning Tower (Albany, NY), 2-79
Cornish, NH, 1-92
Cornstalk (chief), 2-115, 120; 4-101
Cornwallis, Charles, 2-100, 102*; 3-88, 102, 105
"Cornwallis surrenders at Yorktown" (painting), 2-102*
Coronado, Francisco Vasquez de, 4-85; 5-29, 38, 85, 114; 6-17, 36, 87
Coronado Nat. Mem., 6-24
Corporation laws, 2-22
Corpus Christi, TX, 5-121
Corpus Christi Bay (TX), 5-114
Cortereal, Miguel, 1-101
Corundum, 6-64
Corydon, IN, 4-33
Coshocton, OH, 4-101
Cotton, 3-23, 50, 51, 78, 79, 89, 104, 106, 121; 5-21, 47, 50, 93, 121; 6-22, 92; 7-30
Cotton Carnival, 3-123
Cotton Exchange (Savannah, GA), 3-51
Cotton gin, 1-48; 3-0
Cotton mills, 1-93
Cotton plantation, 3-73*
Cotton seed oil, 3-48
Cougars, 5-49
Council of New England, 1-87
Count of Monte Rey, 7-25
Country Club Plaza (Kansas City, MO), 4-94*
County War Mem. (Milwaukee, WI), 4-122
Coureurs de bois (trappers), 4-58
Courtroom, "Hanging Judge" Parker's, 5-18*
Coventry, CT, 1-48
Coventry, RI, 1-106
Covered Bridge Festival, 4-38
Covered wagons, 4-93
Covington, KY, 3-60, 64
Covington House (Vancouver WA), 7-77
Cowboy Hall of Fame (OK), 5-9*
Cowpens Nat. Military Park, 3-109
Cowtantowit (Indian god), 1-100
Coxey, Jacob, 2-34
Coxey's Army, 2-34
Coyotes, 1-11; 5-100
Crabs, 2-51, 106; 7-58
Crafts, Polynesian, 7-80

Craig, Charles, 6-8
Cranberries, 1-59, 79; 2-65; 4-121
Cranberry Glades (WV), 2-121
Cranberry Islands (ME), 1-57
Crater Lake, 1-10; 7-51, 54*, 63
Craters of the Moon Nat. Mon., 6-44, 48, 52, 53
Crator of Diamonds State Park (AR), 5-24
Crawford Notch, 1-83
Crazy Horse (chief), 5-60, 104, 105, 107; 6-118
Creek Confederacy, 2-18; 3-17
Creek Council House (Okmulgee, OK), 5-94
Creek Indian Mem. Assn., 5-94
Creek Indians, 3-18, 22, 33, 44, 74, 115; 5-86, 93, 94
Creole Ball (Vincennes, IN), 4-38
Creosote bushes, 1-11; 7-30
Cretacean Uplift (ID), 6-44
Crickets, 6-103
Crime rates, 1-15
Cripple Creek, CO, 6-34
Crittenden, Robert, 5-21
"Croatoan", 3-87
Crocker, Charles, 7-29
Crockett, David (Davy), 3-119, 123; 5-115, 118
Croghan, George, 4-100
Cromwell, Oliver, 2-44
Crosby, Harry Lillis (Bing), 7-72
Cross Timbers (OK), 5-83
"Cross of Gold" (Speech), 5-63
Crossing of the Fathers (UT), 6-101
Crossing the Delaware, 2-58
Crotchet Mt., 1-93
Croton Alabamensis, 3-23
Crow Indians, 6-58, 64, 115
Crowley, LA, 5-50
Crowley's Ridge (AR), 5-15
Crown Center (Kansas City, MO), 4-91, 94
Crown Point (OR), 7-63*
Cruise ships, 7-19, 91
Cryptovolcano, 3-57
Crystal Court Square (Minneapolis, MN), 4-80
Cuba, 1-90; 3-34, 35
Cuban missile crisis, 3-34
Cucumbers, 7-83
Culebra Island (Caribbean), 7-87
Culpeper, John, 3-87
Culpeper's Rebellion, 3-87
Cultural Gardens (Cleveland, OH), 4-109
Cumberland (Earl of), 7-88
Cumberland Falls, 3-67
Cumberland Gap, 2-97
Cumberland Mts., 3-57
Cumberland Plateau, 3-15
Cumberland River, 3-57, 111
Cumberland parrot, 3-121
Cuming, Alexander, 3-114
Cuomo, Mario, 2-76
Curie, Marie Sklodowska, 6-36
Curie, Pierre, 6-36
Currier Gallery of Art (NH), 1-95
Currier and Ives, 3-9, 74; 4-8
Curry, John Steuart, 1-27; 5-32, 38
Curtin, Andrew, 2-91
Curtis Charles, 5-35
Cusabo Confederacy, 3-99
Cushnoc Island (ME), 1-57
Custer, George Armstrong, 4-62; 5-57, 74, 75, 79, 81, 97, 101, 105; 6-60, 61
Custer, SD, 5-101, 106
Custer Battlefield Nat. Mon., 6-66
Custer State Park (SD), 5-108
Custer massacre, 5-57, 75, 79
Custer's Last Stand, 5-57, 75, 79; 6-62, 63*
"Custer's Last Stand" (painting), 6-63*
"Custer's Last Stand" (panorama),

6-63
Custis-Lee Mansion (VA), 2-108
Customs, Hawaiian native, 7-39, 43, 46, 48
Customs, Indian, 1-43, 44, 59, 71, 100, 101; 2-43, 56, 57, 71, 85, 92; 3-44, 45, 72, 99, 114; 4-16, 28, 44, 57, 72, 85, 100, 114; 5-44, 57, 58, 73, 85, 86, 87, 88, 89, 93, 94, 99, 100; 6-16, 31, 58, 107, 115, 117; 7-12, 25, 67, 93
Customs, prehistoric, 1-59; 2-113; 4-28, 99, 113, 114; 5-16; 6-85, 115; 7-39, 43, 46, 48
Cutler, Lyman, 7-69
Cuyahoga River, 4-97
Cuyuna Range, 4-79
Cyclorama, 3-53
Cypress, 3-36
Cypress, Monterey, 7-30, 33
Cypress Gardens (Charleston, SC), 3-108
Cyripedium reginae (orchid), 4-78
D'Augilar, Martin, 7-53
D'Iberville, Sieur de, 3-73
D-Day, 4-62
Dacotah Indians, 4-6*, 71
Dadeville, AL, 3-25
Dahlonega, GA, 3-51, 53
Dairy products, 2-65, 78; 3-65, 77; 4-19, 22, 120, 123; 7-60
Dakota Indians, 5-78
Dakota Territory, 5-100
Daley, Richard J., 4-20
Daley Plaza (Chicago, IL), 4-24*
Dall, W. H., 7-16
Dall sheep, 7-16
Dallas, TX, 1-19, 27; 5-117, 122*, 123
Daly, Marcus, 6-63
Damien, de Veuster, 7-44
Danish settlements, 4-76
Danville, VA, 2-105, 107
Dare, Virginia, 3-86
Darling, J. N. "Ding", 4-49
Darrah, Lydia, 2-88
Darrow, Clarence, 3-117; 6-49
Dartmouth College, 1-89, 94, 95
Dat-So-La-Lee, 6-75, 76
Dat-So-La-Lee Basket, 6-76*
Date Festival, 7-32
Dates, 7-30
Datura plant, 6-107
Daughters of Charity in America, 2-51
Daughters of the American Revolution, 4-33
Dauphin Island, (AL), 3-15
Davenport, Homer, 7-58
Davenport, IA, 4-52
Davenport, John, 1-44
Davenport, Thomas, 1-121
David (Michaelangelo statue), 5-108
David Crockett Tavern and Museum, 3-123
Davidson, Jo, 5-94
Davis, Herman, 5-19
Davis, Jefferson, 1-26; 2-116*; 3-19, 24, 59, 62, 63, 67, 75, 76, 81; 4-61
Davis, Varina, 3-81
Dawson, Richard, 2-106
Day, John Other, 4-75
"Day After, The" (TV Movie), 5-32
Days of '76 Festival, 5-108
Dayton, George Nelson, 4-77
Dayton, OH, 4-106, 107
Dayton Central High School (OH), 4-107
Daytona Beach, FL, 3-39
De Aylon, Lucas, 3-109
De Bienville, Le Sieur, 3-17, 58
"De Braak", HMS (ship), 2-19
De Courcey, Henry, 2-45
De Gautier, Dona Felisa Rincon, 7-90

De Gourgues, Dominique, 3-32
De Hostos, Eugenio Maria, 7-90
De La Harpe, Bernard, 5-85
De Longueil, Charles, 3-57
De Mille, Cecil B., 7-30
De Narvaez, Panfilo, 3-31; 5-44, 114
De Niza, Marcos, 6-87
De Rouge, Etienne, 7-71
De Smet, Pierre Jean (Peter John), 5-58, 59, 101; 6-60
De Smet, SD, 5-104, 108
De Soto, Hernando, 3-16, 17, 31, 44, 45, 72*, 73, 86, 100, 114; 4-85, 86; 5-16, 22, 44, 85
De Soto Caverns, 3-25
De Soto Nat. Mem., 3-30
"De Soto discovers the Mississippi" (painting), 3-72*
De Tonti, Henri, 5-16
De Vaca, Nunez Cabeza, 6-87
De Vargas, Don Diego, 6-87
De Voto, Bernard, 6-106
De la Warr, Lord (Thomas West), 2-15, 56, 85, 99
Deadwood, SD, 5-101, 105, 108
Dearborn, MI, 4-66
Dearborn Inn (MI), 4-66
Deasonville people, 5-44
"Death Comes for the Archbishop" (book), 6-106
Death Valley (CA), 7-23, 32
Death Valley Scotty (Walter E. Scott), 7-23
Deborah of Hawaii, 7-45
Decatur, AL, 3-22
Decatur, IL, 4-24
Decatur, Stephen, 2-50
Declaration of Independence, 1-48; 2-38, 45, 87, 100, 104, 106; 3-46, 91
Declaration of Independence, Texas, 1-27
Decoration Day, 3-81
Dedham, MA, 1-81
Dedication, national capitol, 2-31
Deep Creek Lake, 2-41
Deer, 1-120; 2-52; 4-22, 50, 101; 5-49; 6-21, 46, 64, 77, 91, 107; 7-72, 84, 94
Deer Creek (SD), 5-105
Deer Creek (WY settlement), 6-116
Deer Island (ME), 1-57
Deere, John, 1-119
Deere and Co., 4-22, 51
Defense Atomic Support Agency, 6-95
Defoe Co., 4-62
Deidesheimer, Philip, 6-78
Dekanawida (chief), 2-71
Delamar House (Boise, ID), 6-53
Delaware (main article), 2-13
Delaware Bay, 2-13, 85
Delaware City, DE, 2-22
Delaware Indians, 2-56, 71, 83; 4-32, 87, 100
Delaware Mem. Bridge, 2-18
Delaware Opera, 2-24
Delaware River, 2-13, 15, 17, 23, 55, 56, 57, 58, 61, 62, 66, 69, 83
Delaware State Museum, 2-25
Delaware Theatre Co., 2-24
Delaware Water Gap, 2-58*, 67, 83
Delaware ox, 2-23
Delisle, MS, 3-71
"Deliverance" (movie), 3-109
Delmar, DE, 2-25
Delmar, MD, 2-25
Delmarva Peninsula, 1-7; 2-13, 23, 97
Deming, W. Edwards, 4-49
Democratic Party, 1-46, 90, 117; 3-20, 48, 90, 104; 5-33, 63, 118; 7-28
Democratic donkey, 2-63
Demopolis Dam, 3-15
Denali (Mt. McKinley), 1-6; 7-9,

12*, 21
Denison, TX, 5-118
Denny, Mary, 7-73
Denver, CO, 1-29; 2-111, 122; 6-28*, 29, 32, 34, 36, 37, 39
Denver Mint, U.S., 6-39
Denver Symphony, 6-39
Depression of 1887, 5-33
Depression of 1893, 1-62; 4-46
Depression of 1929, 1-76, 104; 2-34, 118, 122; 3-89; 4-47, 61, 76, 104; 5-19, 75, 88, 102; 6-33, 61, 74; 7-28, 89
Derby (horse race), 2-60
Derby Line, VT, 1-123
Des Moines, IA, 1-26; 4-42*, 45, 51, 52*, 53
Des Moines River, 4-41, 44
Des Plaines River, 4-16
Deseret (proposed state), 6-103
Desert Botanical Garden (AZ), 6-25
Desert of Maine, 1-58
Deserts, 6-83, 100, 107, 123; 7-31, 32, 46, 55, 65
Detroit, MI, 1-19; 2-97; 4-31, 55, 56*, 58, 59*, 60, 62, 63, 64, 65, 66, 67, 92
Detroit Civic Center, 4-64
Detroit River, 4-55, 65, 67
Deutsch, PA, 2-87
Devil's Gate (WY), 6-113
Devil's Postpile Nat. Mon., 7-23
Devil's Tower Nat. Mon., 6-113, 117, 121
Dewey, George, 1-117, 119; 2-34
Dewey, Thomas E., 2-76; 4-62
DiPrete, Edward, 1-105
Diamond, MO, 4-82
Diamond (elephant), 4-39
Diamond Head (HI), 7-37, 47*, 49
Diamonds, 5-18, 19, 24; 6-64
Dickey, W. A., 7-21
Dickinson, Angie, 5-78
Dickinson, Charles, 3-118
Dickinson, Emily, 1-77
Dickinson, John, 2-17
Dickson, John, 1-89
Digital Computer Co., 1-93
Dillon, Lyman, 4-45
Dingley Brook, ME, 1-63
Dinosaur Nat. Mon., 6-29, 39, 109
Dinosaurs, 1-49, 71; 2-28; 5-57, 85, 99, 107; 6-29, 30, 62, 85, 113
Disasters, 7-62, 70
Disasters, natural, 1-46; 2-18, 48, 90, 118, 122; 3-61; 4-13, 20, 25, 34, 46, 47, 59, 61, 75, 76, 87, 89, 104, 117; 5-17, 19, 33, 36, 43, 47, 60, 61, 75, 88, 93, 102, 103, 117; 6-30, 33, 48, 61, 77, 85, 105, 121; 7-14, 15, 20, 28, 56, 58, 62, 70, 76, 80, 83
Dismal Swamp (NC/VA), 2-109; 3-85
Disney, Walt, 4-91
Disney World (FL), 3-37, 38, 39
Disneyland (CA), 7-33
Disston, Henry, 3-34
Distinguished Service Medal, 5-91
District of Columbia (creation), 2-46
District of Columbia (main article), 2-27
Dix, Dorothea Lynde, 1-77; 3-91
Dix, Dorothy, 3-120
"Dixie" (song), 4-107
Dobbins, Daniel, 2-89
Dochet Island (ME), 1-60
Dock Street Theater, 3-108
Dodge City, KS, 5-32, 33, 36, 39
Dodgers (baseball), 7-28
Doe, Mary Elizabeth McCourt (Baby), 6-34
Dog sleds, 7-18
Dogs, 3-85; 7-93
Dole, James, 7-44, 46

Dole, Sanford, 7-41
Dole Corp., 7-46, 48
Dolly Sods (WV), 2-121
Dolomite, 1-120; 6-108
Domes, capitol, 1-20, 24, 29, 80, 109, 110, 123; 2-37, 54; 4-67, 80, 122; 6-24, 67, 122; 7-35
Dominguez, Francisco Atanasio, 6-101
"Don Pedro" (Merino sheep), 2-23
Don's Club of Phoenix, 6-25
Doolittle, James H., 4-89
Door County, WI, 4-111, 123
Dorchester Heights Nat. Hist. Site (Boston, MA), 1-80
Dorion, Pierre, 5-100
Dorr, Thomas Wilson, 1-104
Dorrance, John T., 2-63
Dorset, VT, 1-121
Douglas, David, 7-58
Douglas, Frederick, 2-21, 49
Douglas, James, 3-57
Douglas, Stephen A., 4-19, 21
Douglas, William O., 4-77
Douglas MacArthur Mem. & Tomb, 2-109
Dousman, Hercules, 4-124
Dover, DE, 1-25; 2-16, 17, 22, 25
Dover, NH, 1-87, 88
Dover Air Force Base, 2-19*
Dover Days celebration, 2-17*
Draft riot, 1-75
Dragon flow (Craters of the Moon Nat. Mon.), 6-44
Drake, Edwin L., 2-93
Drake, Francis, 3-32; 7-25, 83, 88
Dred Scott decision, 4-88
Dresser, Bertha Menzler, 6-2
Drexel, NC, 3-93
Drift Prairie (ND), 5-71
Droughts, 3-35; 4-47, 76; 5-33, 60, 61, 75, 88, 93, 102; 6-30, 33, 61, 85
Drummond, William, 3-87
Dry Falls (WA), 6-44; 7-65
Dry Tortugas (FL), 3-31, 37
Du Gay (Catholic priest), 4-73
Du Lhut, Sieur (Daniel Greysolon), 4-73
Du Pont, Alfred I., 2-20, 24
Du Pont, Coleman, 2-20, 24
Du Pont, E. I., 2-23
Du Pont, Ethel, 2-18
Du Pont, Henry A., 2-24
Du Pont, Henry Francis, 2-10
Du Pont, Pierre Samuel, 2-19
Du Pont companies, 2-19, 22, 64
Du Pont family, 2-18, 19, 24
Du Ru (Catholic priest), 5-45
Du Tisne (explorer), 5-85
Dubuque, IA, 4-45, 51, 52
Dubuque, Julien, 4-44
Ducks, 2-78
Dudley Island (ME), 1-61
Duke, B. N., 3-91
Duke, James B., 2-63; 3-91
Duke Univ., 3-95
Duke of Alburquerque, 6-87
Duke of York, 2-57, 72, 81
Dulles International Airport, 2-107
Duluth, MN, 4-75, 81
Duluth (Sieur du Lhut), 4-73
Dumas, TX, 5-121
Dunbar, Paul Laurence, 4-107*
Dunkards, 2-87
Dunmore, John, 2-100, 115
Dunmore, Lord, 4-101
Dunn, Harvey, 5-108
Dunns Falls, 3-69
Dunraven, Earl of, 5-60
Dunton, Herbert W., 6-88
Duppa, Darrel, 6-19
Durango, CO, 6-39
Durham, NC, 3-95
Durham, NH, 1-88
Duryea, Charles Edgar, 1-79

Duryea, James Franklin, 1-79
Dust storms, 4-47, 76; 5-102; 6-33
Dustin, Hannah, 1-88
Dutch Alley, 5-52
Dutch settlements, 1-44; 2-15, 57, 72, 85; 4-45*, 67
Dutchman mine (AZ), 6-22
Dvorak, Antonin, 4-49
EROS Data Center, 5-106
Eagle Cliff (NH), 1-94
Eagle Island (ME), 1-64
Eagle Point Park (Dubuque, IA), 4-51
Eagle River, 4-122
Eagles, 1-31*; 4-117; 5-78; 6-120
Earhart, Amelia (Putnam), 5-34, 36
Early, Jubal A., 2-33, 89
Early Farmers, 3-85
Early Man, 4-85
Earp, Wyatt, 5-32, 33, 102, 116; 6-20
Earthquakes, 1-43, 51; 3-18, 59, 60, 103, 121; 4-87; 5-17, 36; 6-45, 61, 71, 77, 121; 7-15, 20, 23, 28, 51, 70, 91
East Barnet, VT, 1-114
East Cleveland, OH, 4-107
East Hampton, CT, 1-50
East Orange, NJ, 2-65
East River, 2-71
East Room, White House, 2-31, 38
East St. Louis, IL, 4-23
Easter lily bulbs, 7-60
Easter rabbit, 2-87
Eastern Hemisphere, 7-9
Eastman, George, 2-78
Eastport, ME, 1-10, 67
Eastwood, Clint, 7-28
Eaton, Theophilus, 1-44
Ebenezer Bar (Salmon River), 6-45
Eberhart, Mignon G., 5-63
Economy, 1-20, 38, 39, 51, 52, 65, 79, 93, 104, 108, 122; 2-11, 23, 52, 65, 78, 93, 107, 122; 3-11, 24, 37, 51, 65, 79, 93, 106, 121; 4-9, 23, 37, 51, 65, 79, 93, 108, 121; 5-11, 22, 38, 52, 65, 79, 93, 107, 121; 6-8, 37, 51, 65, 79, 93, 120; 7-19, 31, 46, 60, 73, 80
Eddy, Mary Baker, 1-77, 92
Eddy, Nelson, 2-92
Edenton, NC, 3-87, 88
Edenton Tea Party, 3-88
Edgemont, SD, 5-106
Edinburg, TX, 1-20
Edison, Thomas A., 2-60, 61, 62, 65, 67; 3-39; 4-66, 106, 107
Edisto Beach State Park (SD), 3-108
Education, 1-21
Edward of England, 2-51
Edwards, Edwin W., 5-48
Edwards, James B., 3-104
Effigy Mounds Nat. Mon., 4-43, 52
Egg Harbor, WI, 4-123
Egrets, 2-64; 3-36*; 5-50; 6-0
Ehrenberg, Herman, 6-20
Einstein, Albert, 2-62
Eisenhower, Mamie, 4-50
Eisenhower, Milton, 5-34
Eisenhower Mem. Museum, 5-39
El Camino Real (King's Highway, NM), 6-93
El Dorado, AR, 5-19
El Dorado Sapphire Mine (MT), 6-67
El Morro (San Juan, PR), 7-88, 91
El Paso, TX, 5-114, 117, 121, 122
El Pueblo de Nuestra Senora la Reina de Los Angeles de Porci (LA, CA), 7-25
El Yunque (Mt.), 7-87
El Yunque rainforest (PR), 7-91
Elberon, NJ, 2-60
Elberta peaches, 3-48
Electoral College, 2-104

Electric lights, 2-62
Electric motors, 1-121
Electric power, 7-70
Electrical equipment, 2-78
Electrical goods industry, 2-52, 65; 5-0
Electrical industry, 1-93; 3-20, 117; 4-20, 122; 5-106; 6-19
Electricity, 1-93; 3-97, 106, 121; 4-33, 117; 5-103; 6-48, 79
Electronics industry, 4-79; 7-60
Elephant Butte Reservoir, 6-85
Elephants, 4-83
Elevators, fish, 7-72
Eliot, T.S., 1-77
"Eliza" (schooner), 1-62
Elizabeth, NJ, 2-57
Elizabeth I of England, 1-72; 3-86
Elizabeth II of England, 4-118
Elizabethport, NJ, 2-64
Elk, 5-64; 6-21, 37, 46, 91; 7-72, 77
Elk Point, SD, 5-100
Elkhart, IN, 4-37
Elko, NV, 6-81
Ellensburg, WA, 7-70
Ellicot Mill (MD), 2-49
Elliot Hall of Music (Purdue Univ.), 4-39
Elmira, NY, 2-80
Elms, 1-15
Elms, The (Newport, RI), 1-108
"Eloise" (hurricane), 2-90
Elwood, IN, 4-35
Ely, MN, 4-81
Elysian Field (Hoboken, NJ), 2-60
Emerald Bay Nat. Landmark, 7-35
Emerald Mound, 3-80
Emerson, Ralph Waldo, 1-77
Emery, 2-78
Emigrant aid Co., 1-75
Emigration Canyon (UT), 6-106
Emmett, Daniel, 4-107
Emmitsburg, MD, 2-51
Empire State Bldg. (NYC), 1-20
Empire State Plaza, 2-78
Emporia, KS, 5-35
Emporia Gazette (Newspaper), 5-35
"End of the Trail, The" (Monument), 7-63
Engleman, George, 6-35
Engleman spruce, 6-35
English Turn, LA, 5-45
English settlements, 1-60, 114; 2-44, 57, 72, 99, 109; 3-45, 86, 87, 117
English vs. French wars, 1-61, 72, 87, 88, 102, 114; 2-16, 44, 73, 74, 86, 100, 103, 115, 119; 3-73, 101; 4-30, 58, 73, 101
English vs. Spanish wars, 1-102; 3-32, 86, 101
Enid, OK, 5-85
Eniwetok Island (Pacific), 7-85
Enterprise, AL, 3-23, 25
Entertainers, 1-49; 2-92, 106; 3-22, 63, 77, 118, 119, 120, 123; 4-36, 49, 50, 91; 5-63, 78, 89, 119; 6-35, 80; 7-28, 30, 72, 90
Entrepreneurs, 1-50
Environmentalists, 7-18
Epcot Center (FL), 3-34, 37, 38*
Epidemics, 3-117
Epsom Derby (England), 3-66
Equitable Life Insurance Co., 5-62
Erdie, Romeo D., 2-121
Eric the Red, 1-59
Erie, PA, 2-86, 88, 95; 4-100
Erie Canal, 2-74; 4-18, 32, 60, 103
Erie Indians, 4-100
Erie Triangle, 2-88
Erysipelas, 5-78
Escalante, Silvestre Velez de, 6-101
Eskimo customs, 7-12
Eskimo leaders, 7-12
Eskimo settlements, 7-21
Eskimos, 7-12, 16, 17, 21
Estado Libre Asociado, 7-89

Este, Charlotte, 2-92
Estes Park, CO, 6-29, 37, 38
Estevan (former slave), 6-17
Estherville, IA, 4-46
Estuaries, 2-41, 71, 97
Etchimin Indians, 1-59
Ether (anesthetic), 3-48
Etowah Mounds figure, 3-44*
Eufala Lake, 5-83
Eureka, NV, 6-74
Eureka Springs, AR, 1-27; 5-22, 23
European settlements, 1-44, 87; 3-52, 58, 73, 99; 4-86, 115; 5-16, 31, 100, 115; 6-102; 7-25, 53, 69
Eutaw Indians, 6-100
Euthanasia, 2-25
"Evangeline" (poem), 5-49
Evans, Mathilda, 3-105
Evans, Oliver, 2-21
Evans, Polly, 2-115
Evanston, IL, 1-21
Evansville, IN, 4-33
"Evening at Pueblo of Taos" (painting), 6-94*
Everglades, 3-27*, 33, 38
Everglades Nat. Park, 3-38
Evergreen, AL, 3-22
Evergreen Bridge (WA), 7-74
Evergreen State College, 1-21
Evergreens, 1-94
Evinrude, Ole, 4-119
Evolution, 3-117
Executions, 1-48; 4-75
Exeter, NH, 1-88, 92
Exon, James, 5-61
Explorers, 1-44, 49, 57, 59, 60, 62, 64, 66, 71, 72, 87, 101, 113, 114; 2-15, 29, 43, 57, 71, 72, 85, 92, 114; 3-17, 31, 32, 37, 45, 57, 58, 66, 72, 73, 86, 100; 4-16, 28, 30, 43, 44, 57, 58, 69, 72, 73, 74, 85, 86, 91, 97, 99, 100, 114, 115; 5-15, 16, 22, 29, 30, 36, 38, 44, 45, 58, 73, 74, 85, 100, 114; 6-13, 16, 17, 19, 30, 31, 36, 46, 47, 59, 60, 72, 87, 90, 101, 102, 115, 116, 119; 7-13, 16, 25, 29, 40, 67, 68, 72, 82, 88
Factor's Walk (Savannah, GA), 3-51
Fagatogo, AS, 7-80
Fair, James, 6-74, 77
Fair Haven, VT, 1-121
Fairbanks, AK, 7-14, 15, 18, 20
Fairbanks, Thaddeus, 1-121
Fairbanks Homestead Nat. Hist. Site, 1-81
Fairfax, Thomas, 2-100, 114
Fairfield, AL, 3-23
Fairfield, CT, 1-50
Fairfield, VT, 1-117
Fairmont, WV, 2-121
Fairview, KY, 3-62, 63
Fairview (W. J. Bryan home), 5-67
Fairweather, Bill, 6-60
Fairy terns, 7-44
"Faith 7" (space capsule), 5-90
Falkner, William C., 3-76, 77
Fall Foliage Festival (MA), 1-80
Fall Line, 2-41, 52, 97; 3-41, 99
Falmouth, MA, 1-79
Falmouth (Portland, ME), 1-65
Fanalulu, MT (Imaginary town), 6-66
Fanihi bats, 7-84
Fantastic Caverns (MO), 4-94
Far West, MO, 4-88
Fargo, ND, 1-10; 5-81
Farmer-Labor Party, 4-76
Farmington, PA, 2-95
Farmington, UT, 6-104
Farmington (KY mansion), 3-66
Farnsworth, Philo T., 6-106
Farnum, T. J., 6-101
Farragut, David Glasgow, 3-19, 119; 5-47

Farragut Park, ID, 6-48
Faubus, Orval, 5-19
Faulkner, Sandford D. (Sandy), 5-20
Faulkner, William, 3-76
Fayetteville, AR, 5-23
Fearn, Thomas, 3-22
Federal Hall (NYC), 2-74
Federal Hill, 3-66
Federal "Triangle", 2-34
Feldspar, 1-92; 3-93
Felton, Rebecca, 3-48
Fenian "War", 1-117
Fennimore, James, 6-74
Ferber, Edna, 4-120
Ferdinandian (Spanish settlement), 5-85
Ferguson, James E., 5-119
Ferguson, Miriam A., 5-119
Ferguson House (Lincoln, NE), 5-67
Ferraro, Geraldine, 7-28
Ferrello, Bartolome, 7-53
Ferris, George, 4-20
Ferris, Joe, 5-77
Ferryboats, 2-18, 57, 78; 7-19, 73, 74, 76, 91
Festival Theater, 3-24
Festival of the American West, 5-109
Festivals, 1-29, 30, 46, 52, 66, 80, 95, 108, 122; 2-17, 48, 94, 123; 3-24, 39, 108, 123; 4-38, 39, 45*, 66, 80, 81, 94, 123; 5-39, 50, 51, 52, 53, 108, 122, 123; 6-23, 53, 81, 94, 95, 109, 122; 7-20, 21, 32, 49, 62, 76, 84, 90, 91, 96
"Fiddle back" mound, 4-28
Field, Eugene, 4-91; 6-35
Field, Marshall, 4-21
Field Museum of Natural History (Chicago, IL) 4-11*, 23
Fiesta de Santa Fe, 6-95
Fiesta of San Antonio, 5-123
Fifth Avenue (NYC), 2-80
Fig trees, 7-84
Fillmore, Millard, 2-76
Filson Club Museum, 3-66
Finger Lakes, 2-69, 80
Finnish settlements, 4-76
Fir trees, 4-75
Firehole Canyon (WY), 6-123
Firehoses, 4-107
Fires, 1-51; 2-18, 32, 48, 74, 118, 122; 3-47, 61; 4-20, 59, 61, 75, 76, 88, 117; 5-75, 102; 7-28, 58, 62, 70
Fires, forest, 7-58
First Regiment (CT), 1-46
First Regiment (DE), 2-16, 18
First Regiment (IA), 4-46
First Regiment (MN), 4-75
First Regiment (RI), 1-104
First Road West, 6-122
First State Capitol (MO), 4-94
Firsts, Philadelphia, 2-94
Fish, 1-44; 7-18, 44, 49, 58, 83, 94
Fish, Mrs. Stuyvesant, 1-106
Fish elevators, 7-72
Fish farming, 3-37; 5-22; 7-40, 83
Fish ladders, 1-107; 7-72
Fisher, Carl, 3-34
Fisherman's Wharf (Monterey, CA), 7-34
Fisherman's Wharf (San Francisco, CA), 7-34
Fishing, Deep-sea, 5-50
Fishing, commercial, 1-65, 78, 79, 87, 107, 108; 2-16, 22, 23, 44, 48*, 51, 65, 106; 3-79; 5-51; 7-18, 58, 83
Fishing, hukilau, 7-49
Fishing, sport, 1-64, 78, 94, 107, 120; 2-22, 51, 54, 64, 106; 3-108; 4-22, 78; 5-50, 102, 108; 6-78, 81, 91, 123; 7-44, 94

Fitch, John, 1-48; 2-62
Fitzgerald, F. Scott, 4-78
Five Nations, 2-43, 71
Flag, Fort McHenry replica, 2-48
Flagler, Harrison M., 3-34, 35
Flags, 2-17, 18, 26, 44*, 47, 48, 54, 64, 74; 3-19, 77; 4-33, 39, 44, 67, 74; 5-30, 80, 115, 116; 6-74, 89, 95; 7-16, 17, 19, 26, 55, 80
Flagstaff, AZ, 6-23, 24
Flambeau River, 4-113
Flaming Gorge (WY), 6-113
Flaming Gorge Lake, 6-123
Flaming Gorge Nat. Rec. Area, 6-123
Flaming Gorge Reservoir, 6-99, 113
Flamingo, FL, 3-38
"Flamingo" (sculpture), 4-24
Flanagan, Edward J., 5-63
Flat Rock, NC, 3-91
Flathead Indians, 6-58, 115
Flathead Lake, 6-57
Flax, 5-78, 79
Fleete, Henry, 2-29, 44
Fleischmann Atmospherium-Planetarium (Reno, NV), 6-81
Fleming, A. B., 2-117
Flemingsburg, KY, 3-58
Fletcher, Harvey, 6-106
Flint, 5-73
Flint Ridge cave system, 1-10
Flood, James, 6-74
Flood control, 3-117; 4-75, 104
Floods, 2-90, 118; 3-61, 75, 118; 4-13, 25, 34, 104; 5-19, 43, 47, 102, 103, 117; 6-99, 105
Florence, Italy, 1-101
Florida (main article), 3-27
Flounder, 2-64
Flour processing, 4-119
Flourbag Fort, 2-87
Flower bulbs, 7-73
Floyd, Charles, 4-44, 53
Floyd County, GA., 3-50
Flume, The (NH), 1-94
Flumes, 1-86, 94
Fluorite, 1-92
Fluorspar, 4-22
Flushing Meadow (NYC), 2-81
Flying Eagle Goodbear, Paul, 6-91
"Folk Songs of the American Negro" (book), 3-120
Folsom, Frances, 2-33
Folsom people, 1-100; 5-15, 57, 85; 6-0
Fontaine, Edmund, 2-50
Fontana Dam, NC, 3-95
Fontana Lake, 3-95
Forbes, John, 2-86
Ford, Edsel, 4-64
Ford, Gerald R., 2-35; 3-48; 4-62, 67; 5-62, 66
Ford, Henry, 4-63*, 64, 65, 66
Ford Foundation, 2-94
Ford Motor Co., 4-62, 63
Ford Museum, 4-66*
Ford Nat. Hist. Park, 2-67
Ford Peace Ship, 4-63
Ford's River Rouge plant, 4-67
Ford's Theater, 2-33, 39
Forest Products Lab., U.S., 4-121
Forest industry, 3-36, 77, 79; 4-64, 70, 121; 5-21, 50, 120
Forests, 1-50, 92, 94, 120; 2-22, 55, 63, 67, 77, 85, 106, 107, 120, 121; 3-23, 36, 49, 64, 77, 92, 106, 120; 4-22, 64, 76, 78, 81, 92, 99, 117, 120; 5-36, 49, 64, 67, 78, 92, 120; 6-21, 50, 65, 78, 92, 107, 122; 7-58, 87, 90
Forget-me-not (flower), 7-16
Forrest, Nathan Bedford, 3-116, 119
Fort Abercrombie, 5-74
Fort Abraham Lincoln, 5-74, 81
Fort Ancient State Mem. (OH), 4-99

Fort Ancient people, 4-28
Fort Augusta, 3-52
Fort Beauharnois, 4-73
Fort Bedford, 2-87
Fort Bent, 6-31
Fort Benton, 6-65
Fort Boeuf, 2-86
Fort Boise, 6-47
Fort Bridger, 5-59; 6-116, 123
Fort Buenaventura, 6-102
Fort Buford, 5-74, 75
Fort Buford State Hist. Park (ND), 5-81
Fort Caroline, 3-31, 32, 52
Fort Casper, 6-122
Fort Christina Mon., 2-24
Fort Clatsop, 7-53, 62
Fort Conde, 3-24
Fort Constitution, 1-88
Fort Cumberland, 2-44, 45
Fort Dalles, 7-63
Fort Dearborn, 4-17
Fort Dearborn Massacre, 4-17
Fort Defiance, 4-102
Fort Deposit, MD, 2-47
Fort Dummer, 1-114
Fort Duquesne, 2-86
Fort Erie, 2-80
Fort Evans, 2-115
Fort Frederica Nat. Mon., 3-51
Fort Gaines, 3-24
Fort Garland, 6-90
Fort Hall, 6-47, 53
Fort Henry, 2-115, 120
Fort Jefferson, 3-34, 37
Fort Jessup, 5-47
Fort Kearny, 6-116
Fort Knox, KY, 3-61, 67
Fort Laramie, 6-115, 116
Fort Laramie Nat. Hist. Site, 6-118, 122
Fort Lauderdale, FL, 3-38
Fort Leavenworth, 5-31
Fort Leavenworth, KS, 5-38
Fort Lee, NJ, 2-60
Fort Lee (Charleston, WV), 2-122
Fort Loudoun, 2-100
Fort Louis de la Mobile, 3-17
Fort Mackinac, 4-66
Fort Madison, IA, 4-44, 51
Fort Mandan, 5-73, 74
Fort Mandan Hist. Site, 5-81
Fort McHenry, 2-44*, 47, 53
Fort McHenry Nat. Mon., 2-53
Fort McKay, 4-115
Fort Meigs, 4-102
Fort Meyers, FL, 3-39
Fort Miami, 4-30, 31
Fort Michilimackinac, 4-12*, 58, 66
Fort Mims, 3-18
Fort Moultrie, 3-8
Fort Nashborough, 3-115, 123
Fort Necessity, 2-95; 4-101
Fort Niagara, 2-72
Fort Niobrara Nat. Wildlife Refuge, 5-67
Fort Nisqually, 7-74
Fort Nonsense, 2-59, 67
Fort Norman, 6-80
Fort Okonogan, 7-69
Fort Osage, MO, 4-87
Fort Ouiatenon, 4-30
Fort Peck Dam, 6-57, 66
Fort Peck Reservoir, 6-57
Fort Pickens, 3-21
Fort Pierre, SD, 5-100
Fort Pitt, 2-86, 87, 95
Fort Pleasant, 2-44
Fort Prudhomme (TN), 3-114
Fort Pulaski Nat. Mon., 3-51
Fort Raleigh Nat. Hist. Site, 3-3
Fort Recovery, 4-102
Fort Ridgely, 4-75
Fort Ross, 7-26
Fort Sill, 5-87
Fort Sill, OK, 6-18

Fort Sill Nat. Hist. Landmark, 5-94
Fort Smith, 5-18, 21
Fort Smith, AR, 5-23
Fort Smith Nat. Hist. Site, 5-23
Fort Snelling, 4-74, 76
Fort Snelling State Park (MN), 4-76, 80
Fort St. Charles, 4-73
Fort St. Jean Baptiste, 5-45
Fort St. Vrain, 6-32
Fort Stephanson, 4-102
Fort Stevens, 2-33; 7-56, 62
Fort Sumter, 3-19, 102, 103*
Fort Supply, 6-116
Fort Taylor, 3-34
Fort Ticonderoga, 1-48, 118; 2-72
Fort Tubac, 6-17
Fort Union, 5-74; 6-59*, 60, 88
Fort Union Nat. Mon., 6-93
"Fort Union on the Missouri" (painting), 6-59*
Fort Vancouver, 7-69, 77
Fort Washaki, 6-119
Fort Wayne, IN, 4-28, 31, 37, 39
Fort William Henry, 1-61
Fort Wimberley, 3-46
Fort Worth, TX, 1-27; 5-120, 123
Fort de Charters, 4-16, 25
Fort of the Miamis, 4-30, 31
"Fortune" (ship), 1-72
Fortune 500 companies, 2-22; 4-51
Forty-niners, 5-59; 6-47, 103; 7-27
Fossil, OR, 7-63
Fossil, WY, 6-113
Fossil Cycad Nat. Mon., 5-99
Fossils, 1-11, 71, 99; 2-28, 41; 3-57; 4-83, 85; 5-29, 57, 72, 85, 97, 99; 6-15, 29, 39, 44, 85, 109, 113; 7-63
Foster, Stephen C., 2-92; 3-66
Foster Botanic Garden (HI), 7-49
Fountain of Youth at Lewes, DE, 2-26
Four Corners (AZ/CO/NM/UT), 6-15, 24, 83
Fourteen Points, 2-105
Fox, Catherine, 2-21
Fox, George Lansing, 1-117
Fox Indians, 4-16, 17
Fox Movietone News, 3-109
Fox River, 4-113, 115
Fox hunting, 2-51
Francis, Milly, 5-92
Francis Green Airport, 1-104
Franciscans, 6-87
Franconia Notch, 1-83
Frankfort, KY, 1-26; 3-61, 67, 68
Franklin, Benjamin, 1-18, 19, 77; 2-58, 73, 87, 88, 90, 91, 94; 3-64; 4-74
Franklin, Deborah, 2-94
Franklin, ID, 6-47
Franklin, NH, 1-90, 91
Franklin, State of, 3-115
Franklin, VT, 1-117
Franklin, William, 2-58
Franklin Delano Roosevelt Mem. Bridge, 1-67
Franklin tree, 3-64
Frazier, Lynn, 5-75
Frederick, MD, 2-45
Frederick Evangel. Luth. Ch. (Charlotte Amalie, VI), 7-95
Frederick Island (ME), 1-61
Fredericksburg, TX, 5-119
Fredericksburg, VA, 2-101
Frederiksted, VI, 7-96
Fredonia, AZ, 6-18
Free Soil Party, 1-91
Freedom of religion, 1-101, 102, 105; 2-43, 44, 49; 4-88, 94, 103; 6-104; 7-43
Freedom of the press, 2-73
Freeport, ME, 1-58
Freer Gallery of Art (DC), 2-39
Fremont, John C., 5-100; 6-90, 102;

7-26, 29
Fremont, OH, 4-105, 108
French, Daniel Chester, 1-77, 80; 2-39; 5-67
French Canada, 4-58, 73
French Market (New Orleans, LA), -5-52
French Quarter (New Orleans, LA), 5-52
French Revolution, 2-88
French settlements, 1-60, 114; 3-17, 31, 45, 58, 73; 4-16, 30, 57, 86; 5-45, 85, 86
French vs. English wars, 1-61, 72, 87, 88, 102, 114; 2-16, 44, 73, 74, 86, 100, 103, 115, 119; 3-73, 101; 4-30, 58, 73, 101
Frenchtown, MT, 6-61
Freon, 2-22
Freyeburg, ME, 1-64
Freyeburg Academy, 1-64
Frick, Henry Clay, 2-92
Friction clutch, 1-48
"Frieda" (storm), 7-56
Friendship Cemetery (Columbus, MS), 3-81
Frigate bird, 7-44, 94
Fringed gentian, 4-78
Fritchie, Barbara, 4-66
Frog farming, 5-51
Front Range, 6-29
"Front Street, Showdown on" (Dodge City, KS), 5-39
Front Street (Dodge City, KS), 5-39
Front Street (Ogallala, NE), 5-67
Frontier Days (Cheyenne, WY), 1-29
Frontier Days Old West Museum, 6-122
Frontier Days Rodeo, 6-122
Frost, Robert, 1-119; 7-29
Frozen food industry, 5-64
Fruit bats, 7-84
Ft. Randall Dam, 5-97
Fulbright, James William, 5-20
Fulbright Scholarships, 5-20
Fulton, MO, 4-89, 90
Fulton, Robert, 1-48; 2-62, 116
Fundamental Orders, 1-44, 45
Funston, Frederick, 5-36
Fur rendezvous, 7-20
Fur trade, 1-11, 60; 2-21, 23, 57; 4-16, 30, 57, 74, 77, 86, 92, 100, 115, 124; 5-73, 100, 105; 6-31, 47, 59, 60, 101, 116; 7-26, 53, 69
Furniture, 2-65, 107
Furniture industry, 4-64, 67; 6-65
Gable, Clark, 7-30
Gabriel's Rock (IN), 4-38
Gadsden, AL, 3-19
Gadsden Purchase, 1-90
Gadwall birds, 3-91
Galax, VA, 2-106
Gale, Joe, 7-57
Galena, IL, 4-17, 18, 20*, 21
Gallatin, Albert, 2-92
Gallatin River, 6-59
Galloping Gertie (Tacoma Narrows Bridge), 7-76
Galtier, Lucian, 4-74
Galveston, TX, 1-10; 5-114, 115, 117, 123
Galvez, Don Bernardo, 5-49
Gambling, 2-61; 6-74, 80
Gandia, Manuel Zeno, 7-90
Garces, Francisco Tomas, 6-17, 20
Garden, Alexander, 3-105
Garden City, NY, 2-81
Garden State Arts Center, 2-66
Garden of the Gods (CO), 6-38
Gardenia, 3-105
Gardiner, MT, 6-59
Garfield, James A., 1-118; 2-33, 60
Garland, Augustus, 5-20
Garland, Hamlin, 1-77; 4-120; 5-104
Garner, John Nance, 5-119

Garnets, 2-77; 6-64, 77, 107
Garrett, Elizabeth, 6-91
Garrett, John Jr., 2-23
Garrett, Pat, 6-91
Garrison, William Lloyd, 1-75
Garrison Dam, 5-69, 81
Gary, IN, 4-37
Gary, SD, 5-102
Gas and oil, 1-11; 2-65, 77, 80, 93, 121; 3-64, 65, 78, 79; 4-22, 23, 36, 64, 92, 108; 5-19, 36, 37, 49, 50, 64, 75, 78, 79, 83, 92, 93, 95, 96, 106, 113, 119, 120, 121; 6-36, 64, 65, 91, 92, 106, 107, 108, 118, 120; 7-15, 17, 27, 31
Gas station pumps, 4-37
Gasoline engine cars, 4-65
Gasparilla Festival, 3-39
Gaspee Incident, 1-103
Gateway Arch (Jefferson Nat. Expansion Mem.), 4-86*, 89, 93
Gateway Center (Pittsburg, PA), 2-95
Gateway to Gold (CO), 6-37
Gatlinburg, TN, 3-122
Gatling, Richard J., 3-19
Gatling gun, 3-91
Gaultier, Pierre (Sieur de La Verendrye), 4-73; 5-0
Gayarre, Charles, 5-45
Geddes, E. H., 1-94
Geese, 7-72
Gemstones, 1-92; 2-77; 5-78, 106; 6-21, 36, 50, 77, 91; 7-59
General Court (NH legislature), 1-95
General Electric Co., 2-78; 4-107
General Grant tree, 7-35
General Motors Co., 4-65; 5-37
Genessee River gorge, 2-80
Genoa, NV, 6-77
Geo-thermal energy, 6-79
Geodes, 6-77
Geography, 1-6, 7, 10, 11, 41, 43, 55, 57, 58, 69, 83, 85, 86, 97, 99, 111, 113; 2-13, 15, 25, 27, 28, 41, 52, 55, 69, 71, 75, 79, 83, 97, 98, 100, 111, 113; 3-13, 15, 29, 41, 43, 55, 57, 69, 71, 83, 84, 85, 97, 99, 100, 111, 113; 4-13, 15, 22, 27, 28, 31, 41, 55, 57, 69, 71, 93, 97, 99, 111, 113; 5-6, 13, 15, 27, 41, 43, 55, 69, 71, 97, 111; 6-15, 27, 29, 41, 43, 55, 59, 69, 71, 83, 85, 97, 100, 111, 113; 7-9, 23, 37, 39, 46, 51, 65, 79, 82, 85, 87, 93, 98
Geological Survey, U.S., 6-20
Geology, 1-43, 85, 99, 111, 113; 2-27, 28, 41, 69, 97, 113; 3-9, 41, 57, 71, 85, 113; 4-13, 22, 27, 36, 41, 57, 71, 83, 99, 111, 113; 5-27, 41, 43, 57, 71, 83, 85, 97, 99, 111, 113; 6-15, 15, 20, 29, 43, 44, 71, 85, 97, 100, 106, 113, 114; 7-23, 37, 51, 65, 91, 93
George II of England, 3-45
George III of England, 1-115; 2-0
George Washington Bridge, 2-61
Georgetown, CO, 6-37
Georgetown, DC, 2-29
Georgetown, SC, 3-107
Georgetown Loop RR, 6-37
Georgetown Univ., 7-90
Georgia (main article), 3-41
"Georgia's Aesop" (Joel Chandler Harris), 3-48
Gerald Ford Library, 4-67
Gerald Ford Museum, 4-67
German settlements, 2-87, 94, 115; 4-122
Geronimo (chief), 6-18, 88, 89
Gershwin, George, 2-77
Getty, J. Paul, 5-92
Getty Oil, 2-22
Getty art galleries (CA), 7-33
Gettysburg, PA, 2-18, 89, 92

Gettysburg Address, 2-89
Gettysburg Nat. Cemetary, 2-89
Gettysburg Nat. Military Park, 2-94
Gettysburg of the West (Battle of Westport), 4-88
Ghost Town in WY, 6-122*
Giant Sequoias, 7-30
Giant cobra lilies, 7-58
Giant coreopsis (sunflower), 7-30
Gibbsville conglomerate, 2-93
Gibralter of the Pacific, 7-33
Gibson, Charles Dana, 1-92
Gila City, AZ, 6-18
Gila Cliff Dwellings Nat. Mon., 6-93
Gila Nat. Forest, 6-93
Gila River, 6-15, 85
Gila monsters, 6-21, 92
Gilbert, Cass, 1-30; 4-80; 5-25
Gilbert, Humphrey, 1-72
Gilbert, Raleigh, 1-60
Gilcrease Institute (OK), 5-94
Gilcrest, CO, 6-32
Gillespie, Jesse, 3-103
Gilman, Tabitha, 1-92
Gilman, VT, 1-117
Gilsonite, 6-108
Ginaca, Harry, 7-44
Gingerich, Philip, 6-118
"Girl of the Limberlost, A" (book), 4-35
Gist, Christopher, 3-58; 4-100, 101
Gist, George (Sequoyah), 1-19; 3-9*, 22*; 5-86, 90, 91*, 95
Glacial cirques, 1-85
Glacial moraine, 1-99
Glacier Bay (AK), 7-20
Glacier Bay Nat. Mon., 7-20
Glacier Nat. Park, 6-55, 57, 61, 62, 66
Glacier Peak, 7-65
Glacier Priest (Bernard Hubbard), 7-16
Glaciers, 1-43, 57, 58, 69, 85, 86, 99; 2-69, 113; 4-13, 22, 27, 41, 57, 71, 99, 113; 5-29, 71, 99; 6-44, 66, 97, 113; 7-9, 16, 19, 20*, 21, 23, 51, 65
Gladding's Dept. Store, 1-102
Glass, 2-64, 80, 106, 121; 4-22, 37, 107
Glass, Hugh, 6-60
Glass Mts., 5-95
Glass making, 2-52, 64, 78, 106, 122, 123
Glen Canyon Dam, 6-15, 99
Glencoe, MN, 4-75
Glenn, John, 3-34; 4-105
Glens Falls, NY, 1-15
Glenville, WV, 2-123
Glenwood Springs, CO, 6-39
"Gloria" (hurricane), 1-46
"Gloucester Fisherman" (statue), 1-78*
Glover, Joshua, 4-116
Gnaw Bone, IN, 4-38
Gobi Desert, 6-115
Goddard, Robert H., 1-79; 2-50
Goebel, William, 3-60
Going-to-the-Sun Highway (CO), 6-66
Gold, 1-11, 62; 3-51, 53, 92; 5-18, 36, 74, 106; 6-18, 21, 22, 32, 34, 36, 47, 48, 50, 60, 78, 91, 103, 107, 108, 122; 7-13, 14, 15, 19, 20, 27, 29, 31, 35, 55, 62, 70
Gold Discovery State Park (CA), 7-35
Gold Rush of 1869, 5-74
Gold coral, 7-44
Gold panning, 3-50*
Golden City, AR, 5-18
Golden Days Festival, 7-20
Golden Gate (CA), 7-28, 29, 34
Golden Gate Bridge, 7-28, 34
Golden Isles, GA, 3-42

Golden Jubilee of Statehood (WA), 7-70
Golden Spike Nat. Hist. Site, 6-109
"Golden age of prosperity", 3-46
Goldendale, WA, 7-77
Goldfield, NV, 6-74, 81
Goldfish, 2-53
Goldwater, Barry M., 6-19
Goldwater Dept. Store, 6-19
Goleta, CA, 7-28
Golf, 1-104; 3-49; 5-103
Goliad, TX, 5-115
Gomez, Estavan, 2-71
"Gone With the Wind" (book/movie), 3-48
Goodbear, Paul Flying Eagle, 6-91
Goodhue, Grace Anne (Coolidge), 1-118
Goodlet, Caroline Meriweather, 3-120
Goodman, Joseph, 6-79
Goodrich, Benjamin Franklin, 4-107
Goodyear, Charles, 1-48
Goodyear, Miles, 6-102
Gopher trees, 3-121
Gorges, Ferdinando, 1-60, 87
Gorrie, John, 3-36
Gorton, Samuel, 1-102
Gosiute Indians, 6-72, 101
Gosnold, Bartholomew, 1-72
Gottschalk, Louis Moreau, 5-49
Government organization (CT), 1-46
Grace (Kelly) of Monaco, 2-93
Graceland (E. Presley home), 3-120, 123
Grady Gammage Mem. Auditorium (Phoenix, AZ), 1-27; 6-25
Grafton, WV, 2-119, 123
Graham Cave (MO), 4-85
Grain mills, 1-93
Granby, MA, 1-71
Grand Canyon Nat. Park, 6-18
"Grand Canyon Suite" (Ferde Grofe), 6-21
Grand Canyon of Pennsylvania, 2-83
Grand Canyon of the Colorado, 1-10, 12*; 6-13, 15, 16, 17, 18, 20, 21, 23*, 106; 7-39, 48, 51
Grand Canyon of the East, 2-80
Grand Canyon of the Snake, 6-113
Grand Canyon of the Tennessee, 3-113
"Grand Canyon of the Yellowstone" (painting), 6-119
Grand Canyon of the Yellowstone River, 6-113
Grand Coulee Dam, 7-70, 73, 76
Grand Coulee gorge, 7-65
Grand Forks, ND, 5-81
Grand Island, NE, 5-66
Grand Island (LA), 5-50
Grand Junction, ND, 5-81
Grand Lake, 6-29, 38
Grand Mesa (CO), 6-29
Grand Old Oprey, 1-26
Grand Portage, MN, 4-74
Grand Portage Nat. Mon., 4-81
Grand Prismatic Spring (Yellowstone), 6-121
Grand Rapids, MI, 4-64, 65, 67
Grand River, 4-97
Grand Saline (French settlement), 5-86
Grand Strand, 3-108
Grand Teton, 6-111
Grand Teton Nat. Park, 6-121
Grand Village of the Natchez, 3-79, 80
Grandfather Mt., 3-83*, 94
Granite, 1-65, 67, 92, 107, 120, 121; 7-23, 25
Granite Hills (VT), 1-111, 120
Granite Mt., 5-123

Granite Museum, 1-123
Granite Peak, 6-55
Grant, Ulysses S., 1-89, 91; 2-33, 80, 101, 102; 3-75, 116; 4-10, 19, 20, 21, 36, 105, 108; 5-18
Grant's Tomb (NY), 1-65; 2-80
Grants, NM, 6-85
Grapes, 7-30
Grasse, Francois Joseph Paul de, 2-100
Grasshopper Glacier, 6-66
Grasshoppers, 5-60; 6-48
Grasso, Ella T., 1-46
Gravecreek mound, 2-113
Graves County, KY, 3-63
Gray, Robert, 7-53
Great Basin, 6-43, 71, 99, 101, 113
Great Blue Hills of God, 3-97
Great Blue Hills region (MA), 1-7
Great Divide Basin, 6-111, 123
"Great Embarkation", 3-45
Great Falls, MT, 6-56*, 61, 62, 65, 66
Great Falls of the Missouri River, 6-59
Great Falls of the Potomac, 2-53
Great Lakes, 1-7; 2-69, 74, 83, 89, 100; 4-13, 17, 18, 22, 28, 55, 58, 65, 69, 97, 102, 105, 113, 118
Great Lakes of South Dakota, 5-109
Great Miami River, 4-97
Great Plains, 5-6*, 69, 75, 111
Great Plains Gassification Assn., 5-79
Great Platte River Road, 5-66
Great Pocomoke Swamp (DE), 2-18, 22
Great Salt Lake, 6-43, 44, 97, 99, 101, 104, 105, 109
Great Salt Plains (OK), 5-95
Great Sand Dunes Nat. Mon., 6-32*, 39
Great Smoky Mts. Nat. Park, 3-94, 122
Great Spirit (Indian god), 1-83, 86; 2-69
Great Swamp (RI), 1-99
Great Temple Mound (Ocmulgee Nat. Mon.), 3-50*
"Great Train Robbery" (movie), 2-67
Great Unconformity, 1-43
"Great Wall" (SD), 5-108
Greater Antilles, 7-87
Greater New Orleans Bridge, 5-48
"Greatest Show on Earth, The" (circus), 1-49; 4-123
Greeley, CO, 6-35, 37
Greeley, Horace, 1-91, 93; 6-35
Green Animals Topiary Gardens (RI), 1-108
Green Bay, WI, 4-73, 111, 113, 114, 115, 120, 123
Green Bay Packers (football), 4-123
Green Corn Ceremony, 3-44*
Green Lake, 7-74
Green Mountain Boys, 1-115, 119
Green Mts., 1-43, 69, 111
Green Pond, 1-43
Green Pond Mt., 1-43
Green River, 6-99, 106, 109, 113, 116
Green aquamarine, 6-64
Greenbrier, Hotel (WV), 2-118, 123*
Greene, Nathaneal, 1-106
Greeneville, NC, 3-90
Greenfield, IN, 4-35
Greenfield, WV, 2-123
Greenfield Village, MI, 4-66
Greensboro, NC, 3-93, 95
Greenstone, 1-107
Greenville, TN, 3-90, 119, 123
Greenville, VA, 2-107
Greenwich, NJ, 2-58
Greenwich Bay (RI), 1-99

Greenwich Village (NYC), 2-80
Greenwood, MS, 3-77, 79
Gresham, Bethel, 4-33
Gresham, James B., 4-39
Grey, Zane, 4-107; 6-35, 105
Greybeards, 4-46
Greyhound Corp., 6-22
Greysolon, Daniel (Sieur du Lhut), 4-73
Gridley, Reuel, 6-75
Grierson, Benjamin H., 4-19
"Griffon" (ship), 4-58
Grindstone City, MI, 4-65
Grinnell, IA, 4-46
"Grizzly Bear" (locomotive), 7-27
Gros Ventres Indians, 6-115
Gros Ventres of the Mountains Indians, 6-58
Gros Ventres of the River Indians, 6-58
Groseilliers, Sieur de, 4-115
Groton, CT, 1-79
Grove Cemetery, 1-52
Guadalupe Hidalgo, Treaty of, 7-26
Guadalupe Mts., 5-111, 122
Guadalupe Mts. Nat. Park, 5-122
Guam (main article), 7-82
Guast, Pierre du (Sieur de Monts), 1-60
Guavas, 7-45, 94
Guaxule (Cherokee village), 3-45
Guernsey, Jess, 1-94
Guggenheim Museum of Art (NYC), 2-80; 4-120
Guilford Court House, NC, 3-88
Guilford Courthouse Nat. Military Park, 3-95
Gulf of Alaska, 7-9
Gulf of California, 1-7; 6-15, 20, 29, 113
Gulf of Mexico, 1-7; 2-83, 116; 3-13, 23, 24, 31, 43, 69, 71; 4-28, 30, 83, 99; 5-41, 69, 99; 6-29, 55, 65, 113
Gulfport, MS, 3-81
Gunnison River, Black Canyon of the, 6-29
Gunpowder, 2-19, 24
Guthrie, OK, 5-88
Guthrie, Tyrone, 4-80
Guymon, OK, 5-92*, 93
Gvozdev, Michael, 7-13
Gypsum, 2-77, 106; 4-50
Gypsum Hills (KS), 5-27
H & R Block, 5-36
H. Roe Bartle Exposition Hall (Kansas City, MO), 4-94
Hackensack, NJ, 2-57
Hackensack Meadowlands, 2-61
Hacksaws, 1-91
Hadley, Paul, 4-33
Hadley Museum (DE), 2-13*
Hafnium, 7-60
Hagenbeck-Wallace circus, 4-39
Haida Indians, 7-37
Hainguypooshies (chief), 2-120
"Hair Buyer" Hamilton, Henry, 4-30, 31, 58, 101
Haiti, 2-93
Hale, Edward Everett, 1-14
Hale, Nathan, 1-48, 53
Haleakala (HI), 7-37
Haleakala Nat. Park, 7-46
Half Dome (Yosemite Nat. Pk.), 7-35
Half King (chief), 2-86
"Half Moon" (ship), 2-71
Halifax, NC, 3-88
Hall, Charles Martin, 4-106
Hall, Dick Wick, 6-12
Hall, James Norman, 4-49
Hall, Joyce C., 4-91
Hall of Fame, U.S., 2-20, 92, 120; 7-29, 57
Hall of Flags, (Concord, NH), 1-95

Hallowell, ME, 1-67
Hallshallakeen (Joseph the Younger), 7-71
Hamblin Jacob, 6-106
Hamilton, Alexander, 2-63, 64, 67; 7-96
Hamilton, Henry (Hair Buyer), 4-30, 31, 58, 101
Hamilton, NV, 6-74
Hamlin, Hannibal, 1-61
Hammond, LA, 5-50
Hampshire County, WV, 2-113
Hampson Museum, 5-16
Hampton, NH, 1-87
Hampton, VA, 2-109
Hampton Institute, 2-106, 120
Hampton Roads, VA, 2-102, 103, 107
Hanapepe River, 7-39
Hancock, Cornelia, 2-60
Hancock, MD, 2-41
Hancock Center., Chicago, 4-11*
Handicrafts, 3-121
Handsome Lake (Indian prophet), 2-77
Handy, W. C., 3-22, 118, 119, 123*; 4-91
Hanks, Nancy, 3-62
Hannibal, MO, 4-89
Hanson, Howard, 5-63
Hanson, John, 2-49
Harbors, 1-57, 65, 97, 99; 2-103; 3-46, 47; 4-81, 111; 7-23, 32, 42, 47, 79, 87, 95
Harding, Warren G., 1-117, 118; 4-47, 49, 106, 108; 6-61; 7-14
Hargems, Charles, 4-88
Harlan County, KY, 3-61
Harlem (NYC), 2-80
Harlem River, 2-71
Harlin, J. J., 6-88
Harmon, Charles H., 6-86
Harmony, MN, 4-81
Harmony, PA, 2-95
Harness racing, 4-46
Harney Peak, 5-99
Harolds Club (Reno, NV), 6-81
Harper, Robert, 2-115
Harpers Ferry, WV, 2-32*, 111, 114*, 115, 116, 117, 123
Harpers Ferry Nat. Hist. Park, 2-123
Harrah's Auto Collection (Reno, NV), 6-81
Harriman, Averell, 2-76
Harris, Joel Chandler, 3-48, 49
Harrisburg, PA, 2-30, 89, 94
Harrison, Benjamin, 4-106; 5-76, 102
Harrison, NE, 5-67
Harrison, William Henry, 2-32, 104; 4-31, 32, 33, 35, 106, 108
Harrod, James, 3-58
Harrodsburg, KY, 3-58
Harrodstown (European settlement), 3-58
Harry S. Truman Sports Complex (Kansas City, MO), 4-94
Hart, Charles W., 4-51
Hart, Gary, 5-34
Hart, Nancy, 2-120
Hartford, CT, 1-42*, 44, 46*, 49, 51*
Hartwell Reservoir, 3-43
Harvard Univ., 1-21, 24, 52, 62, 73*, 81; 2-21
Harvey, Cordelia, 4-117
Harvey, Louis P., 4-117
Haskell Opera House (Derby Line, VT), 1-123
Havana, Cuba, 3-32
Havasupai Indians, 6-16, 20
Hawaii (main article), 7-37
Hawaii Island, 7-37, 39, 42, 47
Hawaii Royal palace and throne room, 7-49
Hawaii Territory, 1-90

Hawaii Volcanoes Nat. Park, 7-47
Hawaii native customs, 7-39, 43, 46, 48
Hawaii native recreation, 7-39
Hawaii native wars, 7-41
Hawaiian Islands Nat. Wildlife Ref., 7-44
Hawaiian gods, 7-37, 40*
Hawaiian goose (nene), 7-44
Hawaiian hulu, 7-49, 81
Hawks, 7-94
Hawthorne, Nathaniel, 1-63, 77, 80, 92
Hawthorne trees, 5-21
Hay, 1-121; 6-37
Hay, Merle, 4-46
Hayes, Rutherford B., 1-104; 4-105, 108
Haystack Rock (OR), 7-51, 62
Haywood, William (Big Bill), 6-49
He Devil Mt., 6-43
Head Tide, ME, 1-63
Health care, 1-15
Heard Museum of Anthropology and Primitive Arts, 6-24
Hearst, George, 6-76
Hearst, William Randolph, 6-77; 7-33
Hearst San Simeon State Hist. Mon. (CA), 7-33
Hebron, ND, 5-72
Hecata Head (OR), 7-59*
Hecht, Ben, 4-120
Hedges, Cornelius, 6-117
Heinz, H.J., 2-92
Heinze, Augustus, 6-63
Helena, MT, 1-29; 6-63, 67
Helium, 5-36, 95, 120; 6-92, 106
Hell's Canyon (Snake River), 1-10; 6-43, 52; 7-63
Hell's Half Acre (WY), 6-113, 122
Helme Snuff Plant, 2-23
Hemingway, Ernest, 4-21; 6-49
Hemisphere Plaza (San Antonio, TX), 5-123
Hennepin, Louis, 4-73
Hennings, E. Martin, 6-24, 30
Henry, Patrick, 1-25; 2-100; 4-16, 30
Henry Doorly Zoo (NE), 5-66
Henry VII of England, 1-60
Hepburn, Katherine, 1-49
Herald Square (NYC), 2-80, 81
Herbert, Victor, 2-92
Heritage Square (Denver, CO), 6-39
Hermitage (Nashville, TN), 1-26; 3-119, 123
Heron, blue, 7-94
Herons, 3-121; 5-50; 7-94
Hershey, Milton, 2-92
Hershey, PA, 2-92
Hershey Bar, 2-92
Hessian troops, 2-59
Hetuck (buckeye), 4-103
Hewes, Joseph, 3-91
Hialeah, FL, 1-15
Hiatt, Jesse, 4-51
Hiawatha (chief), 1-62; 2-71, 77
Hibiscus Alley (Charlotte Amalie, VI), 7-95
Hickock, James Butler (Wild Bill), 5-32, 105, 108
Hickory, WI, 4-123
Hidatsa Indians, 5-72
High Plains (TX), 5-113
High Point, NC, 3-93
High Point Mt., 2-55
High Point State Park (NJ), 2-67
Highlands (NJ), 2-55
Highlands Museum and Biological Lab., 3-91
Highways, 1-29, 30, 94; 2-18, 20, 66, 75, 89, 93; 4-23, 24, 46, 93, 103; 5-107; 6-37, 38, 51, 66, 93, 101,

117, 122; 7-15, 18, 32, 33, 60, 62, 73, 84, 91
Hijacking, 2-35
Hiking, 1-94
Hill, James J., 4-77
Hill, Luther L., 3-22
Hill of Sacrifice (HI), 7-49
Hillerich & Bradsby Co., 3-65
Hillsboro, WV, 2-119
Hillsville, VA, 2-106
Hilo, HI, 1-10; 7-47
Hilo Island (HI), 7-46
Hilton Head Island (SC), 3-106, 108
Hilton Head raccoon, 3-105
Hilton's Point (Dover, NH), 1-87
Hinckley, MN, 4-75
Hindenberg (dirigible), 2-61
Hiram Chittenden Locks, 7-74
Historians, 5-119
Historic districts, 1-66; 3-24; 5-23, 25; 6-81, 94; 7-33, 34, 35
Historical Soc. of Delaware, 2-24
History and Technology Bldg. (DC), 2-39
Hitchcock, Lambert, 1-49
Hitchcock chairs, 1-49
Hitchiti people, 3-44
Hitler, Adolph, 1-117
Hoard, William, 4-119
Hoate, John, 7-71
Hoaxes, 2-74; 4-73
Hoban, James, 2-31
Hobby, Oveta Culp, 5-119
Hoboken, NJ, 2-59, 60, 66
Hockey, 4-24
Hocking Hills State Park (OH), 4-97*
Hocking River, 4-97
Hodgenville, KY, 3-62, 63
Hoe, Rice, 2-114
Hoff, Philip H., 1-117
Hogback ridges, 1-58
Hohokam (ancient ones), 6-16, 25
Hokule, 7-43
Holcomb, KS, 5-37
Holland, John, 2-62
Holland, MI, 4-61, 67
Holliday, Cyrus K., 5-38
Holly, 2-23
Hollywood, CA, 7-28, 31
Hollywood Boulevard (LA, CA), 7-33
Holmes, Oliver Wendell, 1-77, 80
Holmes, William, 1-44
Holo-Holo-Ku Heiau (temple), 7-48
Holton, A. Linwood, 2-103
Holy Trinity (Wilimington, DE), 2-24
"Home Sweet Home" (song), 2-81
Homer, Winslow, 1-64; 2-77
Homestake Gold Mine (SD), 5-106, 108
Homestead Act, 5-60, 66, 101
Homestead Nat. Mon., 5-66
Honaunau, HI, 7-48
Honey War, 4-44, 89
Honey creeper, 7-94
Honolulu, HI, 7-38*, 46, 47*, 49, 82
Honolulu Zoo (HI), 7-49
Hood, Thomas, 3-117
Hood River, 7-60
Hooker, Thomas, 1-44
Hoorn, Netherlands, 2-26
Hoover, Herbert, 4-47, 48; 5-35; 7-28, 94
Hoover Dam, 6-15, 24, 69, 71, 74, 78*, 79, 80
Hoover Library, 4-47, 52
Hope Lodge (PA), 2-94
Hopewell people, 4-28, 99, 100*; 5-44
Hopi Indians, 6-16, 17, 24
Hopi Point (Grand Canyon Nat. Park), 6-23
Hopkins, Mark, 7-29
Hopkins, Samuel, 1-121

Hopkins, Stephen, 1-102
Hopkinsville, KY, 3-67
Horlick, William, 4-120
Horned toad, 6-21
Horse Indians, 7-53, 67, 69
Horse farms, 3-66
Horse racing, 4-46
Horse trailers, 5-93
Horseless Carriage, 2-21
Horses, 1-48, 49, 94, 121; 2-108; 5-29, 73, 85, 102; 6-44, 46, 59, 79, 87, 115; 7-53, 63, 67, 90
Horses, prehistoric, 5-29
Horses, thoroughbred, 3-64, 66, 68
Horseshoe Bend, AL, 3-18
Horseshoe Bend Nat. Military Park, 3-25
Horton, George Moses, 2-91
Hostages, 2-35; 3-48
Hostrom, Buzz, 6-19
Hot Springs, AR, 5-16, 22
Hot Springs Mt., 5-22
Hot Springs Nat. Park, 5-22
Hot Water War, 2-89
"Hot dog" (origin), 4-105
Houdon, Jean A., 2-109
Hough, Emerson, 4-49; 6-119
Houghton, Douglass, 4-60
Houghton, MI, 4-55
Houma Indians, 5-45
Housatonic River, 1-43, 69
Housatonic Valley, 1-52
House of Burgesses, 2-99
House of Representatives, U.S., 2-31
House of Seven Gables, 1-80
"House that Jack (a mule) built" (Bellaire, OH), 4-109
"House that Pa built, The" (Wilder home), 5-108
Houser, Allan, 6-91
Houston, D. H., 5-78
Houston, Samuel, 1-19; 3-119, 123; 5-115, 116, 117, 119*
Houston, TX, 1-15, 19; 5-112*, 117, 121, 123
Houston Schoolhouse, Sam, 3-123
Hovenweep Nat. Mon., 6-109
Howe, Elias, 1-79, 91
Howe, Julia Ward, 2-36
Howe, William, 2-17, 88
Howells, William Dean, 1-77
Hoyt Arboretum, 7-62
Hualpai Indians, 6-16
Hubbard, Bernard, 7-16
Hubbard, Edward, 7-70
Hubbard, Frank McKinney (Kim), 4-36
Hubbard, George, 1-121
Huddleston, John M., 5-24
Hudson, Henry, 1-60; 2-15, 57, 71, 85
Hudson, Joseph L., 4-64
Hudson Bay, 4-69; 5-71, 73; 6-55
Hudson River, 1-30; 2-55, 60, 67, 69, 71, 72, 79
Hudson River School of art, 2-79
Hudson River Valley, 1-30
Hudson's Bay Co., 6-47; 7-53, 69
Hueco Tanks (TX), 5-114
Hughes, Charles Evans, 2-76
Hughes, Howard, 7-32
Huguenots, 1-60; 3-100
Hula Festival, 7-49
Hulu, Hawaiian, 7-81
Human rights, 1-75; 3-49
Humboldt, KS, 5-31
Humboldt Redwoods State Park (CA), 7-30
Humboldt River, 6-69
Humingbird, 7-94
Humphrey, Hubert H., 4-76
Humphreys, Davis, 1-48
Hunt, Wilson Price, 6-116
Hunting, 1-59, 64, 120; 3-64, 92, 121; 4-78; 5-65, 76, 109; 6-46, 77,

78, 87
Hunting Island State Park (SC), 3-108
Huntington, Collis P., 7-29
Huntington, NY, 2-76
Huntington, VT, 1-121
Huntington, WV, 2-122
Huntington Library and Museum (CA), 7-33
Huntsville, AL, 3-10, 20, 23, 25
Huron Indians, 2-85; 4-57, 100
Hurricanes, 1-46; 2-61, 90; 3-30, 32, 34; 5-117; 7-87
Hurst, Fanny, 4-91
Huskies (Univ. of WA football), 7-74
Hutchinson, Anne, 1-102
Hutchinson, KS, 5-36, 37
Hutchinson, MN, 4-75
Hydroelectric power, 1-11; 2-121; 3-97, 111, 117
I B M, 2-78
Iao stream (HI), 7-41
Ibarra, Francisco de, 6-87
Iberville, Sieur de, 5-44, 45
Ice Sweepstakes, 7-22
Ice machine, 3-36
Ice-cream cones, 4-89
Idaho (main article), 6-41
Idaho Batholith, 6-44
Idaho City, ID, 6-53
Idaho Falls, ID, 6-48
Idaho Springs, CO, 6-37
Idaho State Univ., 6-53
Iguanas, 2-88
Illini Indians, 4-16, 28, 43, 44
Illinois (main article), 4-13
Illinois River, 4-13, 16
Ilmenite, 2-106
Impeachment (Andrew Johnson), 1-91; 2-33; 3-90
Impeachment (William Blount), 3-115
Imperial Valley (CA), 7-23, 31
"In His Steps" (Book), 5-35
"In Mountain Heights, Colorado" (painting), 6-30*
Incline railways, 3-122
Independence, IA, 4-46
Independence, MO, 4-90, 94
Independence Hall, 2-87, 94; 5-31
Independence Hall (replica), 4-66*
Independence Nat. Hist. Park, 2-94
Independence Rock (WY), 6-113, 122
Indian Hall of Fame, 5-94
Indian Hill (SC), 3-99
Indian Ice Caves, 6-53
"Indian Lament" (music), 4-49
Indian Peace Mem. Statue, 4-80
Indian River, 2-15; 3-30
Indian River Bay (DE), 2-15
Indian Stream Republic, 1-89
Indian art, 5-100
Indian baby, 6-50*
Indian capitals, 2-71, 99; 5-94; 7-13
Indian constitution, 2-71
Indian customs, 1-44, 59, 71, 100, 101; 2-43, 56, 57, 71, 85, 92; 3-44, 45, 72, 99, 114; 4-16, 28, 44, 57, 72, 85, 100, 114, 124; 5-44, 57, 58, 73, 85, 86, 87, 88, 89, 93, 94, 99, 100; 6-16, 31, 58, 107, 115, 117; 7-12, 25, 67, 93
Indian festivals, 6-95
Indian government, 1-100; 5-57
Indian leaders, 1-43, 44, 62, 86, 100, 101, 107; 2-29, 31, 71, 77, 92, 99, 100, 120; 3-16, 17, 22, 33, 35, 45, 72, 73, 77, 86, 88, 99, 114; 4-17, 35, 58, 75, 101, 114; 5-49, 58, 86, 87, 105, 117; 6-18, 47, 49, 61, 64, 87, 88, 106, 118
Indian legends, 1-87, 100; 2-69; 3-71; 5-99; 6-114
Indian paintbrush, 1-11

Indian pipes (plant), 4-78
Indian population, 7-25
Indian preserves, 3-94
Indian pudding, 1-59
Indian rights, 1-62; 3-16, 19, 46, 73, 88, 99, 113, 114; 4-76; 5-86, 101; 6-33, 60; 7-57, 71
Indian treaties, 2-85, 86, 114; 3-101; 6-47, 60
Indian wars, 1-44, 45, 61, 87, 102; 2-15, 43, 44, 57, 88, 100, 115, 116, 119; 3-16, 17, 18, 31, 33, 35, 46, 58, 73, 74, 76, 101, 114, 115, 118; 4-17, 31, 32, 58, 74, 75, 85, 86, 87, 102, 106; 5-16, 30, 33, 58, 60, 75, 87, 101, 102, 105, 114; 6-18, 47, 87, 88, 104, 107, 116, 118; 7-26, 55, 69
Indian weapons, 1-86; 2-29; 5-73
Indian women, 2-71, 85, 120; 3-114; 6-64
Indiana (main article), 4-27
Indiana Dunes, 4-27, 34
Indiana Dunes Nat. Lakeshore, 4-34
Indiana Univ., 4-38, 39
Indiana World War Mem., 4-39
Indiana limestone, 4-36, 37
Indianapolis, IN, 1-26; 4-29*, 32, 33, 35, 37, 38, 39
Indianapolis 500 race, 1-26; 4-39*
Indianapolis Symphony, 4-39
Indians, 1-11, 18, 24, 43, 45, 59, 60, 61, 71, 72, 73, 86, 100, 101, 120; 2-15, 29, 31, 42, 44, 55, 56, 57, 58, 71, 83, 85, 91, 99, 100, 104, 113, 114, 115; 3-9, 16, 17, 18, 30*, 31, 33, 44, 45, 58, 62, 71, 72, 74, 85, 86, 88, 92, 99, 113, 114, 115, 116, 118; 4-15, 16, 17, 25, 28, 30, 31, 32, 43, 57, 58, 59, 60, 62, 71, 72*, 74, 75, 77, 80, 85, 86, 87*, 99, 101, 102, 114, 115; 5-9*, 16, 17, 29, 30, 31, 33, 34, 44, 55, 57, 58, 60, 63, 65, 66, 67, 72, 73, 74, 85, 86, 88, 92, 94, 95, 99, 100, 101, 102, 114, 117; 6-19, 31, 32, 45, 46, 47, 72, 86, 94, 100, 101, 106, 114, 115, 116, 117, 122; 7-18, 19, 25, 29, 32, 53, 55, 56, 67, 69, 71, 72, 93
Indians, displacement, 2-58; 3-19, 33, 46, 74, 88, 116; 4-16, 28, 43, 57, 71, 87, 100, 115; 5-17, 30, 58, 60, 86, 90, 99; 6-60; 7-58, 69
"Indians Attacking Overland Train" (painting), 6-8*
Indigo, 3-78, 106
Indio, CA, 7-32
Industrial Revolution, 1-106, 107
Industrialists, 1-48, 106, 107; 2-20, 24, 77, 78, 92; 3-34, 35; 4-21, 64, 77, 107; 6-63; 7-29, 30, 44, 71
Industry, 1-50, 64, 75, 76, 93, 94, 106, 107; 2-16, 19, 22, 52, 61, 74, 77, 93, 106, 121; 3-23, 25, 37, 51, 79, 93, 95, 121; 4-34, 37, 51, 65, 79, 107, 117, 119, 121, 123; 5-37, 50, 93, 120; 6-22, 36, 51, 63, 108; 7-30, 42, 60, 73, 80, 89, 90
Inge, William, 5-35
Ingersoll, Simon, 1-48
Ingles, Mary, 2-115
Ingram, Osmond Kelly, 3-20
Inness, George, 2-63, 77
Inscription Canyon (CA), 7-32
Inscription House (Navajo Nat. Mon.), 6-25
Inscription Rock (NM), 6-95
Insects, 2-34, 121; 3-20, 23, 25, 78; 6-48, 103; 7-58
Inside Passage, 7-19
Institute of Paper Chemistry, 4-121
Institute of Texan Culture, 5-123
Insurance, 1-51; 2-94; 4-51; 7-93
Integration, 1-76; 5-19, 34

Interior, U.S. Dept. of, 7-80
International Boundary Commission, 1-113
International Fountain (Seattle, WA), 7-74
International Harvester (Navistar), 4-22
International Museum of Photography, 2-80
International Peace Garden (ND), 5-80*, 81
International Peace Park (MT), 6-61
International Petroleum Exposition, 5-94
International Rose Test Gardens (OR), 7-62
International dateline, 7-9, 82
Interracial commissions, 2-48
Interstate Park (MN/WI), 4-124
Interstate highways, 1-30; 5-107; 6-122
Inventors and inventions, 1-48, 50, 79, 91, 94, 119, 121; 2-21, 36, 50, 60, 61, 62, 64, 67, 91, 104, 107, 108; 3-22, 39, 48, 77, 91, 105; 4-21, 104, 106, 117, 119, 120; 6-78, 106
Ioa Needle (HI), 7-46
Ioa Valley (HI), 7-46
Iolani Palace (Honolulu, HI), 7-49
Iowa (main article), 4-41
Iowa City, IA, 4-45, 53
Iowa State Univ., 4-46, 48, 49
Ioway Indians, 4-43, 85
Ipswich, SD, 5-107
Iran, American Embassy in, 2-35
Iranian hostage crisis, 3-48
Iris, 3-121
Irish patriots, 1-117
Iron County, MO, 4-85
Iron Curtain speech, 4-89, 90
Iron and Steel Museum, 3-25
Iron Man, 3-25
Iron mongering, 2-106
Iron ore, 1-11, 93; 2-64, 77, 93; 3-22, 23; 4-76, 78, 92, 120; 5-49; 6-91, 108
Iron processing, 3-23, 65; 4-64, 76
Iroquois Indians, 1-71, 113, 114; 2-43, 71, 73, 83, 85, 92, 99; 3-113; 4-57, 100
Irrigation, 5-64, 103; 6-18, 36, 50, 61, 69, 102, 108
Irving, John, 4-49
Irving, Washington, 2-76, 79
Isa Lake, 6-111
Island Beach (NJ), 2-66
Islands, 1-6, 57, 69, 85, 89, 95, 97; 2-15, 25, 27, 28, 66, 69, 71, 81, 85, 92; 3-29, 30, 34, 39, 69; 4-64, 66, 75, 99, 111; 5-43, 44, 46, 51, 52; 7-9, 15, 21, 25, 33, 37, 39, 40, 42, 44, 46, 47, 48, 65, 79, 80, 81, 82, 87, 93, 94, 96
Isle Royale, MI, 4-57, 64
Isle Royale Nat. Park, 4-66
Isle au Haut (ME), 1-57
Isles of Shoals archipelago, 1-85, 95
Israel and Egypt peace agreement, 3-48
Itasca Lake, 4-69
Itasca State Park (MN), 4-81
Ithaca, NY, 2-80
Ives, Charles, 1-49
Ivory Soap, 4-108
Ivory-billed woodpecker, 3-77, 78
Iwo Jima Statue, 2-108
J. I. Case Co., 4-22
J. Paul Getty Museum, 7-33
Jacataqua (Indian princess), 1-68
Jacataqua Oak, 1-68
Jackson, Andrew, 1-26, 106; 2-32, 76; 3-18*, 33, 74, 80, 90, 104, 105, 115, 116, 118, 119, 123, 124; 5-20, 46, 117

Jackson, Helen Hunt, 6-35
Jackson, MI, 4-64
Jackson, MS, 1-27; 3-70*, 74, 75, 80
Jackson, Sheldon, 7-17
Jackson, Thomas Jonathan (Stonewall), 2-101, 106, 109, 117, 118, 119
Jackson Hole, WY, 6-113, 118, 120, 121
Jackson Hole (WY valley), 6-113, 119, 120
Jackson Hole Nat. Mon., 6-118
Jackson Lake, 6-113
Jackson Purchase, 3-60
Jackson Square (New Orleans, LA), 5-52
Jacksonian Democracy, 3-118
Jacksonville, FL, 3-34, 38
Jacksonville, NC, 1-14
Jacksonville, OR, 7-55
Jade Cove (CA), 7-33
Jaggers, Charles, 3-105
James, Edwin, 6-31, 32
James, Jesse, 4-89
James Fort, 2-108
James G. Blaine House (Augusta, ME), 1-67
James I of England, 1-87
James II of England, 1-45
James Island (SC), 3-106
James River, 2-97; 5-69, 97
James River Canal, 2-107
Jamestown, ND, 5-81
Jamestown, VA, 2-29, 99, 102, 105, 106, 108
Janklow, William (Wild Bill), 5-106, 109
Japan vs. Russia war, 1-89; 2-76
Japanese-Americans, 7-28, 42
Jarvis, Ann, 2-114
Jasmine Lane (Charlotte Amalie, VI), 7-95
Jasper, 1-86; 6-64, 77, 107
Jasper Cave (NH), 1-86
Javelina (wild pig), 6-21; 7-89
Jax Brewery (New Orleans, LA), 5-52
Jazz, 5-49, 52
Jazz Museum, 5-52
Jeannette Rankin Brigade, 6-64
Jefferson, GA, 3-48
Jefferson, Thomas, 1-11, 25, 77; 2-23, 31, 35, 99, 103, 104, 108, 109, 110, 123; 3-66; 5-104, 107
Jefferson City, MO, 1-27; 4-94
Jefferson County, WV, 2-117
Jefferson Davis Mon., 3-63*, 67
Jefferson Mem., 2-30*, 39
Jefferson Nat. Expansion Mem., 4-86*, 89, 93
Jefferson River, 6-59
Jefferson's Rock (WV), 2-122
Jello, 2-22
Jemez Pueblo, NM, 6-91
Jennings, 4-22
Jenny Lake, 6-113
Jersey, Isle of (England), 2-57
Jersey City, NJ, 1-13; 2-57, 67
Jersey Meadows, 2-55
Jersey Turnpike, 1-25
Jersey-Manhatten ferry, 2-57
Jesse Lee Mission Home (Seward, AK), 7-16
Jesuits, 1-60; 4-86; 6-17, 116; 7-82
Jet (stone), 6-107
Jewel Cave (SD), 5-108
Jewelry, 1-107; 2-65, 121
Jewish congregations, 7-96
Jockey Hollow (NJ), 2-59
John Day Dam, 7-60
John Deere Co., 4-22
John F. Kennedy Center for the Performing Arts, 2-30*, 39
John Herron Art Institute (IN), 4-39
John Paul II, Pope, 4-47

Johnny Appleseed Mem. Park (Fort Wayne, IN), 4-39
Johns, James, 1-121
Johnson, Andrew, 1-91; 2-33; 3-90, 95, 116, 119
Johnson, E. C., 6-34
Johnson, John, 4-22
Johnson, Joseph, 2-114
Johnson, Lancelot, 3-48
Johnson, Lyndon B., 1-117; 5-118; 6-19
Johnson, Robert W., 2-63
Johnson City, TN, 1-14; 3-115
Johnson County, KS, 5-38
Johnson County Cattle War (WY), 6-117
Johnson Library, Lyndon B., 5-123
Johnson Space Center, Lyndon B., 5-123
Johnston, NY, 2-73
Johnstone, Nellie (Oil well #1), 5-92, 94
Johnstown, PA, 2-90
Jolliet, Louis, 3-73, 114; 4-15, 16, 43, 44, 86, 115; 5-16
Jones, John Paul, 1-25; 2-54
Jones, Mary, 3-46
Jones, Robert T. (Bobby), 3-49
Jones Beach State Park (NY), 2-81
Jonesboro, AR, 5-19
Jonesboro, TN, 3-114, 115, 122
Jonesville, LA, 5-44
Joplin, MO, 1-14, 20; 4-94
Joseph the Elder (chief), 6-47; 7-63, 71
Joseph the Younger (chief), 6-45*, 48, 49, 61; 7-57, 58, 63, 71
Joshua Tree Nat. Mon., 7-32
Joshua trees, 6-21, 107; 7-30, 32
Joslyn Art Museum (NE), 5-66
Jousting, 2-53, 108
Juarez, Mexico, 5-121
Judith Basin (MT), 6-62, 64
Juneau, AK, 7-13, 14, 19, 21
Jungle Gardens (FL), 3-39
Jungle Gardens (LA), 5-52
Juniper, 6-21
Jurucan (PR native god), 7-87

Kaahumanu of Hawaii, 7-45
Kahoolawe Island (HI), 7-48
Kaibab Paiute Indians, 6-16
Kaibab squirrel, 6-21
Kaiparowits Plateau (UT), 6-97
Kalakaua (David) of Hawaii, 7-41, 43
Kalanikupule (HI chief), 7-41
Kalapana, HI, 7-48
Kalaupapa, HI, 7-48
Kamehameha I (The Great), 1-19; 7-41, 43, 45, 46, 48
Kamehameha II, 7-41
Kamehameha III, 7-41, 42, 43
Kamehameha IV, 7-41, 44
Kamehameha V, 7-4
Kamiah, ID, 6-47
Kamiakin (chief), 7-71
Kanahele, Benihakaka, 7-44
Kanaloa (Hawaiian diety), 7-39
Kanawha Falls, 2-114
Kanawha River, 2-119, 121
Kancamagus Highway, 1-94
Kane (Hawaiian diety), 7-39
Kaneoho Bay (HI), 7-49
Kanosh (chief), 6-106
Kansas (main article), 5-27
Kansas City, KS, 1-15; 5-37, 38; 6-81
Kansas City, MO, 4-85, 87, 89, 91, 92, 93, 94
Kansas City Chiefs (football), 4-94
Kansas Indians, 5-30
Kansas River, 5-29
Kansas State Hist. Soc., 5-38
Kansas State Univ., 5-37, 38
Kansas-Nebraska Act, 1-90; 5-31, 59

Kantor, MacKinlay, 4-49
Kaolin clay, 3-93
Kapiolani (HI chiefess), 7-43
Kapiolani Park (Honolulu, HI), 7-49
Karankara Indians, 5-114
"Karen" (typhoon), 7-83
Kaskaskia, IL, 4-13, 16, 17, 30
Kaskaskia Bell State Park (IL), 4-25
Kastenbaum, Nancy Landon, 5-35
Katmai Nat. Mon., 7-21, 44
Kauai Island (HI), 1-10; 7-37, 39, 44, 48
Kaumaulii of Hawaii, 7-45, 48
Kaunolu (Lanai), HI, 7-48
Kaw Indians, 5-30
Kealakekua Bay (HI), 7-42, 48
Kearny, Stephen Watts, 6-17, 88; 7-26
"Kearsarge" (ship), 1-62
Keene, NH, 1-89
Keet Seel (Navajo Nat. Mon.), 6-25
Keller, Helen, 3-21
Kelleys Island (OH), 4-99
Kelleys Island State Park (OH), 4-99
Kellogg, Frank B, 4-77
Kellogg, W. K., 4-64
Kellogg-Briand Peace Pact, 4-77
Kelly, Grace, 2-93
Kelly, Pat, 4-120
Kelly, William, 3-63
Kelsey, Nancy, 6-102
Kemmerer, WY, 6-119
Kendrick, John B., 6-118
Kenedy, Mifflin, 5-119
Kennard House (Lincoln, NE), 5-67
Kennebec River, 1-57
Kennebunk, ME, 1-64
Kennedy, Edward (Ted), 1-77
Kennedy, Jacqueline Bouvier, 2-36, 38
Kennedy, John F., 1-76; 2-35, 36, 108; 5-91, 117, 118
Kennedy, Robert, 1-77
Kennedy Center for the Performing Arts, 2-39
Kennewick, WA, 7-77
Kenova, WV, 2-111
Kensington, MN, 4-73
Kensington Runestone (reproduction), 4-73*
Kentucky (main article), 3-55
Kentucky Derby, 3-60, 66
Kentucky Lake, 3-57
Kentucky bluegrass, 3-64
Kentucky rifle, 2-93
Keoua (HI chief), 7-41
Kerr, Robert Samuel, 5-91
Kerrey, Bob, 5-62
Ketchikan, AK, 7-7, 18, 19
Ketchum, Black Jack, 6-90
Ketchum, ID, 6-49
Kette adene (Mt. Katahdin, ME), 1-58
Kettering, Charles, 4-104, 106
Key, Francis Scott, 2-47, 50, 53
Key Largo, FL, 3-30
Key West, FL, 3-34, 35, 36, 37
Key West Island (FL), 3-30
Key deer, 3-36
Keyes, Francis Parkinson, 2-106
Keys (FL), 1-7; 3-37
Kickamuit River, 1-99
Kickapoo Indains, 4-87
Kidd, William (Captain), 1-102
Kidnappings, 1-60
Kies, Mary, 1-50
Kilauea (Mauna Loa), 7-37, 43, 47
Kilgore, TX, 5-119
Kill Devil Hill, NC, 3-93
Killdeer, ND, 5-72
Killdeer Mts., 5-72
Killingworth, CT, 1-43
Kilmer, Joyce, 1-92

113

Kimmswick, MO, 4-83
Kindergarten, 4-116
Kinderhook, NY, 2-76
King, Charles Bird, 3-22, 46; 4-7, 30
King, Charles G., 4-65
King, Martin Luther Jr., 1-19; 3-49, 118
King, Richard, 5-119
King County Stadium (Kingdome, WA), 7-74
King George's War, 1-102
King Philip's War, 1-45, 61, 87, 102
King Ranch (TX), 5-119, 121
King Tascalusa, 3-16, 17
King William's War, 1-61, 102
King crabs, 7-17
King's Highway (MS), 3-79
King's Highway (NM, El Camino Real), 6-93
Kingdome (King County Stadium, WA), 7-74
Kingfish, 7-94
Kings Canyon Nat. Park, 7-35
Kings Mt., 3-87, 88
Kings Mt. Nat. Military Park, 3-109
Kingston, NY, 2-66
Kino, Eusebio Francisco, 6-17, 19
Kinzua Reservoir, 2-83
Kiowa Indians, 5-85; 6-31, 32, 115
Kiowa-Apache Indians, 5-85
Kipling, Caroline, 1-119
Kipling, Rudyard, 1-119; 7-29
Kirkwood, Samuel J., 4-45
Kiska Island (AK), 7-15
Kitchen, Peter, 6-20
Kitsap (chief), 7-67
Kitt Peak, 6-25
Kitt Peak Nat. Observatory, 6-25
Kittamaquund (chief), 2-43
Kittatiny Mts., 2-55
Kittery, ME, 1-93
Kitty Hawk, NC, 3-89
Kivas (religious/activities center), 6-30, 86, 93
Klondike (Canada), 7-13
Klondike miners (1899), 7-14*
Knapp mounds (AR), 5-16
Knott County, KY, 3-64
Knotts Berry Farm (CA), 7-33
Know-Nothing Party, 2-47
Knoxville, TN, 3-115, 118, 122
Kock, Albrecht, 4-85
Kodak cameras, 2-78; 5-0
Kodiak, AK, 7-13
Kodiak Island (AK), 7-21
Kodiak bears, 7-14
Kohler of Kohler, WI, 4-122
Kokomo, IN, 4-28
Kokonee salmon, 7-58
Kootenai Indians, 6-45
Korean War, 3-75; 4-62; 7-42
Kotzebue, AK, 7-21
Koyukuk River, 7-11
Kresge, Sebastian S., 4-64
Ku (HI god of war), 7-39, 48
Ku Klux Klan, 4-119
Kullyspell House (ID), 6-47, 48
Kunin, Madeleine M., 1-117
Kure Island (HI), 7-37
Kuttawa, KY, 3-63
Kutzown Folk Festival, 1-30
Kwajalein Island (Pacific), 7-85
Kyanite, 2-106
L'Enfant, Pierre, 2-30, 31, 35, 64, 108
La Belle Riviere (Ohio River), 2-113
La Carta Autonomica, 7-88
La Crosse, WI, 4-124
La Farge, Oliver, 6-20
La Follette, Philip Fox, 4-119
La Follette, Robert M. Jr., 4-119
La Follette, Robert M. Sr., 4-117, 118*
La Guardia, Fiorello H., 2-75; 5-105
La Jolla, CA, 7-31

La Junta, CO, 6-31
La Plata River, 7-87
La Ramie, Jacques, 6-123
La Salle, Sieur de (Robert Cavelier), 3-73, 114; 4-16, 28, 58, 86, 100; 5-15, 16, 17*, 44, 85, 115
Labich, Emmeline, 5-49
Labor movement, 4-61
Labor relations, 3-61
Laclede, MO, 4-90
Laclede's Landing, MO, 4-93
Ladders, fish, 7-72
Lady of Light Chapel (Santa Fe, NM), 6-95
Lady of the Lake, 4-71
Lady's slipper (cypripedium reginae), 4-78
Lafayette, IN, 4-39
Lafayette, LA, 5-53
Lafayette, Marquis de, 2-32, 47*
Lafitte, Jean, 5-46, 47, 50, 115
Lafitte, Pierre, 5-46, 47
Laguna Beach, CA, 7-32
Lahaina, HI, 7-47
Lake Academy, 5-97
Lake Agassiz (prehistoric), 4-71; 5-0
Lake Aitkin, 4-71
Lake Barkley, 3-57
Lake Canandaigua, 2-69
Lake Cayuga, 2-69
Lake Champlain, 1-112*, 114, 122; 2-69, 71, 73, 74
Lake Charles, LA, 5-51
Lake Chelan, 7-76
Lake Chicago (prehistoric), 4-13
Lake Coeur d'Alene, 6-45*, 53
Lake Country (MO), 4-96*
Lake County, OR, 7-51
Lake Duluth, 4-71
Lake Erie, 2-69, 83; 4-58, 60, 97, 100, 102, 103
Lake Geneva, WI, 4-122
Lake George, 7-11
Lake Hopatcong, 2-55, 67
Lake Huron, 4-58
Lake Iliamna, 7-11
Lake Keuka, 2-69
Lake Lure, 3-95
Lake Marion, 3-97, 108
Lake McDonald, 6-55
Lake Mead, 6-15, 34, 69, 77, 78
Lake Memphremagog, 1-113
Lake Mendota, 4-123
Lake Michigan, 4-13, 17, 18, 22, 23, 27, 34, 65, 111, 113, 122
Lake Michigan dunes, 4-36
Lake Missoula (prehistoric), 6-44
Lake Mohave, 6-69
Lake Monongahela (prehistoric), 2-113
Lake Moultrie, 3-97, 108
Lake Ontario, 2-69
Lake Ouachita, 5-22
Lake Owasco, 2-69
Lake Pend Oreille, 6-43
Lake Pepin, 4-71, 73, 75
Lake Placid, NY, 2-75, 79
Lake Pontchartrain, 5-44, 48
Lake Powell, 6-15, 99, 106
Lake Pymatuning, 2-93
Lake Sakakawea, 5-69
Lake Sam Rayburn, 5-113
Lake Seneca, 2-69
Lake Sherburne, 6-55
Lake Shoup, 5-97
Lake Skaneateles, 2-69
Lake Superior, 4-69, 71, 73, 76, 78, 81, 111, 120
Lake Tahoe, 1-27; 6-69, 71, 72, 77, 78, 79, 81; 7-35
Lake Taneycomo, 4-83
Lake Texoma, 5-83
Lake Waiau, 7-39
Lake Washington, 7-74
Lake Webster, 1-71
Lake Winnebago, 4-113

Lake Winnipeg, 4-73
Lake Winnipesaukee, 1-85, 86
Lake of the Ozarks, 4-83
Lake of the Woods, 4-69, 71
Lakes, 1-27, 41, 43, 57, 71, 85, 99, 113, 114; 2-41, 55, 67, 69, 71, 73, 74, 79, 83, 93, 113; 3-15, 43, 57, 67, 69, 70, 97, 108, 111; 4-13, 28, 41, 55, 69, 71, 83, 94, 96*, 97, 113, 124; 5-22, 29, 44, 48, 69, 71, 83, 97, 99, 103, 113; 6-15, 24, 29, 38, 43, 45, 69, 71, 77, 85, 97, 99, 106, 113, 121; 7-11, 35, 39, 51, 54*, 55, 74, 76, 77
Lakeview, OR, 7-51
Lamar, CO, 6-33
Lamar, GA, 3-44
Lamar, MO, 4-89
Lamy, Jean Baptiste, 6-90
Lanai Island (HI), 7-48
Lanainaluna High School (HI), 7-47
Lancaster, OH, 4-106
Lancaster, PA, 1-30; 2-88, 89
Lancaster, SC, 3-104
Lance Creek, WY, 6-113
Land Between the Lakes, 3-57, 67
Land Rush (OK), 5-33, 87*, 88
Land bridge, 7-11
Land grants, 2-16, 29, 43, 44, 45, 85, 115; 4-44; 7-26
Landon, Alf M., 5-34, 35
Lane, Rose Wilder, 5-104
Lanford Station, SC, 3-107
Langhorne, Nancy, 2-105
Langtry, Lillie, 5-122
Langtry, TX, 5-122
Lanier, Sidney, 2-50
Lansing, MI, 1-30; 4-60, 65, 67
Laona, WI, 4-121
Lapham, Allen, 4-119
Lapwai Mission, 6-47
Laramie, WY, 6-116, 123
Larimer Square (Denver, CO), 6-39
Larson Collection, Arne B. (Musical instrument collection), 5-108
Las Vegas, NV, 1-10, 27; 6-22, 69, 70*, 74, 78, 79, 80, 104
Lassen Volcanic Nat .Park, 7-35
Last Chance Gulch (MT), 6-60, 67
"Laughing Boy, a Navajo Romance" (book), 6-21, 91
Laurel, MD, 3-20
Laurel, MS, 3-77
Laurens, Henry, 3-105
Lava Beds Nat. Mon., 7-35
Lava Falls (rapids), 6-23
Lavalava (garment), 7-48
Lavender pasqueflower, 5-106
Law, John, 5-16
"Law west of the Pecos" (Roy Bean), 5-122
Lawnfield (Mentor, OH), 4-109
Lawrence, D. H., 6-90
Lawrence, KS, 5-31, 34, 38
Lawrenceville, PA, 2-92
Laws of Moses, 1-4
Lawson, John, 3-86
Le Claire, IA, 4-50
Le Fleur, Lewis, 3-80
Le Fleur's Bluff (Jackson, MS), 3-74, 80
Le Mars, IA, 4-46
Le Sueur, MN, 4-77
Lead, 1-11; 2-64
Lead, SD, 5-65, 108
Lead mining, 4-44
Lead smelting, 5-65
Leadville, CO, 1-10; 6-34, 35, 38*, 39
League of Nations, 2-105; 6-49
Leavenworth, Henry H., 4-74; 5-31
Lebanon, DE, 2-15
Lederer, John, 2-114
Ledyard, John, 1-49
Lee, Albert, 4-44

Lee, Charles, 1-103
Lee, Daniel, 7-55
Lee, Francis Lightfoot, 2-106
Lee, Henry (Light-Horse Harry), 2-106; 3-46
Lee, Jason, 6-47; 7-55, 57
Lee, Peggy, 5-78
Lee, Richard Henry, 2-106
Lee, Robert E., 2-18, 60, 89, 101, 102, 106, 109, 116, 119; 3-53, 76; 5-116
Lee, Thomas, 3-106
Lee, William Henry, 2-60
Lee family, 2-106
Leech Lake, 4-74
Leeward Islands (HI), 7-44
Leflore, Greenwood (chief), 3-77
"Legend of the Kanawha, The" (poem), 2-120
Legends, 1-87, 100; 2-15, 26, 69; 3-71; 4-28, 81; 5-99; 6-114; 7-51
Legionnaires disease, 2-90
Legislatures, unicameral, 5-61; 7-83, 94
Leif Erickson, 1-71
Leif the Lucky, 1-59
Leis, 7-45
Lemhi Indians, 6-46, 49
Lemhi Pass (MT), 6-59
Lenni Lenape Indians, 2-55, 56, 58, 83
Lenoir, NC, 3-93
Lenox, Walter, 2-64
Lenox ware, 2-64
Lentil beans, 6-51
Lepidolite, 6-91
Leprosy, 7-44
Leutze, Emanuel, 2-58, 94
Levis (trousers), 2-91*
Levisa River, 2-111
Lewes, DE, 2-15, 17, 18, 19, 23, 25, 26
Lewis, Henry, 3-73; 4-6; 5-46
Lewis, Meriwether, 4-44, 87; 5-30, 58, 74, 81, 100; 6-46, 47, 50, 58, 59, 64, 66, 67, 119; 7-53, 62, 67
Lewis, Sinclair, 4-78
Lewis and Clark Centennial Exposition, 7-56
Lewis and Clark Trail, 6-66
Lewis and Clark expedition, 4-44, 53, 87; 5-59, 81, 100; 6-46, 47, 50, 52, 64, 65, 66, 67, 119; 7-53, 62, 67
Lewis bird, 6-50
Lewiston, ID, 6-46, 47, 48, 51
Lexington, KY, 1-26; 3-62, 64, 66
Lexington, MA, 1-61, 75
Lexington, NC, 3-93
Lexington, OR, 7-53
Lexington, VA, 2-109
Lexington of the Seas, 1-61
Libby, MT, 6-65
Liberty, MS, 3-77
Liberty Bell, 2-91*, 94
Liberty Bell of the West, 4-25
Liberty Park, 2-12*
Liberty Party, 1-91
Library of Congress, 2-23
Life expectancy, 1-14
"Life on the Prairie-The Last of the Buffalo hunters" (painting), 6-12*
Lighthouse, Montauk Point (NY), 2-81
Lignite, 1-11; 5-78, 79
Liguest, Pierre Laclede, 4-86
Lilac Festival (Spokane, WA), 7-76
Lilies, 7-58, 60
Liliuokalani, of Hawaii, 7-41, 49
Lilly family reunion, 2-123
Lily, giant cobra, 7-58
Lima beans, 3-50
Limestone, TN, 3-119
Limestone quarries, 4-65
Lin, Shen, 1-42

Linchester Mill (MD), 2-51
Lincoln, Abraham, 1-19, 26, 27, 46; 2-33, 36, 48, 51, 60, 89, 116, 117; 3-48, 59, 62, 63, 67, 90, 119; 4-13, 18*, 19, 21, 24, 25, 33, 34, 35, 46, 75, 120; 5-31, 32, 67, 104, 107; 6-73, 77, 80, 88; 7-27, 55
Lincoln, Abraham (sculptured head), 6-123
Lincoln, IL, 4-19
Lincoln, Mary Todd, 2-36, 38; 6-80
Lincoln, Mordecai, 3-62
Lincoln, NE, 1-26; 5-56*, 60, 63, 67
Lincoln, Robert Todd, 2-108; 4-25
Lincoln, Sarah, 3-62
Lincoln, Thomas, 3-62
Lincoln, William Wallace, 2-36
"Lincoln" (statue), 2-36; 5-67
Lincoln Boyhood Home, 3-63*
Lincoln Boyhood Nat. Mem., 4-33*
Lincoln Center, 2-80
Lincoln Memorial, 1-77, 121; 2-37, 39
Lincoln Nat. Mem. Highway, 4-24; 6-117
Lincoln Park (Seattle, WA), 7-74
Lincoln Park Zoo (Chicago, IL), 4-23
Lincoln's funeral procession, 4-19*
Lincoln's tomb, 4-25*
Lincoln-Douglas debate, 4-21
Lindbergh, Charles A., 2-34, 75; 4-77
Lindsborg, KS, 5-33, 39
Linotype, 2-50
Lipan Apache Indians, 5-114
Lisa, Manuel, 5-100; 6-59, 116
Litchfield, CT, 1-48, 49, 52
Litchfield, MN, 4-75
Lithium, 3-93
Little Arkansas River, 5-32
Little Big Horn River, 5-105; 6-60
Little Carpenter (Attakullakulla), 3-114
Little Colorado River, 6-15
Little Crow (chief), 4-75
Little Diomede Island (AK), 7-21
Little Falls of the Potomac, 2-28, 53
"Little House on the Prairie" (TV series), 5-104
Little Miami River, 4-97
Little Missouri River, 5-69, 77, 80, 97
Little Narragansett Bay (RI), 1-99
Little Norway, WI, 4-123
Little Pigeon Creek, 4-34
Little Rock, AR, 1-27; 5-14*, 16, 18, 19, 20, 25
Little Salt Lake, 6-19
Little Tennessee River, 3-113
Little TVA, 5-63
Little Turtle (chief Meshekinnoquah), 4-31, 35
Little Wabash River, 4-30
Littlefield, AZ, 6-18
Littleton, NH, 1-94
Live Oak Soc., 5-53
Liverpool, England, 3-46
Livestock, 3-37; 5-31, 92, 116; 6-87
Livestock industry, 1-20, 121; 2-23, 107; 3-79; 4-22, 51, 79, 92; 5-32, 37, 64, 93, 106, 116, 121; 6-22, 37, 48, 51, 60, 61, 64, 91, 106, 117, 120; 7-80, 83
Living History Farms Museum, 1-26; 4-47, 53
Livingston, MT, 6-59
Livingston, William, 2-58
Lizards, 7-84
Lloyd, Harold, 5-63
Lobsters, 1-64, 65, 107
Loch Raven Reservoir, 2-41
Locke, John, 3-87
Locke, NY, 2-76
Lofland, John, 2-21
Log cabins, 2-25

Logan, UT, 6-109
Logan (chief), 2-115, 120; 4-101
Logan County, WV, 2-117
Logans elm, 4-101
Logopedics, Institute of, 5-39
Loisel, Registre, 5-100
Loiza Aldea, PR, 7-91
Lolo Pass (ID), 6-47
Lolo River, 6-46
Lomb, Henry, 2-78
London, England, 1-105, 106; 2-76, 105
London, Jack, 7-16
Lone Mountain Guest Ranch (MT), 6-67*
Long, Crawford W., 3-48
Long, Earl K., 5-48
Long, Huey, 5-47, 48
Long, Russell B., 5-48
Long, Stephen H., 6-31
Long Beach, CA, 7-32
Long Beach, MS, 3-81
Long Beach Harbor, 7-32
Long Island (NY), 1-7, 97; 2-69, 71, 76, 78, 81
Long Island Sound, 1-41, 43
Long Island ducklings, 2-78
Long Town (Chickasaw village), 3-72
Long Trail (Texas Trail), 6-117
Longfellow, Henry Wadsworth, 1-62, 77, 101; 4-72; 5-49
Longfellow Mts., 1-58
Longwood Estates (Natchez, MS), 3-80
Lono (Hawaiian diety), 7-39
Lonsdale Pond, 1-99
Lookout Mt., 3-41, 116, 117*, 122; 6-35
Lord Dunmore's War, 2-115; 4-101
Loretto, Estella, 6-91
Los Alamos, NM, 6-89
Los Alamos School for Boys (NM), 6-89
Los Angeles, CA, 1-14, 15, 19, 57; 3-23; 7-24*, 25, 28, 32
Lost City (Pueblo Grande, UT), 6-71
Lost City Museum, 6-81
Lost Colony (NC), 3-86
Lost Colony (WV), 2-119
"Lost Colony" (pageant), 3-93
Lost Dutchman State Park (AZ), 6-25
Lost River, 4-28; 6-43
Lotteries, 1-96; 2-25
Lotus plants, 2-15
Louis XV of France, 5-45
Louisa, KY, 3-63
Louisiana (main article), 5-41
Louisiana Purchase, 2-104; 4-44, 45, 74, 87; 5-16, 30, 45, 58, 73, 115; 6-31, 34, 87, 111
Louisiana Purchase Expo., 4-89
Louisiana Purchase Hist. Mon., 5-25
Louisiana State Univ., 5-53
Louisiana Territory, 2-104; 3-73; 4-44, 86, 87; 5-16, 58, 85, 115; 6-31, 87
Louisiana muskrat, 5-51
Louisville, KY, 1-13; 3-56*, 60, 62, 63, 65
Louisville Slugger (baseball bat), 3-65
Louisville Symphony, 3-66
Louvre (Paris, France), 7-90
Lovell, WY, 6-121
Lovelock Caves (NV), 6-71
Low, Juliette Gordon, 3-48, 49
Lowell, MA, 1-77
Lower Falls of the Yellowstone River, 6-121
Lower Shawneetown (French settlement), 3-58
Lubbock, TX, 5-121

Lubec, ME, 1-67
Lucas, Robert, 4-44
Ludwig, Mary (Molly Pitcher), 2-59
Lumber and wood products, 1-64, 65, 88; 2-22, 107, 121; 3-51, 65, 79, 93, 106, 122; 4-64, 79, 93, 121; 5-21, 50, 120; 6-50, 65, 91, 92, 120; 7-18, 59, 71
Lumbering, 1-64, 79, 87; 3-23, 36, 77; 4-121; 6-107; 7-58, 59, 71
Lunalilo, of Hawaii, 7-41
Lunar Crater (NV), 6-71
Luray Caverns (VA), 2-109
Lynch, Charles, 2-106
Lynch Law, 2-106
Lynchburg, VA, 2-107
Lynn Riggs Mem. Museum, 5-94
Lynx, 7-72
Maass, Clara, 2-63
Mabila, AL (Indian town), 3-16, 17
MacArthur, Douglas, 5-20, 25
MacDonough, Thomas, 1-46; 2-17
MacDowell, Edward, 1-91
MacDowell, Marian, 1-91, 92
MacDowell Assn., 1-91
MacDowell Colony (NH), 1-91, 92
MacMillan, Donald B., 1-62, 66
MacMillan Arctic expedition, 1-62
MacMonnies, William, 1-92
Macadamia nuts, 7-45
Machiasport, ME, 1-61
Machigonne (Portland, ME), 1-60, 65
Machine gun, 3-91
Mackay, James, 6-58
Mackay, John, 6-74
Mackay School of Mines Museum, 6-81
Mackenzie, Donald, 6-47
Mackinac Bridge, 4-12*, 62
Mackinac Island, MI, 4-57, 66
Macon, GA, 3-44, 50
Macy's (NYC), 2-80
Madison, Dolley, 2-31, 32, 36; 3-91
Madison, GA, 3-48
Madison, James, 2-36, 101, 104
Madison, WI, 1-29, 30; 4-112*, 116, 117, 120, 121, 122, 123
Madison River, 6-59
Madison boulder (NH), 1-86
Madrona tree, 7-30, 58
Magee, Augustus, 5-115
Magellan, Ferdinand, 7-82
Magic Kingdom (Disney World, FL), 3-37
Magna Charta of the Northwest, 4-102
Magnet Cove region (AR), 5-21
Magnolia, 3-77
Magnolia Gardens (Charleston, SC), 3-100, 108
Magnolia grandiflora, 3-23
"Maine" (Battleship), 4-46
"Maine" (main article), 1-55
Maine Festival, 1-66
Maine Maritime Museum, 1-66
Maine State Museum, 1-67
"Maine Woods, The" (book), 1-64
Malad River, 6-43
Malaspina Glacier, 7-9
Malden, WV, 2-120
Mall, Washington, 2-37
Mallett's Bay marble, 1-120
Malmaison plantation (MS), 3-77
Malted milk, 4-120
Mammoth, 5-57, 67
Mammoth Cave, 3-57*, 58, 59, 64, 66
Mammoth Cave Nat. Park, 3-66
Mammoth Hot Springs (SD), 5-107
Mammoths, 6-44
"Man O' War" (horse), 3-64, 66
Manalawny Creek, 2-93
Manchester, NH, 1-84*
Manchester, NY, 1-95
Mandan Indians, 5-72, 73

Manganese, 4-78; 5-120
Mango, 7-94
Mangroves, 7-94
Manhadoe Indians, 2-71
Manhattan, KS, 5-38
Manhattan Island (NY), 2-69, 71, 72, 81
Manhattan-Jersey ferry, 2-57
Manila, AR, 5-19
Manila, Philipines, 1-119
Manistee, MI, 4-61
Manitoba Escarpment (ND), 5-71
Manitou Island (MI), 4-57
Manitou Springs, CO, 6-38
Manned Spacecraft Center, 5-117
Manning's Store (Dingley Brook, ME), 1-63
Mansfield, Mike, 6-63
Mantel, White House, 2-38
Manteo, 3-86
Mantle, Mickey, 5-91
Manu Islands (HI), 7-79
Manufacturing, 1-20, 48, 50, 62, 66, 75, 78, 93, 107; 2-52, 64, 77, 106, 121, 122; 3-23, 50, 65, 79, 91, 93, 121; 4-23, 37, 52, 61, 64, 67, 79, 92, 107, 108, 121; 5-47, 93, 107, 120, 121; 6-37, 65, 89, 93, 108, 120; 7-31, 46, 59, 83, 90
Manzanita, OR, 7-62
Maple, sugar, 1-92, 119
Maple Museum, 1-123
Maple syrup, 1-92, 120, 121, 123; 4-72
Maple trees, 1-92, 119, 121
Maps, 1-2, 4, 16, 22, 32; 2-4
Marble Falls, TX, 5-123
Marble House (Newport, RI), 1-107*, 108
Marbles (game), 2-121
Marchais Center of Tibetan Art (NYC), 2-81
Mardi Gras at Mobile, 3-24
Mardi Gras at New Orleans, 5-51*, 52, 65
Mare Point, ME, 1-62
Mariana Islands (Pacific), 7-82, 84, 85
Marietta, OH, 4-102
Marin, Luis Munoz, 7-89, 90
Marine jewel (fish), 7-94
Marineland (FL), 3-39
Marion, AL, 3-19
Marion, Francis, 3-105
Marion, OH, 4-108
Marion County, WV, 2-113
Mariscal Canyon (TX), 5-122
Maritime Indians, 7-11
"Mark Twain" (river call), 4-91
Market Square (Providence, RI), 1-103
Markham, Edwin, 7-58
Markham, William, 2-85
Marksville people, 5-15, 44
Marland, E. W., 5-91
Marquand, John, 2-21
Marquesas Islands Pacific), 7-39
Marquette, Jacques, 3-73, 114; 4-15, 16, 43, 44, 57, 86, 115; 5-16
Marriage customs, Indian, 2-71
Marsh, Grant, 5-79
Marsh, Othniel C., 1-49
Marsh, Sylvester, 1-94
Marsh Island (LA), 5-44
Marshall, CA, 7-35
Marshall, Edward, 2-86
Marshall, George C., 2-106, 108
Marshall, John, 2-94; 7-35
Marshall, Nichola, 3-19
Marshall Islands and Atolls (Pacific), 7-85
Marshall Plan, 2-106
Marshailtown, IA, 4-51
Marshlands (DE), 2-21
Marsing, ID, 6-45
Marten (sable), 6-107

Martha's Vineyard (MA), 1-69, 72, 82
Martin, James G., 3-90
Martin, Thomas S., 2-105
Martinez, Antonio Jose, 6-89
Martinez, Maria, 6-91
Marydel, DE, 2-25
Marydel, MD, 2-25
Maryland (main article), 2-41
Maryland Jockey Club, 2-54
Maryland Line, 2-45
Maryland Tea Party, 2-45
Mascouten Indians, 4-16
Mason, Charlie, 6-30
Mason, John, 1-60, 87
Mason, John L., 2-63
Mason, Stevens T., 4-60
Mason City, IA, 4-49
Mason jar, 2-63
Mason-Dixon Line, 2-52
Masonic Lodge, 2-31
Massachuset Indians, 1-71
Massachusetts (main article), 1-69
Massachusetts Bay Co., 1-73
Massachusetts Institute of Technology, 1-81
Massacres, 1-44, 80, 114; 2-29, 73, 88, 99; 4-17, 59, 62, 101, 102, 115; 5-75, 79, 102, 103, 105, 122; 6-60, 62, 116; 7-69
Massanet, Damian, 5-115
Master Farmers village, 3-44*
Masters Invitation Tournament, 3-52
Masterson, Bat, 5-32
Mastodons, 3-57; 4-83, 85; 5-57; 6-16, 44, 85
Matabesee Indians, 1-43
Matai (family leader), 7-81
Matanuska Valley (AK), 7-14, 20
Matchless Mine, (CO), 6-34
Mather, Cotton, 1-44
Mattamuskeet Lake, 3-85
Mattoon, IL, 4-22, 23
Maui Island (HI), 7-37, 41, 46, 47
Maumee River, 4-30, 97
Mauna Kea, 7-39, 47
Mauna Loa, 7-37, 39, 42, 43, 47
Maxmillian jay, 6-65
Maxwell House (Fort Sumner), 6-90
May, David, 6-35
May Dept. stores, 6-35
May International Festival, 3-123
Mayaguez, PR, 7-92
Mayan civilization, 7-53
Mayer, Louis B., 7-30
Mayflower, replica, 1-79
"Mayflower" (ship), 1-24, 72, 76; 5-89
Mayflower Compact, 1-72
Mayflower Hotel (DC), 2-28
Mayo, Charles, 4-77
Mayo, Henry T., 1-117
Mayo, William J., 4-77
Mayo, William Worrell, 4-77
Mayo Clinic, 4-77
Mayo Family, 4-77, 81
Maytag Co., 4-51
McAdam, John, 3-63
McAdam road surface, 3-63
McAlester, James J., 5-93
McAlester, OK, 5-93
McAllen, TX, 1-20
McArthur, Duncan, 4-60
McAuliffe, Christa, 1-90; 3-35
McCardle, H. A., 5-116
McClellan, George G., 2-92
McCormick, Cyrus H., 2-107; 4-21
McCoy, Tim, 6-119
McCutcheon,. John T., 4-36
McDonald, William C., 6-89
McDonnell Aircraft Co., 4-92
McGillivray, Lachlan, 3-22
McGinley, Phillis, 6-106
McGregor, IA, 4-43
McGregor Heights, IA, 4-52

McGuffey, William Holmes, 3-64; 4-107
McGuffey Readers, 4-107
McIlhenny, E. A., 5-50
McIlhenny family, 5-51
McIntosh, William (chief), 3-46*
McKinley, William, 2-75, 76; 4-48, 104*, 106, 109; 5-61; 7-21
McKinley Birthplace Nat. Mem., 4-109
McKinly, John, 2-17
McKissick Library Bldg. (Univ. of SC), 3-109
McLean, Evelyn Walsh, 6-35
McLoughlin, John, 7-53, 54, 56, 57, 60, 62, 69, 70, 71, 77
McLoughlin House Nat. Hist. Site, 7-62
Mead, James R., 5-32
Meade, KS, 5-37
Meadowlands Racetrack (NJ), 2-61
Meagher, Thomas Francis, 6-60
Meares, James, 7-67
Medicine Bow, WY, 6-113
Medicine Bow Mts., 6-113
Medicine Lodge, KS, 5-33
Medicine Wheel (WY), 6-115
Medicine men (shamans), 7-67
"Meditation on Rhode Island Coal" (poem), 1-109
Medora, ND, 5-76, 77, 79, 80
Meeker, Nathan C., 6-35
Mellon, Andrew, 2-92
Melville, Herman, 1-77; 2-76
Memorial Park (Osawatomie, KS), 5-39
Memorial Stadium (Univ. of NE), 5-66
Memphis, TN, 3-49, 113, 114, 116, 118, 120, 122, 123
"Memphis Blues" (song), 3-120
Mena, Marcos de, 5-45
Menard, Rene, 4-115
Menasha, WI, 4-121
Mencken, H. L., 2-50
Mendenhall Glacier (AK), 7-20*
Mendocino, CA, 7-35
Menehune (prehistoric Hawaiians), 7-39
Menendez de Vailes, Pedro, 3-31, 32, 45
Menhaden, 2-23, 65, 106
Menlo Park, NJ, 2-61, 62, 67; 4-66
Mennin, Peter, 2-92
Menninger, Karl, 5-35
Menninger, William, 5-35
Menninger Clinic (KS), 5-35
Menninger Foundation, 1-27
Mennonite settlements, 5-33
Mennonites, 2-87; 5-33, 37
Menoken, ND, 5-73
Menominee Indians, 4-57, 114, 118, 122
Menominee River, 4-111
Menton, OH, 4-109
Mepking Estate (SC), 3-105
Mera, Harry, 6-89
Mercer, Asa, 7-74
"Mercer Girls", 7-74
Mercersburg, PA, 2-91
Merck, George B., 2-63
Mercury, 6-78
Mercury ore, 7-59
Mercy killing, first, 2-25
Meredith Pub. Co., 4-51
Mergenthaler, Ottmar, 2-50
Mergers, 2-19
Meridian, MS, 3-75
Merino sheep, 2-19
Merrimack River, 1-69, 85
Merritt, Leonidas, 4-78
Merritt, Darwin R., 4-46
Mesa Verde Nat. Park, 6-30, 39
Mesabi Range, 4-78, 81
Mesas, 6-29, 83, 95
Meshekinnoquah (Little Turtle), 4-

35
Mesilla, NM, 6-92
Mesquakie Indians, 4-43
"Messiah" (Handel's), 5-33
Messiah War, 5-102
Metacom (chief), 1-102
Meteor Crater (AZ), 6-23
Meteors, 4-46; 5-114
Methodist, 2-25; 3-49
Metropolitan Museum of Art, 2-80
Metropolitan Opera, 2-80
Metropolitian Stadium (MN), 4-80
Mexican Hat, UT, 6-99
Mexican Revolution, 6-17, 89
Mexican War, 2-104; 3-116; 5-115, 116
Mexican period (CA), 7-26*
Mexico City, Mexico, 1-117
Miami, FL, 1-15; 3-28*, 30, 34, 35, 38; 7-93
Miami Beach, FL, 3-28*, 34, 38
Miami Indians, 4-28, 31, 43, 57, 100, 101
Mica, 1-92; 4-50, 78
Michaelangelo (Statue reproductions), 5-108
Michener, James, 4-49
Michigamea Indians, 4-87
Michigan (main article), 4-55
Michigan National Guard, 4-62
Michigan State Police Headquarters, 4-66
Michigan's 24th regiment, 4-61*
Micronesia, 7-85
Mid Mississippian people, 5-16
Middle Park (CO), 6-29
Middlebury, VT, 1-122
Middlesex, MA, 1-79
Middleton, TN, 3-77
Middleton Gardens (Charleston, SC), 3-108
Middletown, RI, 1-103
Middletown Woolen Mfg. Co., 1-50
"Midnight Ride of Paul Revere, The" (painting), 1-73*
Midnight Sun baseball game, 7-20
Mies van der Rohe, Ludwig, 4-24
Milan, OH, 4-106
Milford, CT, 1-44
Military Prison Park (Andersonville Nat. Hist. Site), 3-52
Milk River, 6-57
Millay, Edna St. Vincent, 1-63
Milles, Carl, 2-24; 4-80
Milling, 1-87
Mills, 1-48, 79, 93; 2-22, 51; 6-36, 65, 78, 103; 7-35
Millsboro, DE, 2-23
Milwaukee, WI, 1-2; 4-114, 116*, 121, 122
Milwaukee Braves (baseball), 4-118
Milwaukee Public Museum, 4-114
Milwaukee RR, 5-103
Milwaukee Summerfest, 4-122
Miner, Hazel, 5-78
Mineral Point, WI, 4-115, 123
Minerals and mining, 1-11, 14, 20, 52, 65, 78, 79, 92, 107, 121; 2-64, 77, 78, 93, 106, 107, 118, 121; 3-22, 23, 50, 51, 65, 78, 92, 106, 107, 121; 4-18, 22, 36, 37, 50, 64, 78, 79, 92, 93, 108, 115, 120, 121; 5-18, 21, 24, 36, 37, 50, 64, 78, 79, 92, 93, 105, 106, 120, 121; 6-20, 21, 22, 36, 48, 50, 51, 60, 63, 65, 74, 77, 78, 89, 91, 92, 105, 106, 107, 120; 7-27, 59, 72, 90, 94, 95
Mingo County, WV, 2-117
Mink growing, 4-121
Minneapolis, MN, 1-14, 29; 4-70*, 73, 74, 76, 79, 80
Minneapolis-Honeywell, 4-79
Minnehaha Falls, 4-80
Minnesota (main article), 4-69
Minnesota Man, 4-71
Minnesota Minning & Manufactur-

ing (3M), 4-79
Minnesota Symphony Orchestra, 4-80
Minnesota Twins (baseball), 4-80
Minnetaree Blackfeet Indians, 6-58
Minnetaree Indians, 6-64
Minot, ND, 5-81
Mintaka Pass (China), 6-37
Mints, 4-64
Minuit, Peter, 2-15, 72
"Minuteman" (statue), 1-77, 80
Mishawaka, IN, 4-28
Miss America Pageant, 1-25; 2-61
Miss Arctic Circle, 7-21
Mission, TX, 1-20
Mission Hills (Kansas City, KS), 5-38
Mission San Carlos Borromeo de Carmelo (Carmel, CA), 7-29
Mission San Diego Alcala, 7-25, 26
Mission San Diego Alcala (mural), 7-26*
Mission San Francisco de Asis, 7-25
Mission of St. Francis Xavier, 4-115
Missisquoi Bay (VT), 1-114
Missisquoi River, 1-113
Mississippi (main article), 3-69
Mississippi Bubble, 5-16
Mississippi Cultures, 3-16
Mississippi Delta, 1-7; 3-69; 5-41
Mississippi Embayment, 4-83
"Mississippi Queen" (Riverboat), 5-43*
Mississippi River, 1-7, 29, 67; 2-83, 100, 113, 115; 3-13, 55, 57, 59, 69, 71, 72*, 74, 75, 78, 79, 81, 101, 113, 114, 118, 122; 4-8, 13, 15, 16, 21, 30, 41, 45, 51, 52, 55, 69, 70, 71*, 74, 75, 79, 81, 83, 86, 88, 89, 91, 93, 94, 111, 113, 115, 123, 124; 5-13, 15, 16, 39, 41, 43*, 43, 44, 45, 51, 69, 85, 86, 99; 6-29, 57, 85, 111; 7-62
Mississippi River Road, 5-25
Mississippi River Territory, 3-73
Mississippi Valley, 4-44, 85
Missouri (main article), 4-83
Missouri Compromise, 4-87
Missouri Indians, 4-43, 85; 5-57
Missouri Ozarks, 4-83
Missouri Plateau, 5-99
Missouri River, 1-7, 29; 4-41, 44, 53, 83, 86, 87, 93; 5-38, 55, 58, 59, 69, 78, 79, 81, 97, 100, 101*, 102, 109; 6-55, 57, 59, 60, 65, 66, 67, 102, 113
Missouri Valley (SD), 5-99
Mitchell, Margaret, 3-48
Mitchell, SD, 5-102, 108
Mitchell Park Horticultural Conservatory (Milwaukee, WI), 4-122
Mix, Tom, 5-78
Mizen, Frederic, 1-28
Mobile, AL, 3-14*, 18, 19, 23, 24, 119
Mobile Bay (AL), 3-20*, 24
Mobile Point (AL), 3-15, 24
Mobile River, 3-17
"Moby Dick" (book), 1-77
Moccasin Bend (TN), 3-122
Mockingbirds, 1-11
Model T Ford, 4-65
Modoc Indians, 6-115
Modoc War, 7-55
Moffat, David, 6-35
Mohawk Indians, 1-43, 44
Mohican Indians, 1-71
Mojave Indians, 6-16
Mokihana berries, 7-45
Molokai Island (HI), 7-37, 48
Molybdenum, 6-36, 91
Monahans, TX, 5-113
Monarch butterflies, 7-30
Mona Island (Caribbean), 7-87
Mondale, Walter, 2-75; 3-61; 4-76;

7-28
Mongoose, 7-94
Monhegan (ME settlement), 1-60
Monhegan Island (ME), 1-60, 66
"Monkey Trial", 3-117
Monkeys, 7-30
Monks Mound (IL), 4-15
Monmouth, NJ, 2-59
Monocacan Confederacy, 2-99
Monongahela River, 2-96*, 113
Monorails, 7-74
Monroe, James, 2-104; 4-87
Monroe, Marilyn, 7-30
Monroe, WI, 4-123
Monroe Doctrine, 2-104
Monsanto Chemical Co., 4-92
Montana (main article), 6-56
Montauk Indians, 2-71
Montauk Point (NY), 2-71, 81
Montauk Point Lighthouse (NY), 2-81
Montclair, NJ, 2-64
Monte Rey (Count of), 7-25
Monterey, CA, 7-26
Monterey Bay, 7-25
Monterey Peninsula, 7-25, 33
Monterey cypress, 7-30, 33
Monterey pine, 7-30
Montezuma Castle Nat. Mon., 6-16, 25
Montgomery, AL, 1-26; 3-19, 24
Montgomery County, MO, 4-85
Montgomery Ward Co., 4-64
Monticello, UT, 6-100
Monticello (VA), 2-104, 108*
Montour, Andrew, 4-100
Montpelier, VT, 1-31, 119, 123
Montreal, Canada, 1-119
Monts, Sieur de (Pierre du Guast), 1-60
Monument Circle (Indianapolis, IN), 1-26; 4-39
Monument Valley (AZ/UT), 1-28*; 6-24, 99
"Monumental City" (Baltimore, MD), 2-53
Monuments, 1-26, 79, 80, 88, 109, 123; 2-24, 36, 39, 50, 53, 67, 95, 108, 109; 3-15, 23, 25, 44, 51, 63, 67, 71, 80, 88, 93, 123; 4-25, 31, 39, 43, 52, 53, 80, 81, 89, 108; 5-24, 25, 38, 66, 67, 77, 80, 81, 99, 103, 123; 6-23, 24, 25, 38, 39, 52, 53, 66, 67, 93, 104, 106, 109, 117, 121; 7-20, 21, 32, 33, 35, 48, 49, 62, 63, 77, 95
Moodus, CT, 1-43
Mooney, James, 1-18
Moore, Arch A., 2-118
Mooresville, IN, 4-33
Moorhead, MN, 1-10; 4-81
Moose, 1-64, 120; 4-64
Moose Island (ME), 1-61
Moosehead Lake, 1-58, 66
Moraines, 1-58
Moran, Thomas, 1-12; 6-21, 119
Moravians, 2-87
Morehead Planetarium, 3-95
Mores, Marquis de, 5-77, 79
Morgan, J. Pierpont, 1-49
Morgan, John Hunt, 4-33
Morgan, Justin, 1-121, 122
Morgan, Morgan, 2-115
Morgan horse, 1-121, 122
Morgan's Spring, WV, 2-115
Morgantown, WV, 2-123
Mormon Battalion, 6-17, 102
Mormon Pageant, 2-80
Mormon Pioneer Cemetery, 5-66
Mormon Rebellion, 6-104
Mormon Tabernacle (Salt Lake City, UT), 1-29; 6-109
Mormon Tabernacle (St. George, UT), 6-109
Mormon Temple (Salt Lake City, UT), 1-29; 6-109

Mormon Temple (St. George, UT), 6-109
Mormon Trail, 5-66
Mormon leaders, 6-105
Mormon religion, 1-119; 2-77; 4-18, 88, 103; 6-102, 104, 105, 106, 109
Mormon settlements, 4-18, 60, 88; 6-14, 18, 47, 81, 102, 116
Mormons, 1-29; 4-88, 94; 5-59, 60, 66, 86; 6-103, 104, 108; 7-32
Mormons displacement, 4-88, 94, 103
Morrill, John, 1-91
Morris, Charles H., 2-118
Morris, Esther Hobert, 6-119
Morris, Gouverneur, 2-88
Morris, Lewis, 2-58
Morris, Robert, 2-88
Morrisey, Jack, 6-34
Morristown, NJ, 2-59, 62
Morro Bay, CA, 7-33
Morro Castle (San Juan, PR), 7-88*
Morse, Samuel F. B., 2-36, 62
Morton, J. Sterling, 5-62, 64, 66
Morton, Jelly Roll, 5-49
Morton, Joy, 5-62
Morton, Julius, 5-62
Morton, Oliver P., 4-33, 35
Morton Arboretum (IL), 4-24; 5-62
Morton Family, 5-62
Morton Salt Co., 5-62
Morton family, 3-94
Moscow, ID, 6-51, 62
Moses (Michaelangelo statue), 5-108
Mothers Day, 2-119
Motion picture industry, 7-28, 31
Motion picture locations, 6-107
Motion pictures, 2-60, 62, 67
Moto, Mr. (fictional detective), 2-21
Mott, Valentine, 3-35
Mound Builders, 4-15, 113; 5-85
Mound State Mon. (AL), 3-16*, 25
Mounds, prehistoric, 2-85, 99, 113; 3-16, 25, 44, 50*, 58, 71, 80, 113; 4-15, 28, 43, 57, 71, 85, 99, 109, 113; 5-16, 44, 85, 99, 113
Moundville, AL, 3-25
Moundville, WV, 2-113
Mountain, official designation, 2-55
Mountain climbing, 1-94
Mountain goats, 5-106*; 7-19, 72
Mountain laurel, 2-93
Mountain lions, 5-120; 6-21
Mountain sheep, 6-46
Mountains, 1-6, 7, 10, 25, 26, 27, 29, 30, 43, 57, 58, 66, 69, 80, 83, 87, 89, 92, 94, 95, 111, 120, 122, 123; 2-28, 41, 55, 77, 79, 83, 97, 107, 111, 113; 3-41, 43, 53, 57, 85; 4-71; 5-15*, 22, 23, 72, 83, 95, 99, 102, 103*, 104, 107, 111; 6-15, 27, 29, 30, 37, 43, 46, 48, 50, 55, 69, 80, 85, 100, 109, 111, 113, 114*, 121; 7-9, 12*, 14, 21, 23, 25, 28, 31, 35, 37, 39, 40, 42, 43, 45, 47, 51, 53, 62, 63, 65, 67, 70, 74, 76, 77, 79, 81, 82, 90, 91, 867
Mountains, prehistoric, 2-28; 4-71; 7-51
Moyle River, 6-50
"Mr. Racing" (Matt Wilson), 3-66
Mt. Adams, 7-65
Mt. Airy, NC, 3-93
Mt. Baker, 7-65, 76, 77
Mt. Charleston, 6-80
Mt. Chocorua, 1-87
Mt. Desert Island (ME), 1-57, 67
Mt. Diablo State Park (CA), 7-35
Mt. Elbert, 6-29
Mt. Evans, 6-37
Mt. Evans Highway, 6-37
Mt. Everest (Nepal), 7-9
Mt. Greylock, 1-69, 80
Mt. Haleakala, 7-45
Mt. Harvard, 6-29

Mt. Hood, 7-51, 53, 62
Mt. Hope Bay (RI), 1-99
Mt. Ida, 5-22
Mt. Jefferson, 1-83
Mt. Katahdin, 1-58, 66
Mt. Katmai, 7-14, 21
Mt. Kineo, 1-58
Mt. Lata, 7-79
Mt. Madison, 1-83
Mt. Magazine, 5-15*, 23
Mt. Malafao, 7-81*
Mt. Mansfield, 1-111, 120, 123
Mt. Massive, 6-29
Mt. Mazama (prehistoric), 7-51
Mt. McKinley (Denali), 1-6; 7-9, 12*, 21
Mt. Mitchell, 3-85
Mt. Monodnock, 1-94
Mt. Moosilauke, 1-95
Mt. Moran, 6-111, 119
Mt. Olympus, 7-67
Mt. Olympus (Greece), 7-67, 76
Mt. Palomar observatory, 7-28, 31
Mt. Princeton, 6-29
Mt. Rainier, 7-65, 72, 74, 77
Mt. Rainier Nat. Park, 7-70
Mt. Rushmore, 5-102, 103*, 104, 107
Mt. Shasta, 7-35
Mt. Shishaldin, 7-9
Mt. Spokane State Park (WA), 7-76
Mt. St. Helens, 6-48; 7-65, 70, 77
Mt. Tabor, 7-62
Mt. Vernon, 1-25; 2-108
Mt. Waialeale, 1-10; 7-37, 39
Mt. Washington, 1-83, 89, 94
Mt. Yale, 6-29
Mud Island (TN), 3-122
Muir, John, 7-16, 19, 58
Muir Woods (CA), 7-35
Muir Woods Nat. Mon., 7-35
Mulberry Grove Plantation (GA), 3-48
Mulberry trees, 2-64; 7-80
Mulford, Samuel, 2-77
Mullan, John, 6-60
Mummers Theater (Oklahoma City, OK), 5-95
Mummies, 3-58
Mummy Range, 6-29
Muncie, IN, 4-37
Municipal Pier (Milwaukee, WI), 4-122
Munro, Wilfred H., 1-101
Mural (TN life), 3-120*
Murals, capitol, 3-120*; 7-18*, 62
Murfreesboro, AR, 5-18, 24
Murfreesboro, NC, 3-91
Murphy, Audie, 5-119
Murray, Mary Lindley, 2-73
Murray, William H. (Alfalfa Bill), 5-91
Muscogee Indians, 3-17
Museum of Amana History, 4-52
Museum of Art, Sci. & Industry (Bridgeport, CT), 1-53
Museum of Modern Art, NYC, 2-80
Museum of Natural History (Cincinnati, OH), 4-109
Museum of Natural Science (Vicksburg, MS), 3-80
Museum of Northern Arizona, 6-25
Museum of Science and Industry, 4-23
Museum of Western Art, 6-39
Museum of Westward Expansion, 4-93
Museum of the Plains Indians, 6-66
Museums, 1-14, 25, 27, 30, 52, 53, 65, 66, 80, 95, 108, 122, 123; 2-13*, 20, 24, 25, 38, 39, 53, 66, 67, 79, 80, 81, 83, 94, 95, 108, 109, 122; 3-24, 25, 39, 53, 66, 80, 91, 109, 122; 4-23, 24, 39, 52, 53, 66, 67, 80, 93, 100, 101, 109, 115, 122, 123; 5-16, 25, 39, 52, 66, 67,

80, 94, 95, 108, 121, 123; 6-24, 39, 53, 62, 66, 75, 81, 95, 121, 122; 7-19, 33, 47, 63, 76, 96
"Music Man, The" (musical play), 4-49
Musk ox, 5-57; 6-44; 7-17
Muskhogean Indians, 3-71, 113; 5-44
Muskingum River, 4-97
Muskogee, OK, 5-89
Muskrats, 2-23
"My Lost Youth" (poem), 1-62
My Old Kentucky Home (estate), 3-67*
"My Old Kentucky Home" (song), 3-66
Myra, WV, 2-120
Mystic Seaport, CT, 1-52
Mystic Soc., 3-24
Mystic Village, MA, 1-37*
Nacogdoches, TX, 5-115
Naismith, James, 5-38
Names, origin, 1-67, 71, 72, 80, 106, 111; 2-25, 43, 56, 57, 74, 119, 122; 3-16, 43, 45, 49, 55, 63, 66, 101, 105, 106, 111, 116; 4-34, 51, 58, 67, 79, 91, 103, 107, 122, 123; 5-55, 65, 88, 91, 92, 99, 113, 114, 122; 6-19, 20, 43, 46, 55, 87, 100, 101, 115, 123; 7-16, 21, 32, 53, 67, 87, 93
Nampa, ID, 6-45
Nantacook Indians, 1-86
Nantucket Island (MA), 1-69, 80
Napa, CA, 7-35
Napatree Point (RI), 1-97, 101
Napoleon Bonaparte, 3-65, 67
Narragansett Bay (RI), 1-41, 97, 99, 101
Narragansett Indians, 1-44, 101
Nash, Timothy, 1-94
Nashua, NH, 1-91, 93
Nashua Indians, 1-86
Nashua Watch Factory, 1-93
Nashville, IN, 4-36, 38
Nashville, TN, 1-26; 3-112, 113, 115, 117, 119, 123
Nassau Hall (Princeton Univ.), 2-61*, 66
Nassau-Suffolk, NY, 1-13
Nast, Thomas (cartoon by), 2-63
Natchez, MS, 3-72, 73, 74, 75, 77, 79
Natchez Indians, 3-71, 72
Natchez Pilgrimage, 3-80
Natchez Trace, 3-79, 80
Natchitoches, LA, 5-45, 53
Nation, Carrie, 3-64
National Air and Space Museum, 1-25; 2-38
National Airport, 2-108
National Archives, 2-27, 38
National Bison Range, 6-66
National Bowling Hall of Fame, 4-94
National Cathedral, 2-34*, 39
National Collection of Fine Arts, 2-39
National Colonial Park, 2-108
National Coursing Meet (Grayhound racing), 5-39
National Cowboy Hall of Fame, 1-27
National Gallery of Art, 1-25; 2-38, 92
"National Geographic" (Magazine), 5-13
National Geographic Soc., 3-15; 4-41
National Guard (OR), 7-56
National Hall of Fame, 2-20, 92, 120; 7-57
National Institutes of Health, 2-53
National League (baseball), 2-75
National Mall, 2-37
National Mem. Cemetery of the

117

Pacific, 7-49
National Mon. to the Forefathers, 1-79
National Music Week, 6-53
National Reactor Testing Station, 6-48
National Register of Historic Places, 5-23
National Rice Festival, 5-50
National Road, 4-103
National Zoo, 2-39
Natural Bridges, 2-8*, 109, 110; 3-55*; 4-83; 6-99, 109
Natural Bridges Nat. Mon., 6-109
Natural Chimneys, VA, 2-108
Natural History Museum, DC, 2-39
"Nautilus" (submarine), 1-46
Nauvoo, ILL, 4-18
Navajo Bridge (AZ), 6-18
"Navajo Children" (painting), 1-28*
Navajo Indians, 1-28*; 6-16, 18, 24, 25, 86, 87, 92, 101, 105
Navajo Nat. Mon., 6-25
"Navajo Silversmith" (painting), 6-24
Naval Academy (Annapolis, MD), 1-21, 25; 2-54
Naval oranges, 7-30
Navassa Island (Caribbean), 7-96
Nazis, 6-105
Nebraska (main article), 5-55
Nebraska City, NE, 5-62
Nebraska Nat. Forest, 5-64
Nebraska State Hist. Soc., 5-67
Nebraska State Museum, 5-67
Needles Highway, 5-107
Neenah, WI, 4-121
Nemours, France, 2-19
Nemours Foundation, 2-20, 24
Nemours estate, 2-24
Nenana, AK, 7-22
Nene (Hawaiian goose), 7-44
Neo American Culture, 5-114
Netherlands, King of, 1-61
Nevada (main article), 6-69
Nevada Commission on Tourism, 6-69
Nevada Proving Grounds, 6-74
Nevada State Hist. Soc. Museum, 6-81
Nevada State Museum, 6-81
Never Summer Range, 6-29
Neville Museum (Green Bay, WI), 4-115
Nevin, Ethelbert, 2-92
Neviusia Alabamensis, 3-23
New Albany, MS, 3-76
New Amstel (New Castle, DE), 2-15
New Bern, NC, 3-87, 88, 94
New Braunfels, TX, 5-113
New Britain, CT, 1-49
New Brunswick, NJ, 2-60
New Castle, DE, 2-15, 16, 20, 24
New Castle, NH, 1-88
New Castle Hist. Soc., 2-24
New Castle and Frenchtown RR, 2-23
New England Peneplain, 1-43
New Glarus, WI, 4-123
New Hampshire (main article), 1-83
New Harmony, IN, 4-32*, 38
New Haven, CT, 1-44, 45, 48, 50, 53
New Jersey (main article), 2-55
New Jersey Brigade, 2-60
New Jersey Plan, 2-59
New London, CT, 1-18, 48, 52
New London, TX, 5-117
New Madrid, MO, 4-87
New Madrid earthquake, 3-121
New Mecklenburg, WV, 2-115
New Mexico (main article), 6-83
New Orleans, LA, 1-10; 3-24, 119; 4-21; 5-45, 46, 47, 49, 51, 51*, 52
New Orleans Bridge, Greater, 5-48
New Orleans Cotton Centennial of 1884, 5-47

New Orleans Mardi Gras, 5-65
New River, 1-30; 2-113, 114; 3-94
New Salem, IL, 4-24
New Sweden, NJ, 2-57
New Ulm, MN, 4-75
New York, NY, 1-14, 15, 19, 21, 24; 2-6*, 24, 30, 31, 48, 61, 67, 70*, 72, 73, 74, 75, 76, 77, 78, 79, 80; 4-91, 120; 5-38
New York (main article), 2-69
New York Bay (NY), 2-71
New York Cosmos (soccer), 2-61
New York Giants (football), 2-61
New York Philharmonic, 2-80
New York Stock Exchange, 2-22
New York Throughway, 2-75
New York Univ. at NYC, 1-21
Newark, NJ, 2-57, 67
Newburgh, NY, 2-73, 77
Newhouse, Samuel, 6-35
Newport, OR, 7-62
Newport, RI, 1-24, 101, 102, 103, 104, 106, 107
Newport Island (RI), 1-97
Newport Jazz Festival, 1-108
Newport News, VA, 2-109
Newport News Shipbuilding Co., 2-102
Newspaper Rock (UT), 6-100
Newspapers, 1-121; 5-35
Ney, Elizabet, 5-119
Nez Perce Indians, 6-45, 46, 47, 48, 49, 52; 7-57, 69, 71
Nez Perce Nat. Hist. Park, 6-52
"Niagara", ship, 2-88*, 95
Niagara Cave, 4-81
Niagara Falls, 2-69, 72*, 80
Niagara River, 2-69
Niantic Indians, 1-107
Nibrathka River, 5-55
Nichols, J. C., 4-94
Nichols Fountain (Kansas City, KS), 4-94*
Nickel, 7-59, 60
Nicolet, Jean, 4-114, 115
Nigh, George, 5-89
"Night Session of the House in 1822" (painting), 2-36
Niihau Island (HI), 7-48
Niles, John Jacob, 3-63
Niles, MI, 4-64
Niles, OH, 4-105, 106
Nimitz, Chester, 5-119
"Nine Lives of Elfego Baca" (movie), 6-90
Nine Mile Canyon (UT), 6-100
Ninigret (Sachem), 1-107
Niobrara River, 5-57
Nipmuc Indians, 1-43, 44, 71
Nipper (dog), 2-69
Nixon, Richard M., 1-76; 2-35; 4-62, 77; 5-62; 7-28
Niza, Marcos de, 6-16, 17
Nobel Prize, 2-62, 76, 119; 4-21, 63, 77, 78; 6-49, 64
Noble, Seth, 1-67
Nogales, AZ, 6-22
Nola, Charles, 1-62
Nome, AK, 7-13, 19, 21
Norbeck, Peter, 5-105
Norfolk, VA, 2-97, 109
Norman, OK, 5-95
Norman Fort, 6-80
Normandy, France, 4-62
Norris, George W., 5-63
Norris Basin (TN), 3-113
Norris Dam, 5-63
Norris Lake, 3-117
Norse Wall House (Provincetown, MA), 1-71
Norse explorers, 1-59, 60, 87
North Amer. Air Defense Command (NORAD), 6-33
North Bend, OH, 4-106, 108
North Carolina, Battleship, 3-94*
North Carolina (main article), 3-83

North Carolina Zoological Park, 3-95
North Dakota (main article), 5-69
North Dakota Economic Development Commission, 5-75
North Haven Island (ME), 1-57
North Kingstown, RI, 1-106
North Park (CO), 6-29
North Platte, NE, 5-63
North Pole, 2-92
"North State Street, Salt Lake City in the early days", 6-103*
Northampton, MA, 1-80
Northern Pacific RR, 7-70
Northwest Co., 4-74
Northwest Ordinance, 4-31, 102
"Northwest Passage" (book), 1-114
Northwest Territory, 4-31, 59, 74, 115
Northwestern Univ., 1-21
Norwalk, CT, 1-14
Norway pine, 4-78
Norwegian pioneers, 5-104, 105
Norwegian settlements, 4-76
Norwich Univ., 1-117
Notches (mt. passes), 1-86
Notre Dame Univ., 4-38*
Nuclear Power, 2-107
Nuclear Science Center, 1-105
Nuclear energy, 3-106
Nuclear research, 7-73
Nuclear tests, 7-85
Nuuanu Pali cliff (HI), 7-48
Nuuanu Valley (HI), 7-41
Nuuanu (HI), 7-48
Nye, James, 6-74, 77
Nylon, 2-22
Nystrom, Al, 5-103
"O, Fair New Mexico" (song), 6-91
O'Brien, William, 6-74
O'Conner, Flannery, 4-49
O'Hare Airport, 4-23
O'Henry (W. S. Porter), 3-91
O'Keeffe, Georgia, 6-91
O'Leary's cow, 4-20
O'Neill, NE, 5-57
O'Reilly, Marshal Alejandro, 7-90
Oo bird, 7-44
Oahe Dam, 5-97
Oahe Lake, 5-97
Oahu Island (HI), 7-37, 41, 48
Oahu Lake, 5-69
Oak Alley Plantation, 5-12*
Oak Creek Canyon (AZ), 6-15, 24
Oak Ridge, TN, 3-122
Oak Ridge Cemetery, IL, 4-24
Oak Ridge Nat. Lab., 3-118
Oak trees, 5-21, 121
Oakland, CA, 1-8*, 10; 7-35
Oakland Bay Bridge, 7-28, 34
Oakville, IA, 4-43
Oakwood (Raleigh, NC), 3-95
Oats, 4-50
Obsidian (volcanic glass), 6-115
Obsidian Cliff (WY), 6-121
Ocala, FL, 1-14
Ocean City, MD, 2-54
Ocean View Blvd. (Pacific Grove, CA), 7-33
Ocheyedan Mound (IA), 4-43
Ocmulgee Nat. Mon., 3-44, 50*
Oconaluftee Indian Village, 3-95
Oconomowoc, WI, 4-122
Oconto, WI, 4-113, 115
Ocracoke Village, NC, 3-93
Odessa, TX, 5-114
Offutt Air Force Base, 5-66
Ofu Island (SA), 7-79
Ogallala, NE, 5-67
Ogallala Sioux Indians, 5-67
Ogallala aquifer, 5-36
Ogden, Peter Skene, 6-101
Ogden, UT, 6-101, 102, 104, 106
Ogdenburg, NY, 6-62
Ogeechee lime tree, 3-49
Oglebay Park (Wheeling, WV), 2-

122
Oglethorpe, James Edward, 3-45, 52
Ohelo berries, 7-43
Ohio (main article), 4-97
Ohio Co. of Associates, 4-102
Ohio Co. of Virgina, 4-100
Ohio River, 1-7; 2-83, 95, 113, 117, 118, 119; 3-13, 55, 58, 59, 60, 65; 4-13, 16, 17, 18, 27, 28, 30, 32, 37, 83, 97, 100, 101, 102, 104
Ohio River Valley, 2-100; 4-0
Ohio Univ., 4-107
Ohiople (Ohio River), 2-113
Ohman, Olaf, 4-73
Oil and gas, 1-11; 2-65, 77, 80, 93, 121; 3-64, 65, 78, 79; 4-22, 23, 36, 64, 92, 108; 5-19, 36, 37, 49, 50, 64, 75, 78, 79, 83, 92, 93, 95, 96, 106, 113, 119, 120, 121; 6-36, 64, 65, 91, 92, 106, 107, 108, 118, 120; 7-15, 17, 27, 31
Oil industry, 2-65; 4-34; 5-47, 50, 75, 93, 117, 120, 121; 7-28, 90
Oil well, first, 2-93
Ojibwa Indians (Chippewa), 4-28, 43, 57, 71, 72, 74, 76; 5-72
Okanogan, WA, 7-71
Okefenokee Swamp (GA), 3-43, 49*, 52
Oklahoma (main article), 5-83
Oklahoma City, OK, 1-27; 5-84*, 88, 95
Oklahoma Territory, 5-88
Okmulgee, OK, 5-94
Okoboji Lake, 4-41
Okolona, MS, 3-75
Old Abe (eagle), 4-117
Old Dover Days, 2-17*
Old Exchange Bldg. (Charleston, SC), 3-102
Old Faithfaul Geyser (Yellowstone Nat. Park), 6-121
Old Fort DeLaware, 2-18
Old Harbor (Block Island), 1-108
Old Hop (chief), 3-114
Old Indian Agency (NE), 5-67
Old Ironsides (ship), 1-80; 5-38
Old Lyme, CT, 1-18
Old Man of the Mt. (NH), 1-85, 86, 94
Old Mission of the Sacred Heart (ID), 6-53
Old North Church (Boston, MA), 1-80
Old Salem (Winston-Salem), NC, 3-95
"Old Santa Fe Trail, The" (painting), 6-88*
Old Spanish Trail, 6-101
Old Stone Fort, 3-113
Old Stone Mill (Newport, RI), 1-101
Old Swedes Church (Wilmington, DE), 2-24
Old Town Hall, (Wilmington, DE), 2-24
Old Village (prehistoric MO town), 4-85
Old West Museum, 5-123
Old Winnemucca (chief), 6-77
Old Woman of the Mts. (NH), 1-94
Oldest House (St. Augustine, FL), 3-32*
Oldham, John, 1-44
Olds, Ransom E., 4-65
Oldsmobiles, 4-65
Oller, Francisco, 7-90
Olosega Island (SA), 7-79
Olvera Street (Los Angeles, CA), 7-33
Olympia, WA, 1-21, 29; 7-76
"Olympia" (ship), 1-119
Olympic Games, 2-75; 3-48; 7-28
Olympic Mts., 7-65, 74
Olympic Nat. Park, 7-70, 76
Olympic Peninsula (WA), 1-6; 7-67,

72, 74, 76
Omaha, NE, 4-53; 5-58, 59, 60, 62, 65
Omaha Indians, 4-43; 5-57, 58, 65
Onandaga (Indian capital), 2-71
Onate, Don Juan de, 5-85, 114, 115; 6-87, 92
Onions, 2-78
Ontonagon, MI, 4-64
Oolagah, OK, 5-89
Opals, 6-77, 107
Opechancanough (chief), 2-100
Operation Bootstrap, 7-89, 90
Operation Serenidad, 7-89
Opossums, 1-11
Optical industry, 1-107
Orange, OH, 4-106
Orange County, VA, 2-104
Oranges, 3-37; 7-30, 80
Orchid Row (Charlotte Amalie, VI), 7-95
Orchids, 1-120; 2-21, 65, 66, 77; 3-36; 4-78, 92; 5-21; 7-45, 46, 49, 72, 84, 90
Ordway, SD, 5-104
Ore, James, 3-115
Oregon (main article), 7-51
Oregon Caves Nat. Mon., 7-63
Oregon City, OR, 7-55, 56, 62
Oregon Territory, 6-111
Oregon Trail, 4-88; 5-31, 55, 59, 66; 6-47, 53, 116, 122; 7-60, 69, 71
Oregon boundary dispute, 3-90
Organ Pipe Cactus Nat. Mon., 6-24
Organ pipe cactus, 6-21
Orienta, OK, 5-95
Oriental Institute (Chicago, IL), 4-24
Orlando, FL, 3-34, 35
Ormandy, Eugene, 2-92
Orozco, Jose Clemente, 1-95
Orr, Robert D., 4-34
Orrum, Eilley, 6-76
Osage Agency (Pawhuska, OK), 5-94
Osage Indians, 4-43, 85, 87; 5-16, 30, 85, 92, 93, 94; 6-20
Osage River, 4-83
Osage Tribal Museum, 5-94
Osawatomie, KS, 5-39
Osceola (Indian leader), 3-22, 33*, 35
Osceola County, IA, 4-43
Oshkosh, WI, 4-114, 117
Oshkosh (chief), 4-114
Ostner, Charles, 6-53
Oto Indians, 5-57, 58
Ottawa, KS, 5-34
Ottawa Indians, 4-16, 28, 43, 57
Otter Crescent (OR), 7-58
Otter Tail River, 4-69
Ouachita Mts., 5-22, 83
Ouachita River, 5-22
Ouachita province (mts.), 5-15
"Our American Cousin" (play), 2-33
Ouragon (Columbia River), 7-53
Ouray, CO, 6-35
Outboard motors, 4-119
Outer Banks (NC), 1-7; 3-83, 85, 89
Ouzel, water, 6-120
Overton, NV, 6-81
Owen, Robert, 4-32
Owen, Robert L., 5-88
Owl, barelegged, 7-94
Owosso, MI, 4-62
Owyhee Lake, 7-60
Owyhee River, 7-60
Oxbow Lakes, 5-44
Oxford, MS, 3-76
Oxford Univ., 2-91
Oxygen, 2-92
Oyster Bay, NY, 2-81
Oysters, 1-107; 2-23, 51, 52, 56, 106; 7-58
Ozark Airlines, 4-92
Ozark Bluff Dwellers, 5-85

Ozark Mts., 1-27; 4-13, 94; 5-22, 83
Ozark plateau, 5-15, 27
Ozokerite, 6-107
Paca House and Gardens (Annapolis, MD), 2-51*
Pacific Grove, CA, 7-30, 33
Pacific Science Center, 7-74
Pack rat, 6-21
Padre Creek, 6-101
Padre Island (TX), 5-113, 123
Padre Island Nat. Seashore, 5-123
Paducah, KY, 3-67
Pageant of the Sault, 4-57, 58
Pago Pago, SA, 1-10; 7-79, 80, 81
Pago Pago Bay (SA), 7-81
Pago Pago International Airport, 7-81
Pahaquarry, NJ, 2-66
Pahvant Indians, 6-106
Paint Rock (TX), 5-114
Painted Desert, 6-100
Paiute Indians, 6-72, 100
Palace of the Governors (NM), 6-95
Palau Island (Pacific), 7-85
Palisades of the Hudson, 2-60, 67
Palisades of the Potomac, 2-28
Palm Beach, FL, 3-35, 39
Palm Springs, CA, 7-32
Palm trees, 3-106; 5-92, 123; 7-80, 84, 90, 94
Palmer, Potter, 4-21
Palmetto State Park (TX), 5-113
Palmetto palms, 3-106; 5-92
Palmira, NY, 2-80
Palmito Hill (TX), 5-116
Palms, coconut, 7-94
Palms, palmetto, 3-106; 5-92
Palms, royal, 7-94
Palo Duro Canyon (TX), 5-113
Palouse (ID), 6-44, 54
Palusami (food), 7-81
Pamlico Sound (NC), 3-85
Pampa, TX, 5-121
Pan American Airlines, 7-42
Pana, IL, 4-22
Panama Canal, 4-121
Panamint Mts., 7-29*
Pancho Villa (Francisco Villa), 6-89
Panhandle's Square House Museum, 5-121
Pantages Theater (Tacoma, WA), 7-74
Paoli, PA, 2-88
Papago Indians, 6-16, 25
Papago Park (AZ), 6-25
Papaya, 7-45, 94
Paper mills, 1-93
Papermaking, 3-93; 4-121
Papillion, NE, 5-55
Paradise Inn (Mt. Rainier), 7-77
Paria River narrows, 6-6*
Parimaribo, Surinam, 1-50
Paris, France, 1-26; 3-67
Paris, IL, 4-23
Paris, KY, 3-65
Paris Opera House (France), 3-67
Park Range, 6-113
Park Row (Brunswick, ME), 1-66
Parke, Francis L., 3-105
Parke County, IN, 4-38
Parker, Francis L., 3-105
Parker, Isaac C., 5-18, 23
Parker, Quanah (chief), 5-94, 120
Parker, Samuel, 6-116
Parker Ranch (HI), 7-46
Parmley, J. W., 5-107
Parr, Charles, 4-51
Parrant, Pierre (Pig's Eye), 4-74
Parris Island, SC, 3-100
Parrish, Maxfield, 1-92; 2-0
Parthenon (Nashville, TN), 1-26; 3-123
Pasadena, CA, 7-33
Pascagoula, MS, 3-79
Pascagoula River, 3-71
Pasco, WA, 7-77
Paso Robles, CA, 1-27

Paso fino (horse), 7-90
Pass Christian, MS, 3-81
Passaconaway (chief), 1-86
Passaic, NJ, 2-60, 65
Passaic River, 2-62
Passamaquoddy Bay (Canada/ME), 1-57
Passamaquoddy Indians, 1-59, 62
Passenger pigeons, 4-120
Patagonia, Argentina/Chile, 1-52
Paterson, NJ, 2-64, 67
Pathway of the Revolution (NJ), 2-58
Patriots from New Castle, 1-88
Patterson, John, 5-20
Paul Bunyan (statue), 1-67
Paul Bunyan Carnival, 4-81
Paulet, George, 7-43
Pawcatuck River, 1-41
Pawhuska, OK, 5-92, 94
Pawhuska (chief), 5-92
Pawnee Indians, 5-30, 57, 58, 60, 63, 85; 6-31
Pawtucket, RI, 1-102, 106, 108
Pawtucket Falls, 1-107
Pawtuxet River, 1-99
Paxson, Edgar S., 6-62
Payne, John Howard, 2-81
Payson, UT, 6-108
Pea Island Nat. Wildlife Refuge, 3-91
Pea Patch Island (DE), 2-15, 18, 24
Pea Patch Island State Park (DE), 2-24
Pea Ridge Nat. Military Park, 5-23
Peabody Museum (Yale Univ.), 1-53, 80
Peace Bridge (NY), 2-80
Peaches, 2-22; 3-107
Peale, Charles Wilson, 2-50
Peale, Rembrandt, 2-53
Peale Island (Pacific), 7-85
Peale Museum, 2-53
Peanuts, 3-21, 50
Pearl Harbor (HI), 7-42, 49, 56
Pearl River, 3-69, 79; 5-41
Pearls, 2-64
Peary, Robert E., 1-64, 66; 2-92
Peary-MacMillan Arctic Museum, 1-66
Peas, 6-51
Peat, 1-11; 4-64, 78
Pecan Island (LA), 5-44
Pecans, 3-50, 79; 6-92
Peccas Indians, 6-95
Pecos River, 6-85
Pecuris Pueblo (NM), 6-87
Pedro, Dom (of Brazil), 3-60
Peebles, OH, 4-109
Pele (HI goddess of volcanoes), 7-37, 43
Pele's hair, 7-37
Peleliu Island (Pacific), 7-85
Pelican Rapids, MN, 4-71
Pelicans, 3-36; 6-5, 77, 107; 7-94
Pella, IA, 4-45*
Pemaquid (ME trading post), 1-60, 61
Pembina, ND, 5-73
Pembina Mts., 5-72
Pemmican (dried buffalo meat), 4-71; 6-87
Penacook (Concord, NH), 1-95
Penacook Indians, 1-71, 86
Pend Oreille Indians, 6-46
Pend Oreille Lake, 6-50, 53
Pend Oreille River, 6-53
Pendleton, OR, 7-63
Pendleton County, WV, 2-114
Pendleton Roundup (OR), 7-63
Penn, William, 1-19; 2-16, 85, 86, 91, 94, 95
Penn, William Sr., 2-85
Penn Center (Philadelphia, PA,), 2-94
Penn's Woods, 2-85

Penney, J. C., 4-91; 6-119
Penney stores, 6-119
Pennsbury Manor (MD), 2-91, 94
Pennsylvania (main article), 2-83
Pennsylvania Ave. (DC), 2-35, 37
Pennsylvania Dutch, 1-30
Pennsylvania German, 1-30
Penobscot Bay (ME), 1-57
Penobscot Indians, 1-59
Penobscot Island (ME), 1-65
Penobscot River, 1-57, 59, 61
Penrose, Spencer, 6-34
Pensacola, FL, 3-32, 33, 39
Pensacola History Museum, 3-31
Pentagoet Indians, 1-59
Pentagon, 2-29, 108
Peoples, 1-38, 47, 63, 76, 91, 105, 118; 2-21, 49, 62, 76, 90, 103, 118; 3-10, 21, 35, 47, 62, 76, 90, 104, 118; 4-10, 21, 34, 48, 62, 76, 90, 105, 119; 5-19, 34, 48, 62, 76, 89, 104, 118; 6-8, 19, 34, 49, 61, 75, 90, 105, 118; 7-16, 44, 57, 71
Pequawket Indians, 1-87
Pequot Hill (CT Indian village), 1-44
Pequot-Mohegan Indians, 1-43
Peralta, Don Pedro de, 6-87
Perdido River, 3-13
Perfumes, 7-95
Periwinkle shells, 1-101
Perlite, 6-92
Perpetual motion, 3-109
Perry, David, 6-47
Perry, George Sessions, 5-119
Perry, Matthew Calbraith, 1-90, 106
Perry, Oliver Hazard, 1-104, 106; 2-88, 89, 95; 4-102, 103
Perry Mem. House (PA), 2-94
Perry Mem. Statue, 2-80
Perry Monument, 2-95
Perryville, KY, 3-60
Pershing, John J., 2-107; 3-61; 4-89, 90; 6-89
Peru, IA, 4-51
Peru, IN, 4-36, 39
Perz, Juan, 7-67
Peshtigo, WI, 4-117
Peterborough, NH, 1-91
Peters, G. W., 4-104
Petersburg cocktail shrimp, 7-17
Petersburg, VA, 2-92
Petrified forest, 6-113
Petrified wood, 6-21
Petrochemical industry, 5-121
Petroglyphs, 5-72, 99; 6-45; 7-25, 53
Petroleum Expo., International, 5-94
Pfeiffer-Big Sur State Park (CA), 7-33
Phalarope, 6-50
Pheasants, 4-50; 5-65, 105, 109
Philadelphia, PA, 1-19; 2-23, 30, 46, 58, 67, 84*, 85, 87, 88, 89, 91, 92, 94, 95; 4-119; 5-31
Philadelphia Art Museum, 2-94
Philadelphia Symphony, 2-94
Philbrook Art Center, 5-94
Philip (chief/king), 1-87
Philip (prince) of England, 4-118
Philippi, WV, 2-117, 123
Phillips, John (Portugee), 6-116
Philosophers, 5-34, 89
Phoenix, AZ, 1-14, 19, 27; 6-14*, 18, 19, 22, 24, 25
Phoenix (bird), 6-19
Phoenix Art Museum, 6-24
Phonographs, 2-62, 67
Phosphates, 3-121; 6-50, 51
Photography, 1-26; 2-78
Piankeshaw Indians, 4-16, 87
Pianos, 1-91; 2-93
Piasa Bird, 4-15*
"Picasso, Chicago" (sculpture), 4-24*
Picasso, Pablo, 4-24
Pickawillany (OH Indian village), 4-

Pickens County Courthouse, SC, 3-103
Pickersgill, Mary, 2-47, 53
Pickett, George E., 2-88
Pickford, Mary, 7-30
Pickwick Lake, 3-69
Pico, Pio, 7-26
Pictograph Cave, 6-66
Pictographs, 5-72, 99, 114; 6-45, 66; 7-25, 53
Picture Gorge (OR), 7-53
Picurie Indians, 5-30
Piedmont Plateau, 2-27, 41, 55, 97; 3-15, 99
Pierce, E. A., 6-47
Pierce, Franklin, 1-89, 90; 3-76
Pierce, ID, 6-47
Pierpont, Francis H., 2-120
Pierre, SD, 1-29; 5-97, 98*, 100, 102, 109
Pig War, 7-69
Pig's Eye (St. Paul, MN), 4-74
Pigs, 5-37, 57; 7-33
Pigs, prehistoric, 5-57
Pigs, wild, 7-33
Pika, 6-36
Pike, Zebulon, 4-44, 74; 5-30, 38; 6-31
Pikes Peak (CO), 6-27, 31, 35, 38
Pikes Peak (IA), 4-44
Pilgrim monuments, 1-79, 80
Pilgrims, 1-60, 72, 73
Pillsbury, John Sargent, 4-77
Pilot Knob, KY, 3-65
Pima Indians, 6-16
Pimiento peppers, 3-50
Pin coral, 7-44
Pinchot, Gifford, 2-92
Pine, ponderosa, 6-107; 7-58
Pine Barrens, 2-63, 66
Pine Creek, 2-83
Pine Mts., 3-57
Pine cones, 7-60
Pine trees, 3-23; 5-49; 6-21, 107; 7-30, 58
Pineapples, 7-42, 44, 45, 46, 80, 91
Pineda, Alonzo Alvarez de, 5-44, 114
Pines, Monterey, 7-30
Pines, bristlecone, 7-30
Pineville, NC, 3-90
Pink dogwood, 3-49, 50
"Pinkie" (painting), 7-33
Pinon pine, 6-21, 107
"Pioneer" (statue), 7-62
Pioneer Gold Museum, 3-53
Pioneer Mural, 5-61*
Pioneer Square (Seattle, WA), 7-74
Pioneer Trail, 5-66
Pioneer life, 5-33, 65, 66
Pioneers, Hawaiian, 7-41
Piper Bldg. (Minneapolis, MN), 4-80*
Pipestone, 4-72, 78
Pipestone Nat. Mon., 4-80
Pippa Passes, KY, 3-64
Pirates, 1-102; 2-16, 21, 50; 3-23, 32, 101, 105; 4-86; 102; 7-83, 88, 93
Piscataqua Estuary, 1-85
Piscataqua River, 1-57, 85, 87, 95
Piscataway Indians, 2-43
Pitcher, Molly (Mary Ludwig), 2-59
Pitcherplant, 4-36
Pittsburgh, PA, 1-14; 2-83, 86, 87, 95, 96*, 111
Pittsburgh Civic Arena, 2-95
Pittsfield, MA, 1-77
Pixley, Benton, 5-30
"Places Rated Almanac" (book), 1-14, 20; 6-89
Plain people, 2-87
Plains, GA, 3-52
Plains Indian Museum, 6-122
Plains Indians, 4-43
Plainsman Museum of the Prairie

Pioneer, 5-66
Plant, H. B., 3-35
Plantains (bananas), 7-91
Plantation system, 2-29, 44; 3-74
Plantations, 7-94
"Planting the Colony" (painting), 2-10*
Plants, 1-11, 71, 79, 120; 2-21, 57, 93, 106, 120; 3-105, 106, 108, 120, 121; 4-22, 36, 78, 92; 5-21, 64, 92, 106, 120; 6-21, 36, 37, 46, 50, 51, 65, 92, 107, 120; 7-30, 42, 46, 58, 60, 62, 72, 80, 84, 91
Plastics, 1-107
Plates, Celeron exploration, 4-100, 101
Platte River, 1-7; 5-55, 58; 6-29
Platte Valley (NE), 5-63
Plenty Coups (chief), 6-64, 66
Plexiglass, 2-65
Plutonium, 7-70
Plymouth, CT, 1-50
Plymouth, MA, 1-24, 72, 73
Plymouth, NH, 1-92
Plymouth, VT, 1-117, 118
Plymouth Co., 1-87
Plymouth Colony, 1-44
Plymouth Notch, VT, 1-123
Plymouth Rock (MA), 1-24, 72, 79; 2-24
Pocahontas (Rebecca Rolfe), 2-38, 99, 101*, 105; 3-86
Pocahontas County, WV, 2-113
Pocasset (Portsmouth, RI), 1-102
Pocatello, ID, 6-47, 51, 53
Pock-marked Kid, 6-88
Pocomoke Assateague Indians, 2-43
Pocomoke Swamp (DE), 2-18, 22
Pocomtuc Indians, 1-71
Podunk Indians, 1-44
Poe, Edgar Allan, 2-21, 50, 106; 4-66
"Pogamue People" (book), 1-49
Poi, 7-45
Poinciana trees, 7-90
Poinsett, Joel, 3-104
Poinsettias, 3-36, 104, 105, 106
Point Barrow, AK, 5-90
Point Lobos (CA), 7-33
Point Pleasant, OH, 4-108
Point Reyes Nat. Seashore, 7-35
Point Roberts (WA/Canada), 7-65
Pokatello (chief), 6-53
Polar Caves (NH), 1-86
Polar bears, 7-17
Polaris submarines, 1-46
Polio, 2-76; 3-47
Polk, Antoinette, 3-120
Polk, James K., 3-7*, 90; 7-69
Polo, 1-104
Polygamy, 6-104
Polynesian crafts, 7-80
Polynesians, 7-39, 79, 80
Ponca Indians, 4-43; 5-57, 60, 85
Ponce, PR, 7-2
Ponce de Leon, Don Juan, 3-31; 7-88, 91
Ponderosa pine, 6-107; 7-58
Ponds, 1-99
Pontiac (chief), 2-87; 4-30, 58, 101
Pontotoc, MS, 3-77
Pontotoc Ridge (MS), 3-73
Pony Express, 4-88*, 92, 93, 94; 5-66, 105; 6-121, 122
Pootatuck Indians, 1-44
Popcorn, 1-59; 4-50, 108
Pope, John, 3-66
Pope, Nathaniel, 4-17
Popes, 4-47
Popham, George, 1-60
Poplar Bluff, MO, 4-85
Poplar tree, 4-36, 38
Population, 1-15, 16, 18, 19; 2-18, 67, 75, 90, 116; 4-23, 34, 59, 60, 75, 116, 118; 6-19, 60, 75, 89, 117; 7-13, 23, 28, 48, 49, 55, 56, 83, 89
Populist Party, 5-33

Porcelain, 2-64
Porcupine River, 7-11
Porgey fish, 2-64
Porpoises, 1-59
Port Angeles, WA, 7-76
Port Arthur, TX, 5-121
Port Chilkoot, AK, 7-20
Port Conway, VA, 2-104
Port Huron, MI, 2-111; 4-55
Port Royal, SC, 3-107, 108
Port Royale, GA, 3-45
Port Tobacco, MD, 2-49
Port of Chicago, 4-20, 23
Port of New Orleans, 5-51
Port of New York, 2-69, 78
Port of New York Authority, 2-61, 69
Port of Seattle, 7-73
Portage, WI, 4-113
Portage River, 4-97
Portaging, 4-113
Portal, ND, 5-81
Porter, Cole, 4-36
Porter, Gene Stratton, 4-35
Porter, Katherine Anne, 5-119
Porter, W. S. (O'Henry), 3-91
Portland, ME, 1-60, 61, 62, 64, 65
Portland, OR, 1-15; 7-52*, 60, 62
Portland Harbor (ME), 1-62
Portland Head Lighthouse, 1-65
Ports, 1-65, 79, 108; 2-23, 65, 66, 69, 78, 122; 3-94, 107, 122; 4-20, 23, 34, 65, 76, 105, 111, 118; 5-51, 52, 89, 121; 6-51, 65; 7-19, 20, 60, 62, 73, 74, 76, 91, 95
Portsmouth, NH, 1-65, 87, 88, 90, 93, 95
Portsmouth, NY, 1-89
Portsmouth, RI, 1-102, 108
Portsmouth, VA, 2-109
Portsmouth Naval Shipyard, 1-65
Portuguese explorers, 1-101
Portuguese fishermen, 1-60
Post, C. W., 4-64
Post, Wiley, 5-89; 7-14
Poston, Charles D., 6-20
Potash, 6-92, 108
Potassium salts, 5-113
Potassium sulfate, 6-24
Potatoes, 1-65, 67; 6-37, 51; 7-45
Potatoes, sweet, 7-93
Potawatomi Indians, 4-16, 17, 43, 57
Potlach, 7-67, 71
Potomac River, 2-27, 28, 29, 30, 31, 35, 41, 52, 97, 108, 111, 113, 114
Potwin, KS, 5-29
Poughkeepsie, NY, 2-78
Poultry, 1-108; 5-21, 64
Poultry products, 1-108; 2-65; 4-22
Pow-wows, 4-25
Powder River, 5-105
Powell, James, 6-18
Powell, John Wesley, 6-13, 20, 106
Powell, William H., 3-72; 4-103
Powers, Caleb, 3-60
Powhatan (chief), 2-99, 105; 3-85
Poynette, WI, 4-109
Prairie States Forestry Project, 5-36
Prairie chicken, 5-64
Prairie dogs, 5-36, 67, 92, 100, 120; 6-119, 120
Prairie du Chien, WI, 4-115, 123
Prairie fires, 5-30*, 102
Pratt, Jonathan, 3-22, 105
Pratt, Orson, 6-102
Prehistoric agriculture, 3-44; 6-30, 85
Prehistoric art, 5-72
Prehistoric customs, 1-59; 2-113; 4-28, 99, 113, 114; 5-16; 6-85, 115; 7-39, 43, 46, 48
Prehistoric customs (Hawaii), 7-39
Prehistoric dieties (HI), 7-39
Prehistoric mounds, 2-85, 99, 113; 3-16, 25, 44, 50*, 58, 71, 80, 113; 4-15, 28, 43, 57, 71, 85, 99, 109,

113; 5-16, 44, 85, 99, 113
Prehistoric mts., 2-28; 4-71; 7-51
Prehistoric peoples, 1-18, 43, 59, 71, 86, 100, 113; 2-41, 55, 83, 113; 3-15, 16, 25, 30, 44, 58, 71, 80, 85, 99, 113, 114; 4-15, 25, 28, 43, 57, 71, 85, 99, 109, 113; 5-15, 16, 29, 44, 57, 72, 85, 99, 113; 6-16, 30, 39, 45, 71, 85, 100, 115; 7-11, 23, 39, 53, 67, 82, 87, 96
Prehistoric plants, 6-44, 113
Prehistoric settlements, 3-16, 113, 114*; 4-85; 6-24
Prehistoric weapons, 2-41; 3-16; 4-57; 5-113; 6-100, 115; 7-11, 40
Prehistoric wildlife, 4-83, 85; 5-29, 50, 57, 99; 6-44, 85, 113; 7-17
Prescott, AZ, 6-18
Prescott, Richard, 1-103
Presidio, TX, 5-113
Presley, Elvis, 3-77, 118, 120, 123
Presque Isle, MI, 4-65
Presque Isle (Erie, PA), 2-86
Presque Isle Peninsula (PA), 2-89
Press, freedom of the, 2-73
Preston, MD, 2-52
Price, Leontyne, 3-77
Price, UT, 6-100
Priest, Ivy Baker, 6-106
Priestley, Joseph, 2-92
Prince del Drago (monkey), 1-107
"Prince of India, The" (book), 4-36
Prince of Wales, 5-117
Princeton, NJ, 1-25; 2-59, 66
Princeton Battlefield State Park (NJ), 2-66
Princeton Univ., 1-25; 2-60, 61, 62, 66, 105
Pring, Martin, 1-60, 87
Printing and publishing, 1-107
Printing press, 1-11
Printz, Johan, 2-15, 57, 85
Privateers, 2-46
"Pro Patria" (statue), 4-39
Proclamation of 1763, 4-30
Proctor, Henry A., 4-32
Proctor, VT, 1-121
Profile Lake, 1-86
Progressive Republican Party, 4-118
Prohibition, 3-75; 5-33
Promontory Point (UT), 6-107
Pronghorn antelope, 1-11; 6-107
Prophecy of Passaconaway, 1-86
Prophet (Tenskwatawa), 4-30*, 32, 35
Prophetstown, IN, 4-32
Proprietors' Co. for Providence Plantations, 1-102
Prospectors, 7-13
"Prosperity" (statue), 1-29
Protestant settlements, 3-100
Providence, RI, 1-24, 98*, 99, 100, 102, 103, 104, 108, 109
Providence River, 1-99, 101
Provincetown, MA, 1-24, 71, 72, 80
Provo, UT, 6-101, 104, 106, 108, 109
Provo Freedom Festival, 6-109
Provost, Etienne, 6-101
Provost Dungeon (Charleston, SC), 3-102*
Prudhoe Bay (AK), 7-18
Pruntytown, WV, 2-117
Pryor, MT, 6-66
Pueblo, CO, 6-32, 33
Pueblo Bonita (NM), 6-86
Pueblo Grande (UT), 6-71
Pueblo Grande Museum, 6-25
Pueblo Indians, 6-25, 86, 87
"Pueblo of Acoma" (painting), 6-86*
Pueblo people, 5-113; 6-16, 30, 31, 45, 71, 81, 86, 100
Pueblos, 1-27; 6-16, 71, 86, 87, 88, 91, 93, 94
Puerto Grande harbor (Culebra

Island), 7-87
Puerto Rico (main article), 7-87
Puerto Rico archipelago, 7-87
Puget, Peter, 7-67
Puget Sound (WA), 1-6; 7-65, 69, 73, 74
Pulitzer, Joseph, 4-91
Pulitzer Prize, 1-63; 2-21, 119; 3-48; 4-21, 35, 49, 91; 5-35; 6-21, 91
Pullen, Harriet (Mother), 7-15
Pullman, WA, 6-52; 7-76
Pulman, George, 4-21
Pulp and paper industry, 1-64
Pumice, 6-92
Pumpkin Center, MO, 4-91
Pumpkins, 1-86, 120*
Puowaina Crater, 7-49
Purdue Univ., 4-38
Purgatoire River, 6-30
Puritans, 1-44, 73, 77, 101
Purple Heart decoration, 1-45
Purple fringed orchid, 4-92
Put-in-Bay, OH, 4-102
Putnam, Amelia Earhart, 5-34, 36
Putnam, Israel, 1-47
Pyle, Ernie, 6-91
Pyle, Howard, 2-21
Pyramid Lake, 6-69, 71, 77
Pyramid mounds, 3-113
Quadra, Juan de Bodega Y, 7-67
Quadricentennial celebration (NJ), 2-61
Quahaug clams, 1-101, 107
Quake Lake, 6-61
Quaker Oats Co., 4-51
Quakers, 1-44, 106; 2-16, 86, 88, 90, 91
Quality of life, 1-13
Qualla Boundary (NC), 3-94, 95
Quantrill, William Clark, 3-60; 5-31
Quapaw Indians, 1-16, 25, 85
Quapaw Quarter (Little Rock, AR), 5-25
Quarries (Indian), 2-29
Quartz, 6-77
Que Island (PA), 2-92
Queen Anne's War, 1-61, 102
"Queen Mary" (ship), 7-32
Queens, NY, 2-71
Quidnick, RI, 1-101
Quincy, MA, 1-81
Quinnehtukgut (CT River), 1-43
Quito Sueno Bank (Caribbean island), 7-96
Quonset, RI, 1-101
Quonset Point (RI), 1-104
Quonset hut, 1-104
Rabbits (Jackrabbits), 5-36
Raccoon River, 4-97
Raccoons, 1-11
Race relations, 2-48, 102; 3-19, 21; 4-62; 5-19
Racine, WI, 4-116
Raddison, Pierre Esprit, 4-115
Radio, 7-42
Radio transmission, 3-63
Radium, 6-36
Rafting, 1-67; 6-52*
Rafting the Salmon River, 6-52*
Raido, 4-23, 123
Railroad Town (Grand Island, NE), 5-66
Railroads, 1-66, 89, 94; 2-23, 59, 60, 62, 74, 117; 3-34, 35, 51, 77, 107, 122; 4-23, 32, 45, 46, 76, 77, 93; 5-32, 36, 38, 40, 60, 65, 75, 80, 102, 103, 188; 6-23, 35, 37, 38, 39, 48, 51, 65, 66, 79, 81, 93, 104, 107, 109, 116, 117, 122; 7-14, 15, 18, 19, 27, 29, 65, 66, 70, 73
Rainbow Bridge (UT), 6-99, 100, 104
Rainbow Bridge Nat. Mon., 6-19
Rainbow Canyon of the Badlands

(WY), 6-113
Rainbow Row (Charleston, SC), 3-108
Rainforest (OR), 7-61*
Raisin River Massacre, 4-59
Rajneesh, (Bhagwan) Shree, 7-56
Raleigh, NC, 1-25; 3-84*, 90, 95
Raleigh, Walter, 3-86
Raleigh-Durham, NC, 1-14, 25
Ramsey, Alexander, 4-74
Ranchos, 7-26
Ranchos de Taos, NM, 6-93
Randall, Alexander, 4-117
Randolph, Peyton, 2-106
Randolph Center, VT, 1-121
Rangeley Lakes, 1-66
Rangers, Ethan Allen's, 1-48
Rankin, Jeannette, 6-61, 64
Ransom, Truman, 1-117
Rapid City, SD, 5-103
Rapp, George, 2-95
Rappahannock River, 2-97
Rashford, Coles, 4-116
Ravens.wood, WV, 2-117
Ray, Robert, 4-47
Rayburn, Sam, 5-119
Razerback hog, 5-21
Razor clams, 7-17
Razorbacks (AR football team), 5-23
"Reader's Digest" (magazine), 5-13
Reading, PA, 2-94
Reagan, Ronald, 1-105; 2-35; 3-48, 61, 90; 4-105; 5-76, 89, 104; 6-19, 118; 7-28
Ream, Vinnie, 2-36; 4-120
Reapers, 2-107
"Rebecca of Sunnybrook Farm" (book), 1-63
Reclamation, 7-73
Reconstruction, 3-19, 75, 89, 102, 104, 117; 4-89; 5-18, 47
Recreation, 1-14, 80; 2-55, 37, 38, 53, 67, 111, 117; 4-65, 66, 81; 5-67, 103, 109; 6-23, 52, 77, 80, 81, 93, 121, 123; 7-23, 33, 39, 62, 76, 84
Red Banks (WI), 4-114
Red Cloud, NE, 5-63, 67
Red Cloud (chief), 5-57, 105; 6-116, 118
Red Desert, 6-123
Red Lake, 4-69, 73
Red Lake River, 4-69
Red Mt. Museum, 3-25
Red Oak, IA, 4-46
Red Paint (Ochre) people, 1-59, 113
Red River, 1-7; 5-15, 41, 44, 53, 71, 79, 81, 83, 113
Red River Campaign, 5-47
Red River Revel, 5-53
Red River Valley, 4-73, 79, 81; 5-71, 72, 79
Red River of the North, 1-29; 4-69, 79, 81
Red River oxcart, 5-80
Red Rock Amphitheater (CO), 6-39
Red Rock Canyon (NV), 6-81
Red Room, White House, 2-38
Red cedar, 6-50
Red granite, 4-121
Redbud (tree), 5-92
Redfield, SD, 5-109
Redwood cypress, 6-44
Redwood trees, 7-30, 35, 58
Redwoods, coastal, 7-30
Reed, Thomas Brackett (Czar), 1-64
Reelfoot Lake, 3-121
Reeves, Bud, 5-78
Reeves, Isaac, 2-22
Reform movements, 2-60
Reformed Dutch Church, 1-31
Regulators, 3-88

Rehoboth, DE, 2-22, 25
Rehoboth Bay (DE), 2-15
Rehoboth Beach (DE), 2-25
Reindeer, 7-16, 17
Religious beliefs, 1-15
Religious co-op, 4-52
Religious freedom, 1-101, 102, 105; 2-43, 44, 49; 4-88, 94, 103; 6-104; 7-43
Remington, Frederic, 2-77; 5-94; 6-62, 63
Remington Art Museum, 6-62
Renaissance Center (Detroit, MI), 4-62, 67
Renaissance Center Project (Kansas City, KS), 5-38
Rendezvous of the trappers, 6-102, 116
Reno, Marcus, 6-60
Reno, NV, 6-69, 71, 74, 78, 79, 81
Reorganized Church of Jesus Christ of Latter Day Saints, 4-94
Republic of West Florida, 3-73
Republican Party, 4-60, 116; 7-28
Republican River, 5-58; 6-29
Republican elephant, 2-63
Research, 1-11, 92, 107, 120, 121; 2-21, 51, 63, 77, 93, 106, 120, 121; 3-50, 51, 78, 92, 93, 106, 119, 121; 4-22, 36, 50, 60, 64, 78, 79, 92, 101, 108; 5-21, 36, 49, 64, 78, 79, 92; 6-22, 36, 64, 65, 77, 78, 79, 91, 92, 106, 107, 120; 7-18, 30, 31, 57, 58, 59, 60, 72, 83, 90, 94
Restoration, 1-66, 80; 2-24, 39, 53, 94, 95, 108, 109, 122; 3-41, 95, 108, 122; 4-25, 93, 94, 108; 5-23, 25, 52, 80, 81, 122; 6-37, 39, 122; 7-32, 33, 62, 74, 76, 77, 91, 95
Revere, Paul, 1-77, 88; 2-105; 3-19; 7-27
Revolutionary War, 1-45, 47, 48, 50, 61, 68, 75, 88, 89, 102, 103, 104, 106; 2-16, 29, 30, 45, 46, 58, 66, 73, 88, 91, 100, 102, 106, 109, 115; 3-8, 18, 32, 46, 58, 73, 88, 102, 105, 114, 115; 4-16, 30, 31, 58, 74, 86, 101, 115; 5-49, 58; 7-25
Reynolds, R. J., 3-91
Rhine River (Europe), 5-43
Rhinebeck, NY, 1-31
Rhinelander, WI, 4-124
Rhode Island (RI), 1-99, 102
Rhode Island (main article), 1-97
Rhode Island Heritage Week, 1-103
Rhode Island Opera Guild, 1-105
Rhode Island Philharmonic Orch., 1-105
Rhode Island red chicken, 1-105, 108
Rhododendrons, 3-94; 7-61, 72
Rib Mt., 4-113, 120
Ribaut, Jean, 3-31, 32, 45
Rice, 3-106; 5-21, 47, 50
Rice, David, 4-91
Richard, Gabriel, 4-59, 63
Richford, NY, 2-77
Richland, WA, 7-70, 73, 77
Richland Center, WI, 4-119
Richmond, VA, 1-25; 2-98*, 101, 109, 111, 119
Riggs Mem. Museum, Lynn, 5-94
Riley, James Whitcomb, 4-35
Ring-tailed cat, 6-36
Ringing Rocks (PA), 2-94
Ringling Brothers, 4-123
Ringling Museum, 3-39
Ringneck Chinese pheasant, 5-109
Rio Brazos de Dios (stream), 5-113
Rio Grande River, 1-7; 5-113, 114, 116, 117, 119, 122; 6-29, 83

Rio de Janeiro, Brazil, 1-57
Rio de las Palmas, (TX), 5-114
Rische, Auguste, 6-35
Ritty, James, 4-104, 106
River Walk (San Antonio, TX), 5-122
River of No Return (Salmon River), 6-43, 52
Rivera, Juis Munoz, 7-90
Riverbend Music Center, OH, 4-109
Riverfront Park (Little Rock, AR), 5-25
Riverfront Park (Spokane, WA), 7-76, 77*
Riverfront Stadium (OH), 4-109
Rivers, 1-6, 7, 10, 27, 29, 30, 41, 43, 57, 69, 85, 99, 113; 2-13, 15, 27, 28, 41, 52, 55, 58, 66, 69, 71, 83, 97, 111, 112; 3-15, 30, 43, 55, 57, 69, 71, 97, 99, 113, 114, 122; 4-13, 16, 27, 28, 41, 55, 69, 71, 83, 93, 97, 111, 113; 5-13, 15, 16, 17, 18, 19, 22, 27, 28, 31, 32, 38, 39, 41, 43, 44, 45, 49, 51, 53, 55, 58, 59, 69, 71, 83, 97, 100, 108; 6-29, 35, 41, 43, 46, 47, 52, 55, 59, 69, 71, 85, 99, 106, 113, 119, 121; 7-11, 19, 22, 39, 48, 51, 55, 56, 60, 63, 65, 71, 77, 87
Riverton, CT, 1-49
Riviera of America (Atlantic City, NJ), 2-66
Riviera of the South (MS Gulf Coast), 3-81
Roadrunners, 6-91
Roan Mt., 3-94, 122*
Roan Mt. State Park (TN), 3-122*
Roanoke Island (NC), 3-86
Roberts, Kenneth, 1-64, 114
Robidoux, Antoine, 6-102
Robin Hood, 1-118
Robinson, Bill (Bojangles), 2-106
Robinson, Edwin Arlington, 1-63
Robinson family (HI), 7-44, 48, 49
Roc River, 4-113
Rochambeau, Jean Baptiste (Comete de), 1-103
Rochester, MN, 4-77, 81
Rochester, NY, 2-78, 80, 111
Rock, Howard (Skivoan Weyahok), 7-16
Rock City (KS), 5-27
Rock Creek (DC), 2-27, 28
Rock Creek Park (DC), 2-34
Rock of Ages Co., 1-121
Rockaway, OR, 7-62
Rockefeller, John D. IV., 2-118
Rockefeller, John D. Sr., 2-77, 79; 4-104
Rockefeller, Nelson A., 1-30; 2-76, 78; 5-19
Rockefeller, Winthrop, 5-19, 22
Rockefeller Center (NYC), 2-80
Rockefeller Park (Cleveland, OH), 4-109
Rocket power, 2-50
Rockport, MA, 1-80
Rockwell, KY, 3-89
Rockwell, Norman, 4-63
Rocky Brook, RI, 1-106
Rocky Butte (OR), 7-62
Rocky Mountain elk, 7-58
Rocky Mountain goats, 6-64
Rocky Mountain sheep, 6-107
Rocky Mt. Nat. Park, 6-38
Rocky Mts., 1-6; 4-99; 5-57, 77; 6-27, 29, 46, 55, 83, 85, 111, 113
Rocky Point, RI, 1-104
Rodeos, 5-94, 121; 6-80, 122
Rodney, Caesar, 2-16*, 20, 24
Rodney Square (Wilmington, DE), 2-24
Roebling, John A., 2-63; 3-60
Roger Williams Bandstand, 1-109

Roger Williams Landing Place Mon., 1-109
Roger Williams Museum of Natural History, 1-109
Roger Williams Nat. Mem., 1-109
Roger Williams Park (Providence, RI), 1-109
Roger Williams Zoo, 1-109
Rogers, Robert, 1-114; 4-58
Rogers, Will, 1-27; 5-89, 94, 95; 6-35, 38; 7-14
Rogers Mem., Will, 5-94
Rogers Rangers, 1-114
Roggeveen, Jacob, 7-79
Rogue River War, 7-55
Rolfe, John, 2-99, 105
Rolfe, Rebecce (Pocahontas), 2-38, 99, 101*, 105; 3-86
Rolfe, Thomas, 2-105
Rolla, ND, 5-72
Rolvaag, Ole Edvart, 4-78; 5-104
Romain Nat. Refuge, 3-106
Rome, GA, 3-19
Romney, WV, 2-117
Roncador island (caribbean), 7-96
Roofless Church (IN), 4-32*, 38
Roosevelt, Eleanor, 2-36, 77
Roosevelt, F. D., 1-67; 2-18, 24, 35, 36, 75, 76, 77; 3-47, 53; 4-35, 49, 89, 90; 5-34, 48, 103; 6-106, 119
Roosevelt, F. D. Jr., 2-18
Roosevelt, John, 2-105
Roosevelt, Theodore, 1-89; 2-75, 76, 77, 78, 81; 3-34; 4-48, 76, 106, 118; 5-62, 64, 69, 76, 77, 80, 81, 94, 104, 107; 6-33, 61, 117
Roosevelt Campobello International Park, 1-67
Roosevelt Dam, 6-20
Roosevelt Field (airport), 2-75
Roosevelt Nat. Mem. Park, Theodore, 5-71*, 80, 81
Roosevelt elk, 7-72
Root, Jim, 4-76
Rosado, Julio, 7-90
Rose Bowl Parade, 7-33
Rose Bowl football game, 7-33
Rose Festival (Portland, OR), 7-59*, 62
Rose Island (IN), 4-28
Rose Island (SA), 7-79
Rose Mantle (HI), 7-47
Rosebud River, 5-105
Rosecliff (Newport, RI), 1-108
Roses, 1-11
Ross, Betsy, 2-94
Ross, Nellie Tayloe, 5-119; 6-118, 119
Ross, Robert, 2-47
Rothermel, Peter F., 1-30; 2-95
Rough Rider Hotel (ND), 5-77, 80
Rough Riders, 3-34; 5-77, 80, 81
"Rounding a Bend" (print), 3-9*
Roundup Cavalcade, International, 5-94
Royal Canadian Air Force, 3-76
Royal English Rangers, 4-58
Royal Gorge, 6-31, 33
Royal Gorge Bridge, 6-33
Royal palace and throne room (HI), 7-49
Royal palms, 7-94
Royall, Ann, 2-119, 120
Royalton, VT, 1-119
Rubber, 1-48
Rubber products, 4-107
Ruby Falls, 3-122
Ruckersville, VA, 2-99
Rug weaving, mechanical, 1-79
Rugby, ND, 5-81
Ruidoso, NM, 6-95
Rum, 7-95
Rumph, Samuel H., 3-48
Rumsey, James, 2-50, 116
Running Antelope (Indian), 5-78
Ruscarora Indians, 2-71

Rushmore, Charles E., 5-107
Rushmore Mem., 5-102, 103*
Russell, Charles M., 5-94; 6-62, 66, 67
Russell, Lillian, 4-5C
Russell Cave Nat. Mon., 3-15, 16, 25
Russia vs. Japan war, 1-89; 2-76
Russian Fort, 7-48
Russian grain embargo, 3-48
Russian settlements, 5-33; 7-13, 23
Russian wild boars, 3-121
Russin, Robert, 6-123
Rutgers Univ., 2-60, 62, 66
Ruth, George Herman (Babe), 2-51
Rutherford, NJ, 2-63
Rutherford B. Hayes Lib. and Mus. State Mem. (OH), 4-108
Rutland, VT, 1-119, 122
Rye, NH, 1-87
Sabin, J. C., 4-46
Sabine River, 5-41, 115
Sacajawea (Indian guide), 6-46, 64
Sachems (chiefs), 1-100
Sackett's Cave, 1-43
Saco, ME, 1-60
Sacramento, CA, 1-8*, 27; 7-29, 35
Sacramento Peak, 6-95
Sacramento Valley, 1-8*
"Sacred Cod" (carving), 1-78
Sacred Heart Mission, 6-47
Sagamore (Indian title), 1-100
Sagamore Hill, 2-81
"Sagebrush Rebellion", 6-75
Saguaro Nat. Mon., 6-24
Saguaro cactus, 6-21
Sailboats, 7-76
Saint Maries, ID, 6-47
Saint-Gaudens, Augustus, 1-92, 95
Saint-Gaudens Museum, 1-95
Sainthood, 2-51
Sakonnet River, 1-99
Salal berries, 7-72
Salem, IL, 1-26
Salem, MA, 1-73, 80
Salem, NH, 1-93
Salem, OR, 1-29; 7-55, 57, 60, 62
Salina, KS, 5-29
Salina, OK, 5-86
Salisbury, NC, 3-90
Salisbury, NH, 1-90
Sallisaw, OK, 5-90
Salmon, 1-64, 67, 120; 4-22; 6-46, 77; 7-15, 17, 53, 56, 58, 72, 73, 76
Salmon Falls River, 1-57, 85
Salmon River, 6-43, 45, 52
Salt Lake City, UT, 1-29, 53; 6-19, 97, 98*, 102, 104, 105, 106, 107
Salt Lake City, UT (North State St. in early days), 6-103*
Salt Lake Valley, 6-102
Salt Museum, 2-80
Salt Palace Center (Salt Lake City, UT), 6-109
Salt River, 6-18
Salt and salt mining, 2-78, 80, 113, 121; 4-22, 64, 108; 5-5, 36, 49; 6-91, 92
Salton Sea State Park (CA), 7-31
Sam Houston Schoolhouse (TN), 3-123
Samoset (chief), 1-60, 73
San Antonio, Fiesta of, 5-123
San Antonio, TX, 1-10, 19, 21; 3-22; 5-10*, 115, 117, 119, 122, 123
San Bernardino, CA, 6-104
San Cristobal (San Juan, PR), 7-88, 91
San Diego, CA, 1-19; 7-23, 25, 31, 32
San Diego Bay (CA), 7-23, 25, 31
San Diego Zoo, 7-31
San Elizario Presidio chapel (El Paso, TX), 5-122
San Felip de Neri Church (Albuquerque, NM), 6-94
San Felipe de Austin, TX, 5-115

San Francisco, CA, 1-8*, 13, 14, 51; 4-106; 5-36; 6-77; 7-27, 28, 35, 41
San Francisco Bay (CA), 7-23, 28, 34
"San Francisco Peaks" (painting), 6-3*
San Francisco World's Fair, 7-28
San Jacinto Mon. (TX), 5-123
San Juan, PR, 7-87, 88, 90, 91
San Juan County, CO, 6-37
San Juan Islands (WA), 7-69, 76
San Juan Mts., 6-29
San Juan River, 6-85, 99
San Luis (park), CO, 6-29
San Luis Valley (CO), 6-31, 37
San Marino, CA, 7-33
San Miguel de Guadalup (SC), 3-100
San Rafael Swell (UT), 6-100
San Xavier Indians, 6-24
San Xavier del Bac (White Dove of the Desert Mission, AZ), 6-17, 18, 24, 25
Sand Hills (NE), 5-57, 67
Sandburg, Carl, 3-91; 4-21
Sandhills State Park (TX), 5-113
Sandia Base (NM), 6-95
Sandia Mts., 6-85
Sandia Nat. Labs., 6-95
Sandia people, 6-85
Sandoz, Mari, 5-63
Sandpoint, ID, 6-53
Sandusky, OH, 4-99
Sandusky River, 4-97
Sandwich Islands (HI), 7-40
Sandy Point, NJ, 2-57
Sangre de Cristo Mts., 6-30, 83
Sanibel Island (FL), 3-30, 39
Santa Anna, Antonio Lopez de, 5-115, 116
Santa Barbara, CA, 7-33
Santa Barbara Channel (CA), 7-25
Santa Barbara Islands (CA), 7-25
Santa Catalina Island (CA), 7-25
Santa Catalina Mts., 6-15
Santa Clara, 2-63
Santa Cruz, CA, 7-30
Santa Fe, NM, 1-27; 6-31, 84*, 85, 87, 88, 89, 91, 95, 101
Santa Fe Opera Assn., 6-95
Santa Fe RR, 5-40; 6-93
Santa Fe Southern Pacific Corp., 6-8
Santa Fe Trail, 4-88; 5-30, 38; 6-31, 88, 93
Santa Rosa Island (CA), 7-25
Santee River, 3-105
"Sap's a runnin", 1-121
Sapphire, NC, 3-92
Sapphire Pool (Yellowstone), 6-121
Sapphires, 3-92; 6-64
Sarasota, FL, 3-39
Saratoga (Schuylerville, NY), 2-73
Sargent, Winthrop, 4-31
Saroyan, William, 7-29
Sarpy, Peter, 5-58
Sassafras, 1-87
Satellites, 2-65
"Saturday Review" (magazine), 2-21
Sauk Centre, MN, 4-75, 78
Sauk Indians, 4-16, 17
Sault Sainte Marie, MI, 4-57, 66
Sausalito, CA, 7-34
Savannah, GA, 3-45, 46, 47, 51, 52*, 102
"Savannah" (steamship), 3-46
Savannah River, 3-43, 45, 51, 97, 99
Sawatch Mts., 6-29
Sawdust Charlie, 6-88
Sawmills, 6-92
Sawtooth Mts., 6-43
Sawyer, Henry W., 2-60
Saye (Viscount), William Fiennes, 1-44
Scandinavian settlements, 4-76

Scarborough, ME, 1-61
Scheffer, George, 7-48
Schenectady, NY, 2-72, 78
Scheyichbi Indians, 2-56
Schiffli embroidery, 2-65
Schoolcraft, Henry R., 4-69
Schurz, (Mrs.) Carl, 4-116
Schuyler, Claude, 2-21
Schuyler, Philip J., 1-119; 2-73
Schuylerville, NY, 2-73
Schwab, Charles M., 2-92
Scioto River, 4-97
Scituate Reservoir, 1-99
Scopes, John T., 3-117
Scopes "Monkey" trial, 5-63
Scott, Dred, 4-88
Scott, Walter E. (Death Valley Scotty), 7-29
Scott, Winfield, 2-51; 3-88
Scotts Bluff Nat. Mon., 5-67
Scrimshaw, 7-12
Sea Lion Point (OR), 7-58
Sea grapes, 7-94
Sea lions, 7-19, 30, 58, 62
Sea otters, 7-17, 19, 26, 30, 58
Sea turkeys, 7-58, 62
Sea turtles, 3-50
Sea-Arama Marineworld (TX), 5-123
Seabees, Navy, 1-104
Seabrook Nuclear Power Plant (NH), 1-93
Seaford, DE, 2-25
Seagull Mon. (UT), 6-104, 106, 109
Seagulls, 6-103, 104, 107
Sealing, 1-52
Seals, 1-59, 64; 7-17, 19, 58
Sears Tower (Chicago, IL), 4-20
Seattle, WA, 1-14; 7-66*, 69, 70, 73, 74
Seattle (chief), 7-71
Seattle Art Museum, 7-74
Seattle Center, 7-74
Seattle Mariners (baseball), 7-74
Seattle Seahawks (football), 7-74
Seattle Supersonics (basketball), 7-74
Seattle Symphony, 7-74
"Seawing" (steamer), 4-75
Sebago Lake, ME, 1-65
Sedona, AZ, 6-24
Seekonk River, 1-99
Seely, John Henry, 6-106
Seely, Martin, 7-30
Seewee Indian Shell Mound (SC), 3-99
Seewee Indians, 3-99
Selfridge, Harry Gordon, 4-64
Selma, AL, 2-18
Seminole Indians, 3-33, 35, 118; 5-86, 94
Seminole War, 3-33; 5-20
Senate, U.S., 2-31, 59; 5-20, 118
Senate Foreign Relations Committee, 5-20; 6-49
Seneca Falls, NY, 2-80
Seneca Indians, 2-85
Seneca Lake, 2-80
Seneca Trail, 2-114
Sequin (River) Indians, 1-43
Sequoia Nat. Park, 7-30, 35
Sequoia trees, 7-30
Sequoyah (George Gist), 1-19; 3-9*, 22*; 5-86, 90, 91*, 95
Sequoyah (proposed state), 5-88
Sequoyah Caverns (AL), 3-25
Serpent Mound State Mem. (OH), 4-109
Serra, Junipero, 7-25, 28, 29
Serrana Island (Caribbean), 7-96
Sesquicentennial (AR), 5-19, 25
Sesquicentennial (TX), 5-117
Seton, Elizabeth Ann, 2-51
Settlements, American, 3-33; 4-31; 5-115; 6-60; 7-69
Settlements, Danish, 4-76

Settlements, Dutch, 1-44; 2-15, 57, 72, 85; 4-45*, 67
Settlements, English, 1-60, 114; 2-44, 57, 72, 99, 109; 3-45, 86, 87, 117
Settlements, Eskimo, 7-21
Settlements, European, 1-44, 87; 3-52, 58, 73, 99; 4-86, 115; 5-16, 31, 100, 115; 6-102; 7-25, 53, 69
Settlements, Finnish, 4-76
Settlements, French, 1-60, 114; 3-17, 31, 45, 58, 73; 4-16, 30, 57, 86; 5-45, 85, 86
Settlements, German, 2-87, 94, 115; 4-122
Settlements, Mennonite, 5-33
Settlements, Mormon, 4-18, 60, 88; 6-14, 18, 47, 81, 102, 116
Settlements, Norwegian, 4-76
Settlements, Protestant, 3-100
Settlements, Russian, 5-33; 7-13, 23
Settlements, Scandinavian, 4-76
Settlements, Spanish, 2-99; 3-17, 31, 32, 45, 58, 73, 99, 100; 5-30, 31, 85, 114; 6-17, 87; 7-25, 88
Settlements, Swedish, 2-15, 18, 24, 57, 85; 4-76; 5-33
Settlements, Swiss, 4-123
Settlements, Welsh, 4-123
Settlements, prehistoric, 3-16, 113, 114*; 4-85; 6-24
Settlers, 1-11; 5-74, 75
Seven Cities of Cibola, 6-87
Seven Falls (CO), 6-38
Seven Hills of Taos (NM), 6-92
"Seventeen" (book), 4-35
Seventeen Mile Drive (CA), 7-33
Sevier, John, 3-115
Sevier Lake, 6-99
Sevier River, 6-99
Sewanee sandstone, 3-121
Seward, AK, 7-16, 18, 20
Seward, William H., 2-76; 7-13
Seward's Folly, 7-13
Sewing machine, 1-91; 2-64
Shadwell, VA, 2-108
Shaker Museum, 1-66
Shaker Village Hist. Dist., 1-66
Shakespeare Festivals, 1-122; 3-24, 108
Shakos (headdress), 3-65
Shamans (medicine men), 7-67
Shanks, Charles B., 4-107
Sharon, VT, 1-119
Sharp, Louis H., 6-11
Sharpsburg, MD, 2-48
Shaw, Ervin, 3-104
Shaw Air Force Base, SC, 3-104
Shawnee, OK, 5-91
Shawnee Indians, 2-85; 4-28, 35, 100, 101
Shawneetown, AR, 5-20
Shay, Daniel, 1-75
Shay's Rebellion, 1-75
Sheaffer Pen Co., 4-51
Sheboygan, WI, 4-122
Shedd Aquarium, 4-23
Sheep, 1-48
Sheepeater Indians, 6-46, 47, 58, 115
Shelburne Museum (VT), 1-122
Sheldon, Charles M., 5-35
Sheldon Mem. Art Gallery, 5-67
Shell Canyon (WY), 6-113
Shellfish, 1-44
Shelling (sea shells), 3-40
Shenandoah, VA, 2-101
Shenandoah Nat. Park, 2-102, 109
Shenandoah Valley (VA), 2-97
Sheperdstown, WV, 2-115, 123
Shepherd, Alan, 3-34
Shepherd, Thomas, 2-115
Sheridan, Philip H., 4-106
Sherman, Robert, 1-48
Sherman, William T., 3-47, 75, 109; 4-106

Sherman Hill (Laramie, WY), 6-123
Sheyenne River, 5-71
Shikellamy (chief), 2-92
Shiloh, TN, 3-113
Shiloh Church (TN), 3-116
Ship Island (MS), 3-73, 74
Shipbuilding, 1-46, 51, 60, 62, 65, 66, 93, 107; 2-16, 61, 66, 89, 102; 3-23, 47, 79; 7-56, 57
Shiprock (NM), 6-95
Sholes, Christopher L., 4-117, 119
Shortia plant, 3-91
Shoshone (Snake) Indians, 6-45, 49, 58, 72, 100, 118
Shoshone Nat. Forest, 6-122
"Shot heard round the world", 1-75
Shoup, ID, 6-45
Shreve, Henry, 5-53
Shreveport, LA, 5-47, 53
Shrimp, 7-17
Shrine to the Sun (Will Rogers Mem., CO), 6-35, 38
Siamese Twins (Eng & Chang), 3-92
Siberia, 7-12, 16
Sibley, Henry Hastings, 4-75, 77
Siboney Indians, 7-93
Sideburns, 1-106; 4-34
Sieber, Al, 6-20
Sierra Mts., 1-8*
Sierra Nevada Mts., 6-69; 7-23, 25, 35
Silk industry, 2-64
Siloam Springs, AR, 5-23
Silver, 1-11; 4-92; 6-20, 21, 22, 36, 48, 50, 51, 81, 91, 107, 108
Silver Bluff, SC, 3-100
Silver City, ID, 6-53
Silver Dollar City, MO, 4-94
Silver Spring, MD, 2-48
Silversmith, 1-77
Silversword plant, 7-46
Silverton, CO, 6-39
Silverware, 1-107
Simpson, John, 1-89
Simpson, Wallis Warfield, 2-51
Sinagua Indians, 6-25
Sinclair, Elizabeth, 7-43
Singer, Isaac M., 2-64
Singer sewing machines, 2-64
Singing River, 3-71
Single Tax Theory, 2-25
Sioux City, IA, 4-44, 53
Sioux Falls, SD, 5-99, 104, 106, 108
Sioux Indians, 2-71, 99; 4-71, 72*, 74, 75, 77, 114; 5-60, 67, 72, 99, 100, 103, 105; 6-31, 115
Sioux Lookout (NE), 5-60
Sisseton, SD, 5-99
Sisseton Indians, 4-43
Sitka, AK, 7-13, 19
Sitka Indians, 6-13
Sitting Bull (chief), 5-74, 75, 81, 102, 105; 6-61
Siva (dance), 7-35
Six Nations, 2-43, 71, 83, 85
Skagit River, 7-65
Skagway, AK, 7-15, 20
Skamania, WA, 7-65
"Skeleton in Armor, The" (poem), 1-101
Skenandoah (chief), 2-77
Skicoworos (Indian), 1-60
Skiing (snow), 1-66, 94, 122, 123
Skitswish Indians, 6-45
Skokomish River, 7-8*
Skyline Drive (Charlotte Amalie, VI), 7-95
Skyline Drive (Shenandoah Nat. Park), 2-109
Skyscrapers, 2-55, 95; 3-52; 4-20; 6-33, 105; 7-33, 74
Slab-House people, 5-85
Slade, KY, 3-55
Slater, Samuel, 1-106

Slater's Mill, 1-106, 107, 108
Slavery, 1-18, 46, 61, 75, 78, 89, 90, 91, 104, 117, 118; 2-17, 29, 32, 44, 47, 49, 51, 74, 89, 100, 101, 102, 116, 119, 120; 3-31, 46, 59, 60, 62, 74, 102, 116, 117; 4-18, 33, 60, 75, 87, 88, 89, 103, 116; 5-31, 49, 86; 6-31, 74, 101; 7-55, 67, 88, 94
Sleepy Hollow Cemetery (NY), 2-79
Slim Buttes fossil beds (SD), 5-99
Slope, The (ND), 5-71
Smackover, AR, 5-19
Smallpox epidemics, 5-63, 73, 74
Smedley, Samuel, 1-50
Smith, Alfred E., 2-75
Smith, Harry Lewis, 3-91
Smith, Hiram, 4-120
Smith, James, 2-87
Smith, Jedediah Strong, 6-101
Smith, John, 1-72, 87; 2-29, 43, 85, 99, 105
Smith, Joseph, 1-119; 2-77; 4-18, 103; 6-105
Smith, Kate, 2-87
Smith, Kirby, 5-18
Smith, Samantha, 1-62
Smith, Samuel Francis, 1-63
Smith Brothers (cough drops), 2-77
Smith Center, KS, 5-27
Smithsonian Institution, 2-29, 38; 6-20, 76
Smoke tree, 4-92
Smoky Mt. Nat. Park, 3-94, 122
Smyth, Thomas A., 2-18
Snake (Shoshone) Indians, 6-45, 49, 58, 72, 100, 118
Snake River, 6-41, 43, 44, 45, 46, 47, 52, 69, 113, 119, 121; 7-51, 63, 65, 70, 77
Snake River Navigation Project, 6-48
Snake River Plain, 6-44
Snake-Columbia Waterway, 6-51
Snelling, Josiah, 4-74
Snowmobiling, 6-109
Snowshoes, 4-57
Snowy Heron, 5-50
Snowy Range, 6-123
Snuff, 2-23, 122
Soccer, 4-24
Society for Establishing Useful Manufacturers, 2-64
Sod houses, 4-75; 6-60
Soda ash, 6-120
Sodium sulphate, 5-78
Soldiers and Sailors Mon. (IN), 4-39
Solomon, Haym, 2-88
Somerset, OH, 4-106
Somerville, NJ, 2-59
"Song of Hiawatha, The" (poem), 4-72
Sonoma, CA, 7-35
Sons of Daniel Boone (club), 3-64
Sons of Liberty, 1-88
Soo Canal, 4-65
Sorghum, 6-37, 92
Sotol, 4-92
Soulier Rouge (chief), 5-49
Sousa, John Philip, 2-36
South Amherst, OH, 4-108
South Battery (Charleston, SC), 3-108*
South Bend, IN, 4-28, 37, 38
South Boston, VA, 2-107
South Carolina (main article), 3-97
South Dakota (main article), 5-97
South Fork Dam, 2-90
South Killingly, CT, 1-50
South Kingstown, RI, 1-101, 106
South Mt., 2-94
South Orange, NJ, 2-62
South Park, CO, 6-29, 31, 34
South Pass, WY, 6-119
South Pole, 1-64
South Seaport (NYC), 2-81

Southern Baptist Theological Seminary, 3-66
Southern Christian Leadership Conference, 3-49
Southern Ozarks, 4-13
Southern Plains Indian Museum & Craft Center, 5-94
Southern Univ. of Baton Rouge, 5-53
Southern hemisphere, 7-79
Southgate, KY, 3-61
Southington, CT, 1-41
Southwest Territory, 3-115
"Sower, The" (statue), 5-67
Soybeans, 3-107; 4-50, 92, 108; 5-21, 50
Space Center, Lyndon B. Johnson, 5-123
Space Museums, 3-10*, 37
Space Needle (Seattle, WA), 7-74
Spalding, ID, 6-50, 52
Spanich settlements, 6-17, 87
Spanish Diggings, (WY), 6-115
Spanish Landing, 3-31*
Spanish moss, 3-79; 5-50
Spanish settlements, 2-99; 3-17, 31, 32, 45, 58, 99, 100; 5-30, 31, 85, 114; 7-25, 88
Spanish vs. English wars, 1-102; 3-32, 86, 101
Spanish-American War, 1-117, 119; 2-34
Spartanburg, SC, 3-107
Spavinaw, OK, 5-91
Spears, Jacob, 3-65
Spelman, Harry, 2-29
Spencer, Benjamin, 1-115
Spies, 3-120
Spillville, IA, 4-49
Spindletop wells, 5-117
Spirit Lake, 4-41
"Spirit of '89" (painting), 5-87*
Spiro Temple Mound (OK), 5-85
Split Rock Lighthouse (MN), 4-78*
Spokane, WA, 7-65, 69, 70, 76, 77
Spokane Falls (WA), 7-69
Spokane House (trading post), 7-69
Spokane Interstate Fair (WA), 7-76
Spokane River, 7-65, 76
Spoleto Festival, 3-108, 109*
Sports, 1-66, 80, 94, 104, 108, 120, 122; 2-53, 60, 61, 79, 80, 81; 3-65, 66; 4-24, 38, 46, 80, 91, 93, 94, 104, 109, 118, 123; 5-38, 66, 67, 91, 109, 123; 6-48, 77, 78, 80, 91, 123; 7-20, 28, 39, 49, 62, 74, 91
Spotswood, Alexander, 2-100, 114
Sprague, William, 1-104
"Sprague" (steamboat), 3-81
Spring Green, WI, 4-120, 123
Springfield, IL, 1-14, 26; 4-24, 25
Springfield, MA, 1-80
Springfield, MO, 4-94
Springfield, VT, 1-121
Springs, natural, 2-114; 3-29, 29*; 4-83; 6-39, 53, 71, 113, 121; 7-59
Sproat, Ebenezer, 4-103
Spruce, 6-21
Spruce Goose (airplane), 7-32
Spuyten Devil Creek, 2-71
Spy charges, Mary Lincoln, 2-36
Squamscott Indians, 1-87
Squando (chief), 1-61
Squanto (Indian), 1-73
Squash, 1-86; 2-57
Squibb, E. R., 2-63
Squirral Cage Jail (Council Bluffs, IA), 4-53
St. Albans, VT, 1-117
St. Anthony's Falls, 4-69
St. Augustine, FL, 3-31, 32, 33, 35, 38, 39
St. Castin, Baron de, 1-60
St. Charles, MO, 4-94
St. Clair, Arthur, 2-92

St. Clair River, 4-55
St. Croix Island (VI), 7-93, 96
St. Croix River, 1-57, 67; 4-69, 81, 111
St. Denis, Juchereau de, 5-45
St. Francis (Indian village), 1-114
St. Francis Indians, 1-86, 114
St. Francis River, 3-15; 4-83; 5-16
St. Francis Xavier Cathedral (Vincennes, IN), 4-83
St. Francis Xavier Mission (MO), 4-86
St. Francisville, LA, 5-49
St. Francois Mts., 4-85
St. George, UT, 6-99, 109
St. Helena Cathedral (Helena, MT), 1-29; 6-67
St. James Court (Louisville, KY), 3-66
St. Joe River, 6-43, 44
St. John Island (VI), 7-93, 95
St. John River, 1-57
St. John's Church (Richmond, VA), 1-25
St. John's Parish, SC, 3-105
St. Johns Episcopal Church (Portsmouth, NH), 1-95
St. Johns River, 3-30
St. Johnsbury, VT, 1-121, 123
St. Joseph, MI, 4-58
St. Joseph, MO, 4-87 88, 89, 94
St. Joseph River, 4-28
St. Joseph's College for Women, 2-51
St. Lawrence River, 2-69, 79; 4-69, 76
St. Lawrence Seaway, 2-75; 4-20, 23, 65, 76, 104, 118
St. Louis, MO, 1-14; 4-84*, 85, 86, 87, 88, 89, 91, 92, 93, 94; 6-59, 88; 7-55
"St. Louis Blues" (song), 4-91
St. Louis Cardinals (baseball), 4-91, 93
St. Louis Cathedral (New Orleans, LA), 5-52
St. Louis Center (MO), 4-93
St. Louis River, 4-69
St. Louis Symphony Orchestra, 4-89
St. Luis, CO, 6-39
St. Marks, FL, 3-32
St. Martin, Alexis, 4-63
St. Martinville, LA, 5-49, 52
St. Mary's Lake, 6-55
St. Mary's MD, 2-44, 53
St. Mary's Mission (MT), 6-60
St. Mary's Mission (WA), 7-71
St. Mary's River, 4-55, 66
St. Marys River, 3-43, 45
St. Patrick's Cathedral (NYC), 2-81
St. Paul, MN, 1-29; 4-73, 74, 79, 80
St. Peter's Bacillica (Rome, Italy), 1-24, 29, 109
St. Petersburg, FL, 3-30, 39
St. Stephen, New Brunswick (Canada), 1-67
St. Thomas, VI (Charlotte Amalie), 7-86*, 94
St. Thomas Island (VI), 7-93, 95
St. Thomas synagogue (Charlotte Amalie, VI), 7-96
Stackpole, Ralph, 7-58
Stagecoaches, 4-93; 5-22, 80, 102, 107; 6-37, 116
Stamford, CT, 1-48
Stamford, TX, 5-121
Stamp Act, 2-16, 45
Standard Oil Bldg. (Chicago, IL), 4-24
Standard Oil Co., 4-104
Standard Time, 2-62
Standing Peachtree (Cherokee village), 3-51
Standish, Miles, 1-73
Stanford, Leland, 6-107; 7-29

Stanford Univ., 1-21; 7-29
Stanley, F. O., 1-89
Stanley Steamer, 1-89
Stanton, Edwin M., 2-92
"Star Spangled Banner" (song), 2-47, 48, 50
Star Spangled Banner Festival, 2-48
"Star of Oregon" (ship), 7-57
Starr, Belle, 4-89
"Starship" (Aircraft), 5-37
State Capitol Museum (WA), 7-76
State Dining Room, White House, 2-38
State Folk Festival, 2-123
State Hist. Museum (NV), 6-71
State Hist. Museum (OK), 5-95
State House, Old (AR), 5-25
State House (DE), 2-25*
State Library (NH), 1-95
State Library (WA), 7-76
State Library and Archives Bldg. (TX), 5-123
State Museum (NY), 2-79
State School for the Blind (SD), 5-102
State Wildlife Museum (MS), 3-80
State of Deseret (proposed state), 6-103
State of Franklin (proposed state), 3-115
Statehouse, Old (CT), 1-40*
Statehouse, Old (MA), 1-80
Staten Island (NY), 2-69, 81
Statesville, NC, 3-93
Statuary Hall (U.S. Capitol), 2-37, 38
Statue of Freedom, 2-33, 37
Statue of Liberty, 1-24; 2-2*, 12*, 74, 75*, 80
Staunton, VA, 2-105, 108
Ste. Genevieve, MO, 4-86, 89, 93
Steam automobiles, 1-89
Steam locomotives, 2-23, 66, 93; 3-107; 5-66
Steam power, 1-79
Steam shovels, 4-121
Steamboats and steamships, 1-48, 122; 2-22, 50, 62, 93, 107, 116; 3-18, 46, 59, 65, 66, 79, 81; 4-8*, 17, 44, 52, 74, 93, 103, 117; 5-17, 38, 43*, 47, 51, 65, 78, 79, 100, 119; 6-22, 51, 60, 65; 7-60
Steel industry, 2-93, 95, 122; 3-23, 65; 4-34, 37, 64; 6-36
Steel processing, 6-108
Steele, Franklin, 4-74
Steele, Theodore, 4-36
Steelhead trout, 7-58
Steeple Bldg. (Christiansted Nat. Hist. Site), 7-96
Steinbeck, John, 7-29
Stephen Collins Foster Mem. Day, 3-66
Stephens, Alexander H., 3-48
Steunenberg, Frank, 6-48
Stevens, Harry M., 4-105
Stevens, John, 4-119
Stevens, S. K., 2-89
Stevens Village, AK, 7-16
Stevenson, Adlai E., 4-21
Stevenson, Robert Louis, 1-10; 7-29, 37
Stevensville, MT, 6-60
Stewart, Anthony, 2-45
Stewart, William Morris, 6-74, 77, 80
Stikine (John Muir's dog), 7-16, 19
Stikine River, 7-19
Stiles, Ezra, 1-119
Still, William Grant, 3-77
Stjukson (prehistoric AZ village), 6-24
Stogies, 2-122
Stokowski, Leopold, 2-92
Stoley, William, 5-64
Stoley State Park (NE), 5-64

Stone, Edward Durell, 5-67
Stone Age, 6-115
Stone Mt., 1-26; 3-3*, 41, 52, 53
"Stone bones" (Fossils), 5-57
Stonehenge (Britain), 6-115; 7-77
Stonewall, TX, 5-118
Stonington, CT, 1-46, 49
Stonington Point (RI), 1-97
"Storm on the Prairie" (painting), 5-2*
Storms, 2-18; 4-46
Stowe, Harriet Beecher, 1-49, 64; 4-104
Stowe, VT, 1-123
Straits of Mackinac, 4-58, 62
Strang, James Jesse, 4-60, 66
Strategic Air Command Museum, 5-66
Stratton, Winfield Scott, 6-35
Strauss, Levi, 7-31
Strawberries, 1-95; 5-50; 7-18, 30
Strawbery Banke (Portsmouth, NH), 1-87
"Street Scene Hopi Pueblo" (painting), 6-17*
Strikes, 1-76; 5-19
Strong, Phil, 4-49
Struck-by-the-Ree (Indian Leader), 5-100
Stuart, Gilbert, 1-24, 103, 106, 109
Stuart, J. E. B., 2-18, 89
Stuart, Robert, 6-116
Stubblefield, Nathan, 3-63
Studebaker automobiles, 4-37
Sturbridge Village, MA, 1-80
Sturgeon, 1-120; 7-72
Sturgeon Bay, WI, 4-123
Sturgis, SD, 5-105, 108
Stuttgart, Germany, 5-21
Stuyvesant, Peter, 2-15, 72, 85
Submarines, 2-62
Subways, 2-35; 7-34
Suckiagu (Hartford, CT), 1-44
Suckow, Ruth, 4-49
Sugar, 5-50; 7-90
Sugar Loaf Monolith (MN), 4-81
Sugar beets, 6-120
Sugar maples, 1-94
"Sugar-on-snow", 1-121
Sugarcane, 5-50; 7-42, 46, 94, 95
Sugarloaf Mt., 1-66
Sughkonet Indians, 1-102
Sullivan, Anne, 3-21
Sully, Thomas, 2-46
Sulpher, 5-49, 50, 92, 120
Sulphur Spring Valley (AZ), 6-16
Sultan of Swat, 2-51
Sumla Cave Shelter people, 5-113
Summerfest, Milwaukee, 4-122
Summersville, WV, 2-120
Summersville Reservoir, 2-113
Summit House Resort (Mt. Washington), 1-94
Sumter, SC, 3-103, 104
Sumter, Thomas, 3-103
Sun Valley, ID, 6-48, 53
Sunapee, NH, 1-90
Sundance, WY, 6-121
Sundew plant, 2-121; 4-36
Sunflowers, 5-79; 7-30
Sunnyside (Washington Irving's home), 2-79
Sunset Crater, 6-15, 23
Sunshine Mine, (ID), 6-51
Sunspot on Sacramento Peak, 6-95
Superdome (New Orleans, LA), 5-48
Superior Nat. Forest, 4-76
Superior-Duluth harbor, 4-111
Superior-Quetico primitive region, 4-81
Superstition Mt., 6-25
Superstition Mt. Lost Gold Trek, 6-25
Supreme Court, U.S., 1-89; 2-31, 38, 52; 5-33

Supreme Courts, state, 2-18
Suquamish Museum, 7-69, 75
Susquahannock Indians, 2-43, 85
Susquehanna River, 2-83, 85, 92
Sutro, Adolph, 6-78
Sutter, John, 7-26, 29, 35
Suttlers Store (Fort Laramie), 6-122
Swain Island, 7-80
Swallows, 6-50; 7-31
Swamp Fox (Francis Marion), 3-105
Swamp Park, 3-52
Swamp pink, 2-22
Swamps, 1-99; 2-18, 22, 28, 55, 109; 3-36, 43, 49*, 52; 7-39
Swan, Whistling, 4-1
Swan Valley, DE, 2-15
Swans, 6-120
Swans Island, 1-57
Swanson, Gloria, 7-30
Swanton, VT, 1-113, 114
Swanzey, NH, 1-92
Swastika, 6-105
Sweat Mansion Museum, 1-65
Swedish Festival, 5-39
Swedish settlements, 2-15, 18, 24, 57, 85; 4-76; 5-33
Sweet potatoes, 3-21; 7-93
Swilling, Jack, 6-18
Swiss Settlements, 4-123
Sycamore trees, 2-120; 4-36
Syracuse, NY, 1-10; 2-80
Syringa, 6-50
TVA (Tennessee Valley Authority), 3-20, 111, 117; 5-63
TWA (Trans World Airlines), 2-35
TWA hijacking, 2-35
Ta'u Island (SA), 7-79
Tabasco sauce, 5-51
Tabor, Augusta, 6-34
Tabor, H. A. W., 6-34
Tabor Opera House (Leadville, CO), 6-38*, 39
Tacoma, WA, 7-70, 74
Tacoma Narrows (WA), 7-74
Tacoma Narrows Bridge, 7-74
Taconic Mts., 1-69, 111
Taconite, 4-76, 79
Taffy, 2-66
Taft, Robert, 4-106
Taft, William Howard, 2-34, 108; 4-48, 106; 5-63
Taft Nat. Hist. Site, 4-108
Tahiti Island (Pacific), 7-43
Tahlequah, OK, 5-94
Taliesin, 4-120, 123
Tallahassee, FL, 1-26, 27; 3-31, 33, 34, 39
Tama, IA, 4-43
Tama County, IA, 4-47, 48
Tamique Indians, 5-114
Tampa, FL, 3-34, 39
Tampa Bay, FL, 3-32
Tampanogos Cave Nat. Mon., 6-109
Tanana River, 7-11, 22
Tanglewood (Berkshire, MA), 1-80
Taniers, 7-91
Tank Cottage (Green Bay, WI), 4-123
Tannehill Hist. State Park (AL), 3-25
Taopi (chief), 4-75
Taos, NM, 6-31, 90, 91, 92, 93
Taos Pueblo, NM, 6-93, 94
Tapa cloth, 7-80
Tappen, ND, 5-74
Tappen Zee Bridge (NY), 2-79
Tarantulas, 6-21
Tarkington, Booth, 4-35
Tarleton, Banastre, 3-102
Taro plants, 7-81
Tarpon, 7-94
Tarrytown, NY, 2-79
"Tascalusa's Revenge", 3-17
Tatnall, Henry Lea, 2-21

Taughannock Falls, 2-80
Taxes, 1-90; 2-44, 45, 58, 77, 87
Taxes, colonial, 2-44, 45, 58, 77, 87
Taylor, Moulton B., 7-71
Taylor, Robert, 5-63
Taylor, William S., 3-60
Taylor, Zachary, 2-76, 104; 3-62; 4-91; 5-17
Tchaikovsky Award, 5-119
Tchefuncte people, 5-44
Tea, 1-103
Tea parties, revolutionary, 1-130; 2-45, 58
Teapot Dome (MT), 6-61
Teapot Dome scandal, 6-61, 118
Tecumseh (chief), 3-18, 73; 4-31, 32, 35, 102
Teflon, 2-22
Telegraphy, 2-37, 62, 89; 4-45; 6-107, 120
Telephones, 1-50, 104; 2-90; 4-37; 5-87; 6-48; 7-19
Television, 2-35; 4-23; 7-19, 31, 80
Temple Square (Salt Lake City, UT), 6-104, 109
Ten Thousand Islands (FL), 3-31
Tendoy (chief), 6-49
Tenino, WA, 7-65
Tennessee (main article), 3-111
Tennessee Dept. of Tourist Devlop., 3-118
Tennessee Life (mural), 3-120
Tennessee River, 1-7; 3-13, 15, 57, 60, 69, 71, 111, 122; 4-117
Tennessee River Valley, 2-51
Tennessee State Museum, 3-123
Tennessee Valley Authority (TVA), 3-20, 111, 117; 5-63
Tennessee marble, 3-121
Tennessee volunteers, 3-116
Tennessee-Tombigbee Waterway, 3-23, 25
Tennis, 1-104
Tenskwatawa (The Prophet), 4-30*, 32, 35
Tensleep, WY, 6-115
Tensleep Canyon (WY), 6-113
Tepees, 5-57, 73
Tercentenary celebration (DE), 2-18
Tercentenary celebration (Jamestown, VA), 2-102
Tercentenary celebration (MD), 2-48
Terlingua, TX (Ghost town), 5-122
Terns, 6-50
Territorial Capitol, Old (AR), 5-25
"Territorial Enterprise" (newspaper), 6-79
Territory of Minnesota, 4-74
Terrorism, 2-16, 32, 35, 50, 116
Terry, Eli, 1-50
Tertiary period, 2-113
Tesuque Pueblo, NM, 6-95
Teton Dam, 6-48
Teton Mts., 6-111, 113, 114, 114*, 116, 119, 121
Teton Pass (WY), 6-116
Teton Sioux Indians, 5-100
Teton Uplift (WY), 6-113
Texan Culture, Institute of, 5-123
Texarkana, AR, 5-23
Texarkana, TX, 5-23
Texas, Battleship, 5-123
"Texas" (Pageant), 5-121
Texas (main article), 5-111
Texas City, TX, 5-121
Texas Declaration of Independence, 1-27; 5-123
Texas Longhorns, 5-92
Texas Republic, 5-116
Texas annexation, 6-111
Textile industry, 1-106, 107
Textiles, 2-22, 64, 106; 3-50, 91, 93, 106; 7-95
"Thaddeus" (ship), 7-42

Thames River (CT), 1-43, 52
Thanksgiving, 1-59, 73
Thanksgiving, first, 1-73
Thaquamenon Falls, 4-55*
That's Curious, 1-1, 7, 11, 14, 18, 20, 21, 26, 27, 31, 43, 45, 48, 49, 51, 52, 53, 57, 59, 60, 61, 63, 64, 67, 68, 71, 72, 77, 80, 85, 86, 88, 89, 90, 91, 93, 94, 96, 99, 100, 102, 103, 107, 109, 114, 115, 119, 121, 123; 2-15, 16, 19, 24, 25, 27, 31, 33, 36, 38, 39, 41, 47, 50, 52, 53, 57, 59, 60, 62, 72, 74, 77, 79, 86, 89, 94, 97, 100, 103, 105, 110, 111, 117, 119, 121; 3-16, 17, 18, 19, 22, 23, 30, 32, 34, 35, 36, 40, 45, 46, 47, 49, 53, 58, 59, 64, 65, 66, 71, 72, 75, 77, 81, 85, 86, 87, 88, 91, 95, 99, 100, 103, 104, 105, 107, 110, 113, 117, 119, 120; 4-13, 15, 19, 23, 25, 28, 31, 32, 34, 36, 38, 41, 44, 46, 48, 49, 50, 53, 57, 58, 59, 60, 63, 67, 69, 74, 77, 79, 85, 86, 89, 90, 91, 92, 101, 102, 105, 106, 108, 109, 113, 115, 117, 120, 123; 5-16, 18, 19, 20, 22, 24, 26, 31, 32, 33, 36, 37, 44, 47, 48, 49, 50, 51, 53, 57, 58, 59, 61, 64, 65, 72, 75, 76, 77, 78, 79, 81, 83, 85, 86, 88, 90, 92, 94, 95, 96, 99, 100, 101, 102, 103, 105, 108, 114, 115, 117, 119, 120, 12 "The Chasm of the Colorado" (painting), 6-21
The Oaks (Booker T. Washington's home), 3-25
Theodore Roosevelt Birthplace Nat. Hist. site, 2-18
Theodore Roosevelt Island (DC), 2-27, 28
Theodore Roosevelt Lake, 6-18
Theodore Roosevelt Nat. Mem. Park, 5-71*, 80, 81
Thermopolis, WY, 6-113
Thermopolis Hot Springs State Park (WY), 6-121
Theropod dinosaur, 1-71
"This Is the Place" (monument), 6-106
Thom, Robert, 4-91
Thomas, Lowell, 6-35
Thomas Gilcrease Institute of American History and Art, 5-94
Thomasville, NC, 3-93
Thompson, Charles, 2-20
Thompson, David, 5-73; 6-47, 48; 7-69
Thompson, John, 6-77
Thompson, Virgil, 4-91
Thomson, David, 1-87
Thone, Charles, 5-62
Thoreau, Henry David, 1-64, 77, 78
Thornton, William, 2-31
Thorp, Freeman, 5-19
Thorpe, Jim, 5-91, 95
Thousand Islands (NY), 2-79
Thousand Springs (ID), 6-43, 53
Three Brother Island (WV), 2-120
Three Forks, ID, 6-55
Three Forks, MT, 6-64
Three Springs Fisheries (MD), 2-51
Thumb, Tom, 1-53
"Thumb Grant", 2-45
Thunderbolt, GA, 3-44
Thunderbolt Run (Mt. Greylock), 1-80
Ti plant, 7-45
Tiber Creek, 2-27, 31
Tibet, 2-67, 81
Tidal waves, 7-15
Tiffany, Louis C., 1-29; 7-76
Tiffany's (NYC), 2-80
Tilden, Samuel J., 2-76; 4-89, 105
Tilghman, Tench, 2-47*
Timberline Lodge (Mt. Hood), 7-62
Times Square (NYC), 2-80

Tinicum Island (PA), 2-85
Tippecanoe, IN, 4-35
Tippecanoe River, 4-32
Tires, 4-107
Tishomingo, OK, 5-94
"Titanic" (ship), 6-36
Titanium, 2-77, 78, 106; 6-78; 7-59
Titanotheres, 5-57
Titusville, PA, 2-93
Tlingit Indians, 7-9, 12
To-pa-tu (Indian leader), 6-87
Toadstool Park, (NE), 5-67
Tobacco, 1-51, 86; 2-29, 44, 52, 63, 107, 121; 3-50, 64, 78, 89, 107*, 121; 4-92; 7-90, 91, 93
Tobacco auction, 3-107*
Tobacco industry, 3-91
Todt Hill, 2-69
Tohoga (Indian village), 2-29
Tokyo, Japan, 7-21
Toledo, OH, 4-60, 97, 103, 108
"Tom Sawyer" (book), 2-80
Tomatoes, 7-30, 83
Tomb of the Unknown, 1-25; 2-108; 6-64
Tombigbee River, 3-15
Tombstone, AZ, 6-20
Tomochichi (chief), 3-45, 51
Tompkins, Sally, 2-105
Tonkawa, OK, 5-87
Tonkawa Indians, 5-114
Tonopah, NV, 6-74
Tonto Nat. Mon., 6-25
Topaz, 1-92; 6-64, 107
Topeka, KS, 1-27; 5-28*, 35, 36, 38
Topeka High School, 5-38
Torchwood tree, 3-36
Tories, 3-18
Tornadoes, 4-46; 5-19
Totem poles, 7-7*, 19, 75*
Touro Synagogue Nat. Hist. Site, 1-108
Tower of the Americas (San Antonio, TX), 5-123
Town Creek Mound State Hist. Site (NC), 3-85
Town Hall of Hoorn (reproduction), 2-26
Tractors, 4-51
Trade winds, 7-79, 93
Tradelphia Reservoir, 2-41
Traders, 3-86, 114; 4-30, 100; 5-29, 37, 58, 73, 74, 100; 6-31, 59, 116, 122; 7-53, 67
Traer, IA, 4-49
Traffic circles, 2-66
Trail Ridge Road (Rocky Mt. Nat. Park), 6-37, 38
Trail of Tears, 3-19, 74, 88, 116; 5-23, 86
Tramsways, 7-81
Trans Pecos Region (TX), 5-111
Trans-Mississippi International Exposition, 5-61
Trans-World Airlines (TWA), 4-92
Transfer Day (VI Festival), 7-96
Transportation, 1-62, 93, 122; 2-18, 22, 23, 55, 59, 61, 74, 75, 78, 93, 107, 116, 122; 3-20, 23, 34, 35, 38, 46, 51, 65, 79, 111, 117, 122; 4-18, 23, 37, 38, 45, 46, 65, 66, 78, 91, 93, 97, 103, 105; 5-22, 38, 45, 47, 51, 60, 65, 79, 80, 107, 123; 6-22, 23, 37, 51, 65, 79, 101, 104, 107, 108, 120, 122; 7-14, 15, 18, 19, 27, 32, 42, 55, 60, 73, 74
Transylvania Univ., 3-62
Trappers and trapping, 2-23; 3-114; 4-58; 5-51, 58; 6-12, 31, 116; 7-20
Traverse City, MI, 4-66
Travis, William Barrett, 3-22; 5-115, 119
Travois, 4-72
Treaties, 1-44, 61, 73, 77, 89, 91; 2-20, 46, 85, 86, 91, 105, 114; 3-101, 114; 4-32, 74, 101, 102, 103; 6-47,

60, 116; 7-26, 57, 80
Treaties, Indian, 2-85, 86, 114; 3-101; 6-47, 60
Treaty of Green Ville (Greenville), 4-102
Treaty of Guadalupe Hidalgo, 7-26
Treaty of Paris, 2-46, 91; 4-74
Treaty of Portsmouth, 1-89
Tree Trail (Arbor Lodge, NE), 5-66
Tree frogs, 7-90
Trees, 1-11, 15, 19, 29, 88; 3-64, 77; 4-36, 41; 5-21, 49, 53, 62, 78, 92, 120, 121, 123; 6-21, 50, 92, 107; 7-30, 35, 58, 62, 80, 84, 90, 94
Trees, prehistoric, 6-44
"Trees" (poem), 1-92
Trenton, NJ, 1-24, 25; 2-56*, 59, 66
"Triangular Trade", 1-78
Trinity College, Hartford CT, 1-53
Trinity College, San Antonia TX, 1-21
Triple Divide Peak, 6-55
Tropical rain forests, 7-46
Troup, George M., 3-46
Trout, 1-67; 5-102; 6-50, 77; 7-58, 72
Troy, ID, 6-49
Truck farming, 1-108
Truckee, NV, 6-79
Truckee River, 6-69, 81
Truk Island (Pacific), 7-85
Truman, Harry S., 2-35; 3-63; 4-49, 89, 90, 91, 94
Truman Library, 4-87*
Truman Sports Complex (Kansas City, MO), 4-94
Trumbull, John, 1-49; 2-102
Trumbull, Jonathan, 1-45, 47
Trump Tower (NYC), 2-81
Trumpeter swans, 6-50, 120
Trunk Bay (St. John Island, VI), 7-95
Trustees Gardens (Savannah, GA), 3-51
Tsa-La-Gi (recreated Indian village) OK, 5-94
Tsali (Indian leader), 3-88
Tslalakum (chief), 7-71
Tsunami (tidal wave), 7-15
Tubac, AZ, 6-20
Tubbs, Poker-Alice, 5-105
Tubman, Harriet, 2-49
Tucker County, WV, 2-115
Tucson, AZ, 6-17, 18, 19, 22, 24
Tug Fork River, 2-111; 3-55
Tule Lake, 7-58
Tule Lake Nat. Wildlife Refuge, 7-58
Tule Springs (NV), 6-71
Tulip Grove, TN, 3-123
Tulip poplar tree, 4-36
Tulsa, OK, 5-89, 94
Tumwater Falls Park (WA), 7-76
Tuna, 1-107; 2-64; 7-94
Tuna Tournament, U.S. Atlantic, 1-107
Tung nut, 3-79
Tunica Hills, LA (Indian village), 5-45
Tunican Indians, 5-44
Tupelo, MS, 3-75, 77
Turkey red wheat, 5-37
Turkeys, 1-11, 59; 3-121; 6-21, 120
Turquoise, 6-77, 91, 92
Turtle Mt., 5-72
Turtle effigies, 5-72
Turtles, 7-88
Tuscarora Indians, 3-85
Tuscumbia, AL, 3-20
Tuskegee Institute, 2-106; 3-21, 24
Tutuila Island (SA), 7-79
Tuxedo, NY, 2-79
Tuzigoot Nat. Mon., 6-25
Twain, Mark (Samuel L. Clemens), 1-49, 53; 2-80; 3-65; 4-89, 91, 119; 5-15, 53; 6-76, 77, 79; 7-29
Twenty-fifth anniversary celebra-

125

tion (HI), 7-43
Twenty-mule teams, 6-22
Twin Cities, MN, 4-79
Two Bar Cattle Co., 6-117
Two Ocean Pass (WY), 6-111
Twok (George Aden Ahgupuk), 7-16
Tying machine (grain), 4-119
Tyler, John, 2-104; 4-33
Tynes, Molly, 2-105
Typewriters, 3-105; 4-117, 119
Typhoons, 7-80, 83
Tyrannosaurus Rex, 5-107
U.S. Air Force, 5-117; 7-85
U.S. Air Force Academy, 6-38
U.S. Atlantic Tuna Tournament, 1-107
U.S. Dept. of Interior, 7-80
U.S. Geological Survey, 6-20
U.S. Military Academy, 1-30; 3-62; 4-90
U.S. Mint (CO), 6-39
U.S. Mint (NV), 6-81
U.S. Naval Academy, 1-21, 25
"U.S. News and World Report" (magazine), 1-21
U.S. Senate, 2-31, 59, 92; 3-48; 5-20, 118; 7-85
U.S. Steel Co. (USX), 2-92; 3-23; 4-37
U.S. Supreme Court Bldg., 1-121
U.S.S. Alabama Battleship Mem. Park (AL), 3-24
UN Human Rights Commission, 2-36
Uinta Mts., 6-29, 100
Ulibarri, Juan, 6-31
Ultralight planes, 3-92*
Umbrellas, 2-52
Umpqua River, 7-51
"Uncle Remus", 3-48
Uncle Sam, 2-74
"Uncle Tom's Cabin" (book), 1-49, 63; 4-104
Underground Railroad, 1-117; 2-17, 116; 4-33
Unicameral legislatures, 5-61, 63; 7-83, 94
Unicycles, 5-93
Union Pacific RR, 6-48, 107
Union Square (San Francisco, CA), 7-34
United Daughters of the Confederacy, 3-120
United Fruit Co., 1-79
United Nations, 2-36, 91; 4-21, 63; 7-28, 85
University Horseshoe (Univ. of SC), 3-109
University of Alaska, 7-20
University of Arizona, 6-24
University of Arkansas, 5-23
University of California, 1-21; 7-27, 35
University of California, Berkeley, 1-21; 7-35
University of Georgia, 3-53
University of Idaho, 6-52; 7-76
University of Iowa, 4-45, 46, 49, 53
University of Kansas, 5-35, 38
University of Louisville, 3-66
University of Maryland, 2-53
University of Michigan, 4-63, 67
University of Minnesota Mines Experiment station, 4-79
University of Mississippi, 3-76
University of Montana, 6-64
University of Nebraska, 5-66
University of Nebraska at Linclon, 5-67
University of Nevada, 6-81
University of New Mexico, 6-95
University of North Carolina, 3-95
University of North Dakota, 5-73
University of Notre Dame, 4-38*
University of Oklahoma, 5-95
University of Puerto Rico, 7-91

University of South Carolina, 3-109
University of South Dakota, 5-108
University of Texas, 5-123
University of Texas, Austin, 1-27
University of Utah, 6-109
University of Vermont, Burlington, 1-122
University of Vermont, Morgan Horse Farm, 1-122
University of Virginia, 2-104, 108
University of Washington, 7-74
University of Wisconsin, 4-118, 123
Unknown, Tomb of the, 1-25; 2-108; 6-64
"Unsinkable Molly Brown, The" (Broadway play), 6-36
"Unto These Hills" (Pageant), 3-92, 95
Upper Black Eddy, PA, 2-94
Upper Falls of the Yellowstone River, 6-121
Upper Priest Lake, 6-43
Upside Down River (Wood River), 6-44
Uranium, 5-76, 106; 6-36, 91, 92, 108, 120; 7-70
Uranium chain reactor, 3-118
Urban Institute of Washington, DC, 4-79
Urban restoration, 4-93, 94; 7-95
Urey, Harold C., 6-64
Utah (main article), 6-97
Utah Lake, 6-99
Ute Black Hawk War, 6-104
Ute Indians, 6-30, 72, 77, 87, 100, 115
Utiangue, AR (Indian town), 5-16
Uto-Aztecan Indians, 6-16
Vaca, Alvar Nunez Cabeza de, 5-114
Vail, CO, 6-39
Valdez, AK, 7-18, 20
Valdez Glacier (AK), 7-13
Valentino, Rudolph, 7-36
Valley Falls, RI, 1-101
Valley Forge (PA), 2-88
"Valley Forge of Connecticut, The", 1-47
Valley Head, AL, 3-25
Valley of Ten Thousand Smokes (AK), 7-14
"Valley of the Vapors" (Hot Springs, AR), 5-22
Valparaiso, IN, 4-37
Values, 1-15
Valverde (Spanish explorer), 6-30
Van Allen, James, 4-49
Van Allen belt, 4-49
Van Buren, AR, 5-18
Van Buren, MO, 4-83
Van Buren, Martin, 2-76, 104
Van Dyke, Henry, 1-67
Van Lew, Elizabeth, 2-105, 106
Van der Stucken, Frank, 5-119
Vanadium, 6-36
Vance, Zebulon Baird, 3-91
Vancouver, George, 7-67
Vancouver, WA, 7-70, 77
Vanderbilt, Cornelius, 1-104; 2-78
Vanderbilt, Mrs. Cornelius, 1-206
Vanderbilt, William K., 1-108
Vardaman, James E., 3-75
Varese, Edgar, 1-92*
Vargas, Diego de, 6-31
Vasquez, Louis, 6-123
Vasquez, Lucas de Ayllon, 3-86
Veblen, Thorstein, 4-78
Veiled Prophet Fair, 4-94
Verendrye, Francois, 5-73, 100; 6-58
Verendrye, Louis-Joseph, 5-73, 100; 6-58
Verendrye, Sieur de La (Pierre Gaultier), 4-73; 5-0
Vermillion, SD, 5-99, 108
Vermillion River, 4-97
Vermont (main article), 1-111

Vermont Marble Co., 1-121
Vermont Marble Exhibit, 1-122
Vermont Wildflower Farm, 1-122
Verrazano, Giovanni da, 1-60, 87; 2-57, 71; 3-86
Verrazano Narrows (NY), 1-25
Verrazano Narrows Bridge, 1-24; 2-75*
Veteran's Mem. Bldg. (Detroit, MI), 4-66
Vicksburg, MS, 2-51; 3-75, 80, 81
Vicksburg, siege of, 3-74*
Vicksburg Nat. Military Park, 3-80, 81*
Victor Records, 2-62
Victoria of England, 4-50
Victorio (chief), 6-88
Vieques Island (Caribbean), 7-87
Vietnam Mem. (The Wall), 2-39, 40*
Vietnam War, 2-90; 4-35; 5-118; 6-64
Vieux Carre (New Orleans, LA), 5-52
Viking explorations, 1-59, 101; 2-57; 4-72
Villa, Francisco (Pancho), 6-89
Villa Louis (Prairie du Chien, WI), 4-124
Villere Plantation, LA, 5-46
Vinalhaven Island (ME), 1-57
Vincennes, Francois de, 4-30, 38
Vincennes, IN, 4-16, 30, 31, 38
Vinegar Bible, 1-95
Vinson, Fred M., 3-63
Virgin Islands (main article), 7-86
Virgin Islands Corp., 7-94
Virgin River, 6-99
Virgin River Canyon, 6-99
Virginia (main article), 2-97
"Virginia" (ship), 1-60
Virginia Beach, VA, 2-99, 109
Virginia City, MT, 6-60, 66
Virginia City, NV, 4-91; 6-74, 76, 77, 78, 79, 81
Virginia Military Institute, 2-109
Virginia Museum of Fine Arts, 2-109
Virginia Street (Charleston, WV), 2-122
Virginia and Truckee RR, 6-79, 81
Virginia-Truckee RR Museum, 6-81
Virgins of St. Ursula, 7-93
Vista House (OR), 7-63
Vitamins, 4-119
Vizcaino, Sebastian, 7-25
Volcano House Hotel (HI), 7-47
Volcanoes, 1-6, 43; 4-71; 6-15, 43, 44, 45, 48, 71, 85, 93, 115; 7-14, 16, 21, 23, 37, 39, 42, 43, 45, 47, 51, 62, 65, 70, 77, 79, 82, 93
Vollrath Co., 4-122
Von Braun, Wernher, 3-20
Vonnegut, Kurt, 4-49
Voyageurs, 4-30, 58, 73, 74, 77
"Vulcan" (statue), 3-25*
Vulture mine, AZ, 6-22
W H A Radio (Madison, WI), 4-123
Wabash, IN, 4-33, 35
Wabash River, 4-13, 28, 30, 32
Wabash and Erie Canal, 4-32
Wadsworth, Joseph, 1-45
Wadsworth, SC, 3-104
Wagner, Richard, 7-74
Wahoo, 7-94
Wahquinnacut (sachem), 1-44
Wahunsonacock (chief Powhatan), 2-99, 105
Waiilatpu Mission (WA), 7-69
Waikiki, HI, 7-41
Waikiki Beach (HI), 7-49
Wailua River, 7-39, 48
Waimea Canyon (HI), 7-39, 48
Waimea River, 7-39
Waipahee Falls (HI), 7-48
"Waiting for a Chinook (The Last

of Five Thousand)" (painting), 6-62
Wake Island (Pacific), 7-85
Waksman, Selman, 2-62
Walastonite, 2-77
Walden Pond (MA), 1-78
Waldron, Lawrence R., 5-78
"Walk-in-the-Water" (steamboat), 4-103
Walker, Thomas, 3-58
Walker (chief), 6-104
Walker Lake, 6-69, 71
Walker River, 6-69
Walker War, 6-104
Walking Purchase, 2-86
Wall, SD, 5-108
Wall, The (Vietnam Mem.), 2-39, 40*
Wall Drugstore (SD), 5-108
Wall Lake, 4-41
Walla Walla, WA, 6-60; 7-76
Wallabout Bay (NY), 2-74
Wallace, "Uncle" Henry, 4-48, 49
Wallace, Ben, 4-39
Wallace, George, 3-20, 21
Wallace, Henry A., 4-49
Wallace, Henry C., 4-49
Wallace, Lew, 2-48; 4-35; 6-90
Wallace, Lurleen B., 3-20
"Wallace's Farmer" (magazine), 4-49
Wallenpaupack Lake, 2-83
Wallowa Lake, 7-63
Wallowa Mts., 7-53
Wallum Lake, 1-99
Walnut Canyon (AZ), 6-23
Walnut Hill, IA, 4-53
Walnut River Valley (KS), 5-30
Walrus, 7-17
Walsh, Thomas F., 6-35
Walsh, Thomas J., 6-61
Walt Disney World (FL), 3-34
Walt Whitman Birthplace Assn., 2-81
Walton, Sam, 5-21
Wamego, KS, 5-36
Wampanoag Indians, 1-71, 73, 100, 102
Wampum, 1-59, 100, 101; 2-57, 83
Wanchese, 3-86
Wannamaker, John, 2-92
Wapiti Valley (WY), 6-122
Wappinger Confederacy, 1-43
War Mem. Mon. (NJ), 2-67
War Sanitary Fund, 6-75
"War is Hell", 3-75
War of 1812, 1-45, 61, 75, 77, 89, 104, 106; 2-17, 31, 46, 47, 59, 74, 89, 101; 3-18, 33, 46, 60, 74, 102, 115, 116; 4-16, 32, 44, 59, 74, 87, 102, 115; 5-20, 46, 47, 100
War of Jenkin's Ear, 3-32
War of the Outbreak, 5-10
War with Mexico, 1-90; 2-104; 3-62, 76; 5-18, 20, 47, 51; 6-17, 73, 88, 90, 102, 111; 7-26, 27
War with Spain, 1-117, 119; 2-34
Waramaug (chief), 1-44
Ward, Aaron Montgomery, 4-21, 64
Waring, Fred, 2-92
Warm Springs, GA, 3-47, 53
Warne John, 5-119
Warner, John William, 2-103
Warner, Seth, 1-119
Warren, A. C., 4-59
Warwick, RI, 1-102
Warwick Airport, 1-104
Wasatch Mts., 6-97
Washakie (chief), 6-106, 118, 119
Washburn, Edward Payson, 5-21
Washburn, ND, 5-73
Washburn family, 1-64
Washington, Booker T., 2-106, 120; 3-21, 25
Washington, D.C., 1-25, 29; 2-20, 25, 28, 47, 48, 53, 55, 60, 64, 88,

102, 107, 108; 4-120; 6-76, 88; 7-57
Washington, George, 1-19, 24, 25, 45, 47, 75, 77, 103*, 106, 109; 2-5*, 24, 30, 31, 36, 44, 45, 47*, 50, 58*, 59, 66, 73, 74, 86, 87, 88, 100, 101, 103, 108, 109, 115, 119, 120, 123; 4-31, 35, 46, 90, 101, 102; 5-104, 107
Washington, George (WA pioneer), 7-72
Washington, George (statue), 6-53
Washington, Harold, 4-21
Washington, Martha, 1-25; 2-108, 110
Washington, NC, 3-94
Washington & Lee Univ., 2-106, 109
Washington (main article), 7-65
Washington County, ME, 1-67
Washington County, SC, 3-114
Washington Crossing State Park (NJ/PA), 2-67*, 94
"Washington Crossing the Delaware" (painting), 2-58*
Washington Island (WI), 4-111
Washington Masonic Nat. Mem., 2-108
Washington Mon. Nat. Mem., 2-37, 39
Washington State Library, 7-76
Washington and Lee Univ., 2-106
Washoe Indians, 6-75
Watauga Assn., 3-114
Water Tower (Chicago), 4-11*
Water routes, 2-116; 3-13, 23, 51, 79, 122; 4-18, 23, 37, 39, 60, 73, 86, 93, 97, 103, 104, 113, 115; 5-22, 38, 45, 51, 123; 6-51, 65; 7-18, 60
Water supply, 1-7, 14, 87; 2-67, 121; 3-22, 29; 4-22, 55; 5-36, 49, 64, 83; 6-21, 36, 50, 69, 99, 107, 120; 7-20, 30, 39, 59, 71, 93, 94, 96
Water turkey (anhinga), 3-27*, 36
"Water war" (AZ vs. CA), 6-18
Waterfalls, 1-43, 107; 2-28, 41, 53, 69, 72, 80, 114; 3-67, 69, 122; 4-55*, 69, 80, 124; 5-67, 108; 6-38, 44, 59, 114, 121; 7-35, 39, 48, 63, 76, 77, 84, 91
Waterford, PA, 2-86
Watergate scandel, 2-35
Waterloo, IA, 4-51, 53
Waterpower, 1-11; 2-121; 3-97, 111, 117; 5-106; 6-19, 51; 7-60, 73
Watersheds, 1-11; 2-113; 3-13, 30, 43, 71; 4-28, 69, 83, 97, 104, 113; 5-55, 69, 71, 83, 99; 6-15, 29, 43, 55, 59, 69, 85, 99, 111, 113; 7-11, 39
Watertown, CT, 1-52
Watertown, WI, 4-116
Watkins Glen, NY, 2-80
Watsonville, CA, 7-30
Wausau, WI, 4-121
Waveland, MS, 3-81
Waxham, NC, 3-90
Waymouth, George, 1-60
Wayne, (Mad) Anthony, 2-92; 3-46; 4-31, 59, 102
Wayne, John, 4-50
Wea Indians, 4-87
Weapons, 5-114; 6-74, 81, 89, 100, 106, 115; 7-11, 40, 70
Weapons, Indian, 1-86; 2-29; 5-73
Weapons, atomic, 6-74, 89; 7-70
Weapons, prehistoric, 2-41; 3-16; 4-57; 5-113; 6-100, 113; 7-11, 40
Weather service, U.S., 4-119
Weaving machine, 1-50
Webb, Walter Prescott, 5-119
Webster, Daniel, 1-61, 63, 64, 89, 90
Webster, Noah, 1-49
Webster-Ashburton Treaty, 1-61, 89, 91
Wedgewood china, 3-93

Weems, Mason Locke, 2-50
Weirton, WV, 2-111, 122
Weirton Steel Co., 2-122
Weiser, Conrad, 2-92; 4-100
"Welcome" (ship), 2-85
Weld County, CO, 6-37
Welk, Lawrence, 5-78
Well number one (OK), 5-92, 94
Wells Fargo and Co., 7-27
Welsh settlements, 4-123
Welty, Eudora, 3-76
Wendover, NV, 6-81
Wentworth, Benning, 1-88, 114, 115
Wentworth, John, 1-88, 94
Wentworth-Coolidge House (Portsmouth, NH), 1-95
Werowocomoco (Indian capital), 2-99
Wesley, Charles, 3-49
Wesley, John, 3-49
West, Benjamin, 2-92
West, Thomas (Lord De la Warr), 2-15, 56, 85, 99
West Branch, IA, 4-47, 48, 52
West Hartford, CT, 1-49
West Indies, 1-78, 99
West Orange, NJ, 2-61, 67
West Plymouth, NH, 1-86
West Point, NY, 1-30, 47
West Point Academy, 1-30; 3-62; 4-90
West Quoddy Head (ME), 1-55
West Virginia (main article), 2-111
Westmoreland County, VA, 2-104
"Western Engineer" (steamboat), 4-44
Western Hemisphere, 7-11, 95
Western Heritage Center, 5-95
Western Reserve, 4-102
Westminster Abbey (England), 1-62
Westminster College, 4-89, 90
Westo Indians, 3-99
Westport, MO, 4-88
Westward Expansion, Museum of, 4-93
Wetherill, Richard, 6-30
Wethersfield, CT, 1-44, 45, 53
Wewoka, OK, 5-94
Weyerhauser, Frederick, 4-77
Weymouth, MA, 1-73
Whaleshead Beach (OR), 7-51
Whaling, 1-52
Whaling Museum, 1-52
Whatcom County City Hall (WA), 7-76
Wheat, 4-79; 5-37, 78, 79, 93, 106, 121; 6-37, 51, 54, 65, 92, 120; 7-60, 73
Wheeler, Burton K., 6-61, 63
Wheeling, WV, 2-115, 117, 122
Wheeling, WV/OH, 1-15
Wheelwright, John, 1-87
Whidbey Island (WA), 7-71
Whipple, Henry Benjamin, 6-101
Whistler, James Abbott McNeill, 1-77
White, Byron R., 6-35
White, Elizabeth, 2-65
White, Jim, 6-93
White, John, 3-85, 86
White, John Blake, 3-8
White, Pearl, 2-60
White, William Allen, 1-118; 5-35
White Dove of the Desert Mission (San Xavier del Bac), 6-17, 18, 24, 25
"White Fox" (locomotive), 7-27
White House, The, 1-25, 27, 77; 2-30*, 31, 32, 35, 37, 38; 5-32; 6-80
White House (Casa Blanco, San Juan, PR), 7-91
White Maine marble, 1-67
White Mt. Nat. Forest, 1-92
White Mts. (AZ), 6-15
White Mts. (NH/ME), 1-31, 83, 87, 111

White Plains, NC, 3-92
White Point Mt., 2-97
White River, 4-83; 5-15
White Sands Nat. Mon., 6-93
White School of Journalism (Univ. of KS), 5-35
White Sulpher Springs, WV, 2-123
White pine, 6-50
White sea lions, 7-58
White water rafting, 6-23
Whiteman, Paul, 6-35
Whitemarsh, PA, 2-88
Whitesbog, NJ, 2-65
Whiting, IN, 4-37
Whitingman, VT, 1-119
Whitman, Marcus, 6-116; 7-69, 71
Whitman, Narcissa, 7-69, 71
Whitman, Walt, 2-36, 63, 76, 81
Whitney, Eli, 1-48, 50; 3-48
Whitney Gallery of Western Art, 6-122
Whittier, AK, 7-18, 20
Whittier, John Greenleaf, 1-77, 92
Whooping cranes, 1-11; 5-120, 123
Wicasset, ME, 1-62
Wichita, KS, 5-35, 37, 39
Wichita Indians, 5-39, 85
Wichita Mts., 5-83, 92
Wichita Mts. Wildlife Refuge, 5-92
Wichita Symphony Orchestra, 5-39
Wickenburg, Henry, 6-22
Wickford Harbor (RI), 1-97
Wickliffe, KY, 3-58
Widow Ford Nat. Hist. Pk., 2-67
Wiggin, Kate Douglas, 1-63
Wigwam (Chicago, IL), 4-18
Wigwams, 4-72
Wilcox, VA, 2-107
Wild Ammonoosuc River, 1-85
Wild Goose RR, 7-19
Wild West Show, Buffalo Bill's, 5-63
Wild West and Rough Riders Show, 4-50
Wild pigs (javelina), 6-21; 7-33
Wild rice, 4-72*, 78, 114, 121
Wild tiger lily, 3-121
Wild turkeys, 1-11, 59; 3-121; 6-21, 120
Wilder, Laura Ingles, 5-104, 108
Wildlife, 1-11, 64, 71, 78, 120; 2-23, 51, 52, 64, 77, 93, 120, 121; 3-23, 36, 49, 64, 77, 78, 106, 121; 4-22, 50, 64, 101, 120; 5-21, 36, 49, 50, 51, 64, 65, 78, 92, 100, 105, 120; 6-21, 36, 46, 50, 64, 66, 77, 92, 93, 103, 107, 119, 120, 121; 7-17, 30, 33, 44, 58, 62, 72, 77, 84, 94
Wildlife, prehistoric, 4-83, 85; 5-29, 50, 57, 99; 6-44, 85, 113; 7-17
Wilkes, John, 7-79
Wilkes Island (Pacific), 7-85
Will Rogers Mem. (OK), 5-94
Will Rogers Shrine to the Sun (CO), 6-35, 38
Willamette River, 7-51, 60
Willamette Univ., 7-57
Willamette Valley (OR), 7-57, 62
Willapa Hills, 7-65
Willard, Jess, 6-91
Willard Hotel (DC), 2-36
William Penn Mem. Museum and Archives, 1-30; 2-95
William Rockhill Nelson Gallery of Art, 4-94
William Tell festival, 4-123
Williams, Andy, 4-50
Williams, Bill, 6-35
Williams, Charles W., 4-46
Williams, Roger, 1-101, 102, 105, 109
Williams, Roger (entertainer), 4-50
Williams, William Carols, 2-63
Williamsburg, VA, 1-25; 2-100, 108, 109
Williamsburg of the Sea (Mystic

Seaport, CT), 1-52
Williamstown, VT, 1-121
Willkie, Wendell L., 4-35
Willow, AK, 7-15, 19
Willow Run, MI, 4-62
Willowbrook, ME, 1-66
Willson, Meredith, 4-49
Wilmette, IL, 4-24
Wilmington, DE, 2-14*, 15, 17, 18, 23, 24
Wilmington, NC, 3-89, 94
Wilson, AR, 5-16
Wilson, Charles Banks, 5-91
Wilson, Edith Bolling, 2-34, 63, 105
Wilson, Emmanuel, 2-117
Wilson, James (Tama Jim), 4-48, 49, 106
Wilson, James Harrison, 2-18
Wilson, John L., 3-105
Wilson, Margaret, 4-49
Wilson, Samuel, 2-74
Wilson, Thomas Woodrow, 2-34, 39, 48, 60, 61, 62, 63, 102, 105, 108; 3-109; 7-28
Winchester, VA, 2-101
Winchester Museum, 6-122
Wind Cave (SD), 5-108
Wind River, 6-119
Wind River Indian Reservation, 6-122
Wind River Range, 6-113
Wind farm, 1-93
Window in the stomach, 4-63
Windsor, CT, 1-44, 53
Windsor, VT, 1-122
Wine industry, 2-78; 5-21
Winn, Matt, 3-64, 66
Winnebago Indians, 4-43, 114
Winnemucca, NV, 6-77
Winnemucca, Old (chief), 6-77
Winnipesaukee Indians, 1-86
Winona, MN, 4-6, 81
Winston-Salem, NC, 3-95
Winter Carnival (St. Paul, MN), 4-80
Winter scene (VT), 1-120*
Winter wheat, 5-37
Winterthur Museum, 2-20, 24
Winterthur gardens (DE), 2-20
Winthrop, John Jr., 1-4, 45, 73
Winyah Bay (SC), 3-100
Wirkus, Faustin, 2-93
Wisconsin (main article), 4-111
Wisconsin Dells, 4-123
Wisconsin Hist. Soc., 4-123
Wisconsin Idea, 4-117
Wisconsin River, 4-43, 52, 73, 113, 115, 123
Wisconsin's Eagle Regiment, 4-117
Wisdom, John H., 3-19
"Wisdom" (statue), 1-24
Wister, Owen, 6-119
Witness trees, 4-120
"Wizard of OZ" (book), 5-105
Wolcott, Oliver Jr., 2-31
Wolfe, Thomas, 3-91, 95
Wollastonite, 2-77
Wolverines, 4-64
Wolves, 1-11, 64; 6-0
Wolz, Jacob, 6-22
Women's Hall of Fame, 2-80
Women's rights, 1-75; 3-74, 117; 4-50; 6-33, 61, 64, 118; 7-28, 56, 90
Wonder stone, 6-77
Wood, Abram, 3-58
Wood, Grant, 4-49
Wood Lake, MN, 4-75
Wood River, 6-44
Woodall Mt., 3-71
Woodburn Estate (DE), 2-20
Woodfill, Samuel, 3-61
Woodland Indians, 4-43
Woodland Man, 4-85
Woodland Park Zoo (Seattle, WA), 7-74

Woodland people, 3-16
Woodpecker, Ivory-billed, 5-49
Woodstock, VT, 1-122
Woodward, Henry, 3-101
Wool, 7-62
Wool industry, 2-23
Woolaroc Museum, 5-94
Woolen mills, 1-48
Woolworth, F. W., 2-92
Worcester, MA, 1-75
Worcester Art Museum, 1-80
Worden Pond (RI), 1-99
Work, John Wesley, 3-120
World Series (baseball), 4-118
World Trade Center (NYC), 2-81
"World Turned Upside Down, The"
    (song), 2-101
World War I, 1-46, 62, 67, 75, 89,
    117; 2-18, 34, 48, 61, 63, 65, 75,
    90, 102, 105; 3-20, 34, 47, 61, 75,
    76, 89, 103, 105, 117; 4-20, 33, 39,
    46, 47, 61, 63, 76, 89, 90, 104,
    118; 5-19, 33, 36, 47, 61, 75, 77,
    88, 102, 117; 6-18, 33, 61, 74, 89,
    104, 117; 7-28, 56, 70, 88, 94
World War II, 1-7, 46, 62, 65, 90,
    104, 117; 2-18, 34, 48, 61, 75, 90,
    102, 106, 118, 120; 3-20, 34, 47,
    61, 75, 89, 104, 118; 4-20, 34, 47,
    62, 76, 89, 90, 104, 118; 5-19, 34,
    47, 61, 75, 89, 117, 118, 119; 6-19,
    33, 48, 49, 64, 74, 89, 91, 104; 7-
    14, 28, 42, 44, 48, 56, 70, 73, 83,
    88
World War Mem. Plaza (IN), 4-39
World's Championship Chili Cook-
    off, 5-122
World's Columbian Exposition, 4-

123
World's Fairs, 2-75, 90; 3-118, 122;
    4-20, 89, 106, 119, 123; 5-39, 48,
    52, 61; 7-28, 56, 70, 74, 76
Worley (pirate), 3-101
Wounded Knee, SD, 5-102, 103
"Wreck of the Hesperus, The"
    (poem), 1-62
Wren, Christopher, 4-90
"Wren's Nest" (Atlanta, GA), 3-49
Wright, Allen (chief), 5-88
Wright, Frank Lloyd, 1-27; 2-80, 95;
    4-24, 119, 120, 123; 6-24
Wright, Harold Bell, 4-91
Wright, Orville, 3-5, 89*, 93
Wright, Wilbur, 3-5, 89*, 93
Wright Brothers, 3-5, 89*, 93; 4-66,
    104, 106
Wright Brothers Nat. Mem., 3-5*,
    93
Wupatki Nat. Mon., 6-23, 25
Wyandot Indians, 4-28, 100, 101
Wyeth, Nathaniel, 6-47; 7-57
Wyoming (main article), 6-111
X-ray photography, 3-91
Xaraname Indians, 5-114
Yakima, WA, 7-70, 77
Yakima Indians, 7-71
Yakima River, 7-65, 77
Yale, Linus, 1-48
Yale Bowl, 1-53
Yale Univ., 1-21, 49, 52, 53, 119
Yale locks, 1-48
Yamacraw Bluff, GA, 3-51
Yamacraw Indians, 3-45
Yamassee Indians, 3-101
Yampa River Canyon, 6-29
Yams, 7-80, 91

Yankton, SD, 5-97, 100
Yankton Sioux Indians, 5-100
Yaocomico (MD Indian village), 2-
    44
Yap Island (Pacific), 7-85
Yazoo River, 3-79, 81
Yeager, Charles (Chuck), 2-120, 123
Yell, Archibald, 5-18, 20
Yellow Bear (chief), 5-120
Yellow fever, 3-75
Yellow magnolia, 3-23
Yellow warbler, 1-11
Yellowstone Lake, 6-113, 121
Yellowstone Nat. Park, 6-55, 61, 66,
    71, 111, 112, 113, 114, 116, 117,
    119, 120, 121, 122
Yellowstone River, 5-69; 6-57, 59,
    113, 114, 118, 121
Yellowstone gateway, 6-66
Yellowstone geysers (Yellowstone
    Nat. Park), 6-71
Yellowtail, Robert, 6-64
Yellville, AR, 5-20
Yerkes Observatory (Lake Geneva,
    WI), 4-122
Yo Semite Indians, 7-23
Yoga tree, 7-84
Yorba Linda, CA, 7-28
York, Alvin C., 3-117
York, ME, 1-60, 63, 65
York, PA, 2-88
York River, 2-97
Yorktown, VA, 2-100, 102, 108, 109
Yosemite Falls (Yosemite Nat.
    Park), 7-32*
Yosemite Nat. Park, 7-23, 32*, 35
Youghiogheny Reservoir, 2-41
Young, Bennett, 1-117
Young, Brigham, 1-19, 119; 6-102,

103, 104, 105, 106, 107, 109
Young, Clara Decker, 6-103
Young, Ewing, 7-57
Young, Levi Edgar, 6-106
Young, Mahonri, 6-106
Young's Bay (OR), 7-53
Young's Mem. Cemetery (NY), 2-81
Younghans, Maria, 3-81
Younghans, Miranda, 3-81
Ysleta, TX, 5-115
Yucca, 5-106; 6-21, 92; 7-30
Yuchi Indians, 3-113
Yukon River, 7-11
Yukon Territory, 7-70
Yukon gold rush, 7-70
Yuma, AZ, 6-18
Yuma (Yuman) Indians, 6-16, 18
Zane, Betty, 2-120
Zanesville, OH, 4-107, 109
Zebulon Pike Locks (IA), 4-52
Zenger, Peter, 2-73
Zinc, 1-11; 2-77, 106; 3-64; 4-92,
    120, 121; 5-37, 92, 93; 6-48, 50,
    51, 91
Zinzendorf, Nicholas, 2-87
Ziolkowski, Korczak, 5-104
Zion Canyon (UT), 6-107
Zion Cliff ruins (UT), 6-100
Zion Narrows (Zion Nat. Park), 6-
    99
Zion Nat. Park, 6-99, 108
Zirconium, 7-60
Zoar, OH, 4-103
Zoos, 1-14, 109; 2-39, 80, 94; 3-24; 4-
    23, 67, 93, 109; 5-39, 66; 6-35, 38;
    7-31, 49, 74
Zuni Indians, 6-17
Zwaanendael, DE, 2-15, 25